JAPANESE PRINTS

I. HARUNOBU: *Girl with Cranes.* See note, page 264

JAPANESE PRINTS

FROM THE
EARLY MASTERS
TO THE
MODERN

by James A. Michener

with Notes on the Prints by
RICHARD LANE

with the cooperation of
THE HONOLULU ACADEMY OF ARTS

CHARLES E. TUTTLE COMPANY: PUBLISHERS

RUTLAND, VERMONT & TOKYO, JAPAN

Published by the
Charles E. Tuttle Company of
Rutland, Vermont & Tokyo, Japan
with editorial offices at
15 Edogawa-cho, Bunkyo-ku, Tokyo

Copyright in Japan, 1959
by James A. Michener
All rights reserved

Library of Congress Catalog
Card No. 59-10410
First printing, 1959

Book design and typography by Kaoru Ogimi
Color plates by the Kyodo Printing Co., Tokyo
Gravure plates by the Inshokan Printing Co., Tokyo
Letterpress by the Kenkyusha Printing Co., Tokyo
MANUFACTURED IN JAPAN

TABLE OF CONTENTS

LIST OF ARTISTS AND PRINTS

Arranged alphabetically according to the names by which the artists are generally known. A star indicates mounted color plates.

7

JAPANESE PRINTS

2. KIYONOBU I: *Seated Courtesan* (half of album page). See note, Page 255

INTRODUCTION

THIS BOOK deals with what have been called "the magnificent scraps of paper," the woodblock prints of Japan, and with their modern successors, the creative prints, of which more later. The proper name for the traditional prints reveals their meaning: ukiyo-e, "pictures of the passing world"; and the three examples which open this essay, Prints 2, 3, and 4, have been especially chosen to illustrate certain basic aspects of this enchanting art.

First of all, each print appears on a sheet of handmade paper, delightful in itself and resembling the end papers of this book. This paper is coarse and absorbent, composed of thousands of interlocking fibers into which the ink has been impressed. It is resilient, glowing, and vibrant. Its recuperative powers are phenomenal and it lends luster to whatever appears upon it. The beginning of any good Japanese print is the unique paper upon which it is printed.

Each of the first three prints is a sumizuri-e, *sumi* meaning "black ink," *zuri* "printed," and *e* "picture." Ukiyo-e prints began with such pictures, and color was a late innovation, so that to understand Japanese prints, one must first learn to enjoy the sumizuri-e; and it is a fact that most collectors prize first the black-and-white prints of the early days. Wherever possible throughout this book, sumizuri-e have been introduced, for I hold them in special affection, and if I were asked to nominate one print which has taught me most about ukiyo-e, it would probably be Print 9, a near-perfect specimen of sumizuri-e, a poetic recollection of one of the supreme moments in Japanese literature, and an intricate work of art whose grandeur derives from the judicious use of black and white.

Prints 2, 3, and 4 also illustrate the flowing line that characterizes ukiyo-e and forms its chief artistic accomplishment. The line is bold yet poetic, strong yet evocative, heavy black yet glowing with light, and above all a joy to look at as it twists and flows across the paper. This soaring line is the soul of ukiyo-e, and in these first prints one can see how effective it is. The second figure from the left in Print 4 is as attractive a bit of art as will appear in this book; yet it is composed principally of bold, strong lines, without any color. In most examples of ukiyo-e, this line dominates, and unless one appreciates its essential Japanese quality he misses the lesson of Japanese prints.

The print on the opposite page is of special interest in that it is the right-hand half of a page from an erotic album; unfortunately, modern publishing standards do not permit reproduction of the left-hand half of the print, which depicts the young courtesan's customer. A great many ukiyo-e prints were frankly erotic in nature – Prints 11 and 13, for example – and others contained esoteric overtones of eroticism that delighted the knowing. Three such different prints as 111, 141, and 145–46 have sexual intimations which were not lost upon their original Japanese buyers. For example, the handsome courtesan opposite has her obi tied conspicuously in front, which signifies that she is an inhabitant of the Yoshiwara, the gay quarter of Edo, now called Tokyo. By looking for obi whose big bows ride in front, the reader will be able to spot some of the famous courtesans featured in this book.

Finally, these first three prints remind us of the fact the women who appear in them lived to provide excitement for the rising merchant class that had

3. STYLE OF SUKENOBU:
Courtesans in Procession.
See note, page 255

sprung up in Japan toward the close of the sixteenth century. In the Genroku period, 1688–1703, when ukiyo-e enjoyed its first great flowering, these wealthy merchants were not yet powerful enough to challenge openly the samurai class that ruled the nation; but they had already carved out for themselves a secure place in Japanese life. By law they were required to wear somber clothing dominated by blacks and grays, but the interior linings of their kimono were apt to be of silver and gold. They were forced to live in houses that were outwardly plain, but the inner quarters were often rich in art. The brothels in which they hid their Yoshiwara mistresses were luxurious and the costumes of the girls were resplendent, as Print 160 shows. It is the *arriviste* world of this rising middle class that ukiyo-e depicted, and in the prints one finds many echoes of that fact. The rowdy, exciting theaters patronized by the merchants occasioned many of the prints reproduced in this book; and it is for this rich record of Edo that the ukiyo-e is today prized by social historians.

Therefore, these first three prints form an appropriate introduction to the art, for without a sound appreciation of sumizuri-e, one's final estimate of ukiyo-e must remain unbalanced; but if one acquires a love of these early prints he can proceed through all the stages of color printing and comprehend what the artist is trying to do, for the basis of ukiyo-e is line, and a print which starts with an evocative line will probably turn out to be a lovely thing, no matter what happens to the colors. I once knew an art dealer who found himself with a stack of faded Japanese prints to peddle, and as each potential customer thumbed them he would chant: "Faded, faded, but as that great collector Frank Lloyd Wright has said, 'All is fled save beauty.' " Actually, it was the poet Arthur Davison Ficke who delivered that line, and although I was always amused when my dealer friend quoted it, trying to lure me into a purchase, I now think favorably of Ficke's statement; when the colors have finally fled we still have the flowing line, and essentially that is what counts.

It seems to me that the chief merit of Japanese prints is their ability to meet the human mind on the simplest level of appreciation and to lure it on, as one's comprehension increases, to successively more complex levels of enjoyment, until the mind is at last brought to contemplate one of the world's more profound problems: What is a work of art?

I now invite the reader to accompany me on a brief reprise of the exciting intellectual journey one undertakes when he first purchases a print. Let us suppose that you have just acquired Print 5, Harunobu's "Girl with Ox," believed to be a portrait of Osen, one of the teahouse beauties of the time, as she sweeps up superfluous love letters. It is easy to believe that this is a work of art. The design is carefully worked out; the coloring is both subtle and appropriate; the total effect is pleasing. If you proceed no further in your investigation than this, you have had a satisfying aesthetic experience, although one of limited scope.

But it is very unlikely that you will be able to stop there. Subtly you are drawn into speculative inquiries that become inevitable, and soon you are asking: "Why is it that Japanese connoisseurs with refined taste refuse to accept woodblock prints as first-class art?" You are now involved in the intricate aesthetic theories of Asia; and no matter how much you originally treasured this Harunobu print, you are forced to confess that it is spiritually on a lower plane than those other works of Asian art which Japanese connoisseurs have generally categorized as first class. For example, it is pretty obvious that prints lack the subtle intellectual content of Asia's famous black-and-white imaginary landscapes. Whether you like it or not, a study of Japanese prints forces you into making value judgments, which is a fine exercise for any mind.

But when you have settled to your own satisfaction the relative position of prints in Asian art, and when you have resignedly come to accept your Harunobu for exactly what it is – no more and no less – you suddenly find yourself asking: "Wouldn't this be a more legitimate work of art if it were a one-copy painting instead of a multicopy print?" This is a most perplexing question, and it has exercised able minds for many years; for when you ask it you are coming perilously close to the heart of aesthetics, and you will never be content until you have penetrated as far into this thrilling field as your mind can take you. For to answer the difficult question of "Can a multicopy print be as legitimate as a one-copy painting?" requires an answer to a much more profound problem: "What is a work of art?" There is no subject matter better suited on which to hang this question than your copy of Harunobu's "Girl with Ox."

You have purchased, for about seven hundred dollars, your original Harunobu, but what, actually, do you have? I should like to analyze rather carefully several possible answers to that question.

First, as we have seen, you have a piece of paper. It is one of the finest papers

4. STYLE OF MASANOBU:
Courtesans in Procession.
See note, page 257

ever constructed by man. Rembrandt saved all he could find and reserved it for his finest prints. Other European artists also loved it. If you examine it under a microscope, you see a surface consisting of thousands of absorbent fibers casually interlocked in haphazard patterns. As centuries pass, ink that once appeared on the surface fibers seems to sink into the hidden interior fibers, so that from one generation to the next the beauty of the print is deepened and mellowed. Two hundred years from now your Harunobu will be different from what it is now, but it will be no less beautiful. But Harunobu himself had nothing to do with the paper. He did not make it, nor select it from others that were available. He probably never touched it and quite possibly did not even see it. Whatever of art he contributed to this print must have been imparted via some other medium than the paper.

Second, you have on the paper some of the most satisfying lines in art. In fact, if from your ownership of this Harunobu you attain only an increased appreciation of line as a component of art, you will have gained the essential lesson of Japanese prints. It is a line that sings, that moves joyously, that evokes empathy, that delights the eye, and no matter how long you own this Harunobu, you will never tire of its gentle, Japanese line. Yet Harunobu himself had nothing to do with the line you see. It is true that he drew a basic sketch for the print, exactly as Giorgione drew a sketch for his "Fête Champêtre" in the Louvre, but there the similarity ends, for when Giorgione's sketch was finished, he went ahead and transferred it onto his canvas; that is to say, Giorgione both drew the sketch and painted the resulting picture. Harunobu did not transfer his sketch onto the wood block from which your print was made; a skilled artisan did that, and often where Harunobu drew thick, he carved thin. Where Harunobu merely suggested an idea, he developed it. In many instances, we suspect that the art-content of a completed wood block depended as much upon the woodcarver as it did upon Harunobu.

Third, your print contains areas of color, skillfully mixed and applied, and the second major lesson which the Japanese print can teach the Western owner is the judicious placement of masses of flat color. But Harunobu neither mixed the colors you see nor applied them to the absorbent paper. That was accomplished by highly trained printers. In fact, Harunobu probably never saw the specific colors that appear on your print. All he did was to obtain from the printer a bundle of key-block proof sheets that looked like the Hokusai key-block proof of Print 6. Picking up one of these proofs, Harunobu indicated the three areas that were to be printed green – panniers, broom, pine needles – but he did not use green ink to do this; he daubed the required areas with an ugly, reddish stain, adding at one corner of the print a swatch of the green he had in mind. This key-block proof was then returned to the woodcarver, who cut the green block. Next Harunobu took another proof and with the same ugly red stain marked the kimono to be printed salmon, and the salmon block was cut. The orange, the reddish brown, and the gray were similarly indicated. When the required color blocks had been cut – in this case, about seven – it was up to the printer to mix the recommended colors, to see that they harmonized, and to apply them to the paper.

By a process of elimination we have now subtracted from your print every tactile component and have proved that Harunobu could not possibly have had anything to do with any one of them. He did not make the paper; he did not cut the lines; he neither mixed nor applied the colors. One further important fact must be borne in mind. At no time in the history of your print did Harunobu ever "paint" it as you see it now. Your print is therefore not a copy of an original work of art, for I must stress that no "original work of art" ever existed, except as a concept in Harunobu's mind. All he did was to set in motion, by means of an idea which he represented in the shorthand of a sketch, the processes which resulted in a work of art. What you have is a scrap of paper to which certain things have been done – but never by Harunobu – and it is interesting that each of the things done to the paper can also be subtracted one by one, for they are tactile accomplishments: the colors can easily be faded out by either sunlight or bleaches; the lines can be removed; and the paper itself can be lifted away strand by strand until mysteriously what was, is suddenly no more.

You are thus driven, whether you like it or not, perilously close to the Platonic concept that your print can be nothing but a constellation of accidental physical components, held together momentarily by their relationship to a master idea. I hold this to be the most logical definition of a Japanese print, and the one that provides the greatest intellectual stimulation.

You are now prepared to face the problem which launched your investigation: "Is a multicopy print in any way inferior to a one-copy painting?" The conclusion you have reached as to what a print is applies equally to a painting, although in the latter case its applicability is not so obvious. One can visit Giorgione's "Fête Champêtre" throughout a lifetime without being forced to consider the conclusions reached above, for one can easily delude himself into believing that, in viewing the canvas upon which Giorgione happened to paint, one somehow or other sees the painting itself, as if the canvas and its accidental pigments were the work of art; but no sensible person can study Harunobu's portrait of Osen without wondering exactly what it is he holds in his hands, for sooner or later he will fall prey to several persistent doubts, which I should now like to express as questions.

Question one: *Since Harunobu issued about two hundred copies of his print, what is the relation of my copy to the ultimate work of art which it represents?* For example, if you could see at one instant all two hundred copies, would you then understand what Harunobu intended his work of art to be? More practically, how many different copies from among the two hundred must you see before you can detect the artist's basic intention, as for example in the case of Prints 183 and 184?

Question two: *Were all two hundred copies of the original printing equal works of art, or was one lucky success the real work of art with the other 199 no better than near misses?* And if the latter is the case, how can you be sure that the copy you have is not one of the failures and therefore of no artistic value?

Question three: *Is it not more logical to think of a print as an original Platonic idea which has been subdivided mechanically into two hundred equal representations, each a reasonably satisfactory approximation of what the artist intended?* Obviously this is the concept upon which the collector or museum has to operate, but to accept the concept as a philosophical principle raises many difficult points, the most perplexing being this: Since it is likely that of the original two hundred prints at least 190 have been destroyed, do the ten surviving now divide among themselves the original reservoir of artistic content, so that each surviving print is now twenty times richer in art-content than it was when issued? Finally, if the day comes when only one copy remains, as seems to be the case with Print 81, does it then absorb the entire art-content with which the original edition was once endowed? You can see that this form of question brings us back once more to where we started: "If you destroy all but one copy of a print, is it then as important a work of art as a painting?"

Question four: *Since in the original edition of the Osen portrait Harunobu had nothing directly to do with the paper, the carving, or the printing of his prints, why are they any more legitimate as works of art than a facsimile copy which you could buy in Japan today, hand-carved on Harunobu's type of wood, hand-printed on his type of paper, and colored with his kind of colors?* And if you conclude that the copy is an adequate work of art, since it is capable of reminding us what Harunobu intended, why wouldn't a good colored photographic reproduction, like Print 5, serve equally well?

Question five: *What is the artistic value of a work like Print 7, which was re-issued in 1916 by printing with certified old paper and old ink from the original wood block preserved since the 1710's?* This problem is most perplexing. It should be noted that when the Art Institute of Chicago issued the first volume of its history-making catalogue it saw fit to include as Kiyonobu I, Number 1, a modern printing, like Print 7, whose block dated back to 1698.

In the years when I was assembling the collection shown here, and helping others to assemble theirs, I was extraordinarily busy with other work, yet I think that a day never passed when I did not for recreation contemplate the intellectual problems posed by these alluring scraps of paper. I have reached the following tentative conclusions, but I could be persuaded by some better informed investigator to surrender them tomorrow if he could show me how to escape certain contradictions.

It seems to me that a work of art consists of two parts, and the fact that they are mutually repellent emphasizes the complexity with which we deal. First, a work of art must exist as an idealistic concept in the mind of a human being, but I shall not argue if you prefer to express the condition as "a felt stimulus within the viscera." It is generated from an intuitive impulse which illuminates in an instant the total ultimate possibilities of which this work of art will be capable. This intuitive impulse may be received either before, during, or after conscious thought processes about the work of art have begun, but for most of us it is not responsive to an act of will; that is, the required intuitive impulses cannot be evoked when needed. There appear to be some men who can consciously generate repeated intuitive impulses, and I suppose that this skill is what we refer to as genius. (It is obvious that the entertainment of intuitive impulses is not restricted to artists; an artist is a man who develops his intuitive impulses within the field of the arts; a general develops his in warfare; a scientist, in the field of science.) When the intuitive impulse has been accepted and understood, it is consciously elaborated into a fully developed master idea for the work of art. For example, the grand design is determined; the meaning is reviewed and organized; the techniques which will be effective are selected. When this elaboration is completed a master plan has been evolved and perfected, and it stands ready to be transformed into a canvas, a statue, a poem, or a woodblock print.

When this master plan has been developed intellectually, or viscerally, the first half of the artistic process has been completed, but observe that it exists only as a potential in the mind, or perhaps being, of an individual. It can exist nowhere else, and unless it has once so existed it can never be transformed into an objective realization. That is why it is ridiculous to call a segment of natural landscape a work of art, or a stone that has been accidentally polished by the sea. Such things are adventitiously appealing, because by accident they conform to definitions which human beings have decided to accept as identifying beauty, but the accidents of nature have nothing to do with art.

A work of art must begin as an intuitive insight which has been consciously elaborated into a master idea capable of being objectified; but a work of art cannot be considered created until it has been transformed into an objective realization. When Keats wrote "Heard melodies are sweet, but those unheard are sweeter," he was referring only to the first half of the artistic process, for unheard melodies may not be considered art. They are something else. Obviously, Harunobu's intuitive impulse regarding what might be accomplished

5. HARUNOBU: *Girl with Ox*. See note, page 264

in a print portraying Osen must have been finer than the master idea which he subsequently developed, and I suppose that in its turn the master idea must have been finer than the end product after it had been filtered through the hands of the papermaker, the woodcarver, and the printer. But in neither of its more perfect ideational forms was it yet a work of art.

The second requirement of a work of art is its realization in some objective form which the human audience can perceive. The audience is not required to understand the objective form; it is required only to perceive it; customarily, understanding comes later. The general public is always tempted to identify this objective realization of the master idea as the work of art, but as Harunobu's Osen portrait proves, that cannot be the case. The objective realization is best comprehended as a convenient and persisting reminder to the perceptive world that the work of art does exist. It is helpful to keep in mind two characteristics of the objective realization of the work of art. It is not required to conform to what society currently considers beautiful, for a moment's analysis will satisfy anyone that beauty is merely an agreed-upon convention at once arbitrary, capricious, irrelevant, and temporary. I am afraid that beauty as defined by popular taste has very little to do with art. It is closer to fashion. More important, however, is the fact that the technical processes whereby the master idea is transformed into an objective realization are relatively unimportant, and the fact that the Japanese Harunobu in the Osen print utilized – or perhaps commandeered – a certain well-defined set of techniques which he himself helped pioneer does not make it binding upon the Japanese Onchi to use the same techniques when he wants to create his objective realization of Print 242, in which Onchi's radically new techniques proved as successful for his purposes as Harunobu's had done for his. If genius consists of the ability to generate or to entertain repeated intuitive impulses upon which a work of art can be elaborated, then talent is the gift which certain men have for selecting and operating the skills appropriate for transforming their master ideas into satisfactory objective realizations. Consequently, whatever technique proves effective for the job in hand is the right technique. There can be no other hierarchy of values, which disposes of the question: "Is an oil painting more important as a work of art than a woodblock print?"

It is apparent that I have maneuvered myself into a difficult dualism: a work of art is both an idealistic concept, never fully realized, plus an objective realization whose function is to remind the world that the complete work of art exists. It is a dualism which contains many perplexing contradictions, but one with which I have been increasingly content to live. It has enhanced a thousandfold the joy I have found in prints, and it has given me a philosophical base from which to conduct my daily work. Few abstract ideas ever give a man so much.

The questions asked earlier may now be answered. The portrait print of Osen which you bought is an objective realization of a master idea which Harunobu the artist developed from an initial intuitive impulse. The realization was accomplished mainly by skilled artisans working upon Harunobu's rough report of his master idea, delivered in the form of a sketch. The print's function is to remind you that a work of art exists.

If all two hundred copies of the original edition were extant, one would in no way diminish the art-content of another. The two hundred would merely be capable of reminding more people that a work of art exists. It is true, however, that of the two hundred prints in the original edition some were better executed than others and can be said to have been materially closer to what Harunobu intended than those with poor registry or smeared colors. That is why, as we shall see later, an amusing argument has arisen over Print 175.

Also, to buy any copy of Print 233 is now risky, because the artist rejected many of his printings as having failed to come up to his demanding standards; but, prudently, he did not destroy the failures; he kept them in the corner and either he or his heirs later peddled them at high prices.

Obviously, when only one copy of a famous print remains, its money value is enhanced, but not its art-content. When only one copy exists, as only one copy of the "Fête Champêtre" has always existed, its responsibility to an appreciative world is increased, but not its art-content. In common sense, it is obvious that since Giorgione may be presumed to have touched the canvas of the "Fête" and to have applied the pigments with his own hand, the "Fête" has a certain souvenir value which your print of Osen, which Harunobu probably never saw or touched, cannot have. But souvenir values are not art values, and when Giorgione started work on the actual painting of the "Fête" he surely came no closer to realizing his master idea than did Harunobu and his team of artisans when they produced the Osen portrait. In Giorgione's case all shortcomings could be attributed to one man; in Harunobu's to a team of men. But the relationship of objective realization to master idea must have been about the same. If this concept seems repugnant – and to some it does, for they insist that a canvas actually touched by Giorgione must be finer art than a print not touched by Harunobu – please consider the roomful of Rubens in the Louvre not far from the "Fête Champêtre"; we know that students applied much of the pigment and some of the underlying drawing; so this leaves a Rubens somewhere between a "Fête" and a "Girl with Ox," and pretty soon we are lost in distinctions which become ridiculous.

There is another way to approach this ticklish problem of objective realization. Of all the world's performances of Beethoven's *Fifth Symphony* no two have ever been identical; they could not be. Nor has any even closely coincided with the master idea evolved by Beethoven, just as his finally developed master idea could not have exhausted the possibilities latent in the initial intuitive insight out of which he built the symphony. The analogy to Harunobu's portrait of Osen is close: an orchestra does for Beethoven's master idea what the woodcarvers and printers did for Harunobu's.

Finally, if all two hundred prints from the original edition of the Osen portrait were destroyed, there would be some merit in having available one of the modern hand-carved, hand-printed facsimiles which you can buy in Japan; its merit would derive from the fact that it was created under almost the same conditions, using almost the same materials as the original. It is therefore slightly closer to the spirit of Harunobu's objective realization of his concept than our color reproduction, Print 5. That is why hand-carved Roman copies of lost Greek statues have a minor artistic value of their own, for they are the only reminders we have of the fact that Greek artists once entertained transcendent intuitions and realized them in majestic form. However, the modern facsimile of the Osen is markedly poorer in evocative power than one of the two hundred original copies issued under Harunobu's direction, but only because cumulative

6. HOKUSAI: *The Poet Abe no Nakamaro Longing for Home* (key-block proof). See note, page 274

errors must have been introduced in paper, wood, carving, pigment, and printing, and these remove the end product a little farther from what Harunobu originally intended. Since I doubt that Harunobu ever saw or touched the original of Print 5, which now rests in Honolulu, I obviously do not love this print because it was ever close to Harunobu; I love it because it represents in objective form a dazzling idea which Harunobu once entertained. However, later in this essay I do admit that I cherish any print a little more if it once belonged to someone like Edmond de Goncourt, Louis Ledoux, or Frank Lloyd Wright, but when I say this I am speaking as an antiquarian interested in the history of collecting and not as an appreciator of art. The fact that De Goncourt once owned a print is as irrelevant artistically as the fact that Giorgione once touched the "Fête Champêtre."

As to the value of Print 7, which was struck off on old paper using old ink applied to an original block carved more than two hundred years ago, I must confess perplexity. I see some merit in having such a print available, especially when all copies of the original seem to have been lost, which is the case of a handsome Kiyonobu block held in the Freer Gallery, but I would not buy such prints myself; the three I have came with another collection. Yet I know that Japanese ink in its solid form retains its properties for centuries and is truly identical with what it was three hundred years ago; the paper is demonstrably the same, for it also is identical; and the wood block is unquestionably ancient; but it seems to me that enough change must have taken place in the latter two components to produce cumulative variations which remove the resulting print some further distance from what the artist originally intended. On the other hand, I confess that frequently the modern printing has been done so adroitly that I cannot distinguish the copy from the original, nor can many others, which is why honorable publishers fasten onto the backs of their copies certificates explaining how they were printed. Intending counterfeiters do not, and I would not care to estimate the number of undetected copies held presently in unsuspecting collections, including my own. In recent times the carved blocks of both Goyo and Onchi have been used posthumously for large editions; the latter bear certificates admitting late origin; the former do not. I say I am perplexed by this problem because I fear that my objection to such prints stems from antiquarian considerations and not from artistic ones. I am perilously close to saying: "I don't like this Goyo copy, made only shortly after his death by the same printer who made the originals, from the same blocks and using the same paper and ink, mainly because Goyo never touched the print." And that of course is, artistically speaking, nonsense.

It comes down to this. Art concerns only two value judgments: "Was the original master idea of merit? Was it effectively realized?" One is not concerned with whether it was tastefully realized or in conformity with prejudicial standards. On the other hand, it is obvious that it will usually be the dedicated and skilled artist who will have the best chance of either generating a good master idea or of effectively realizing it. This is merely to say that professionals create art, not amateurs.

Japanese prints are a joy to those who know them, for by the processes I have briefly summarized, these magnificent scraps of paper lift us from idle contemplation of what was an unimportant plebeian art into the upper realms of speculation, and anything which can do that is good to have around.

At this point the general reader may wish to pass directly to the prints, for what follows is largely an explanation of how the ukiyo-e which appear in this book were assembled, information that may be of more interest to fellow collectors than to others. I would urge, however, that the reader first glance

7. KAIGETSUDO DOHAN: *Courtesan.*
See note, page 255

through those paragraphs below and on page 22 that explain the inclusion of modern prints, to my mind one of the most important features of the book.

In 1942, America's foremost collector of Japanese prints, the successful New York businessman and poet Louis V. Ledoux, started publishing what ultimately became, in five sumptuous volumes, the most handsome catalogue of an ukiyo-e collection ever issued. The work produced two opposite effects, the second of which would have dismayed the author.

On the one hand, it demonstrated to Japan and Europe the high level which American connoisseurship had reached, which was Ledoux's intention. But on the other, it stultified American collecting for a decade, because comments occasioned by it created the impression that this was the last great assembly of Japanese prints that could ever be collected by one man. The international market was supposed to be dried up; Japanese storehouses had no more prints to disgorge; and all previously existing major collections in America had come to permanent rest in museums.

Among the potential collectors who were scared off by the Ledoux catalogue and its attendant rumors was the present author. For some time both my travels and my interests had been concentrating on Japan, and I had often casually considered starting a small personal collection of prints, but I knew, for the experts had told me, that no good ones were available.

Then three unrelated accidents changed my mind. First, while I was exploring in the Afghan desert, a letter arrived advising me that I had unexpectedly inherited from a donor I had not seen in twenty-five years a small, choice collection of Japanese prints. So whether I wanted to or not, I had become a collector.

Second, the trustees of the estate of Charles H. Chandler, of Evanston, Illinois, called upon me to discuss the sale and dispersal of the great Chandler collection, consisting of 4,533 prints assembled mainly in the first two decades of this century, when collecting was at its height. I found to my surprise that there was a possibility that this splendid group, containing many masterpieces, might possibly be sold to a single purchaser.

Third, and as I look back on this fact it seems the most important of all, I discovered the contemporary school of Japanese prints. I grew to know some of the artists and to love their work. From them I acquired many handsome prints that spoke to me in vital, modern accents. I therefore conceived the idea of doing what no one else had done before: building a single, small collection of choice prints that would start with Moronobu and continue right down to the challenging work of today.

When I began collecting seriously I suddenly discovered that many art shops around the world had excellent single prints. In Paris, London, and New York, dealers had surprisingly good, though small, stocks. I also found that Japanese

8. MASANOBU: *Onoe Kikugoro*.
See note, page 257

collectors were willing to sell or trade choice items and that small collections were constantly coming on the market.

However, it was obvious from the start that one could not hope to duplicate or even rival the great Ledoux collection; prints of supreme quality are not coming onto the market rapidly enough. But I found that I could do what Ledoux had not done: I could gather into one small collection representative examples of the exquisite work of the past plus the thundering vitality of the present. It was within those limitations that I worked. The present volume, in its quiet and limited way, demonstrates what any collector can accomplish in today's market. It is, I think, the first private collection that exhibits the entire gamut of Japanese prints. If it has any special merit, this lies in the fact that in the later pages I have chosen from the work of living men, men whom I love as creative brothers, for they have produced a group of prints which illuminate our age and form a worthy capstone to the work of the past. The collection here offered is thus not merely an antiquarian thing, preserving and treasuring past beauties; it is an exploration into the future. It has an intellectual justification of its own.

The critical notes appearing at the end of this book are the work of Dr. Richard Lane and indicate where each print was found. Here the reader will quickly discover that of the 257 prints reproduced in this volume, 166 came from the Chandler collection. This could be construed as proving, not that Japanese prints are available today, but that anyone can have a reasonably good collection if he can stumble upon a treasure trove like Chandler's.

That is not a fair conclusion. When I started collecting I knew what the Chandler collection contained: a wealth of Masanobu, Toyonobu, Harunobu, Utamaro, Sharaku, Hokusai, and Hiroshige prints. Therefore I bought few or no prints by these artists, even though thousands were offered.

Similarly, dealers offered me dozens of fine early prints, but again I elected to gamble on acquiring the Chandler holdings. Had there been no Chandler prints in the offing, and had I been restricted only to the prints available in public shops over the past five years, I would nevertheless have been able to build a collection just about as good as the one here offered. It is interesting to note which Chandler prints would have been unobtainable elsewhere: the Choki snow scene, Print 174; the big Kiyomasu, Print 16; and the Toyonobu puppeteers, Print 81. They are unique treasures. The others could have been duplicated, and still can be, not always in identical subject matter, but in prints of the same relative importance.

Take for example the case of the Kaigetsudo prints, like Print 15. After Ledoux accumulated six of these rare masterpieces, it was confidently assumed that this feat could never be duplicated. In fact, it was doubted that any additional Kaigetsudos would ever appear on the market, and collectors like me accepted the prospect of having no prints by these artists. But in 1957 five different Kaigetsudos came up for sale. Two are still available in Japan. Dealers in that country also have for sale three substantial general collections which, if combined, would surpass what is shown here. From California a marvelous collection will one day be available to the general buyer.

Collectors are repeatedly asked to compare their collections with others, and this provides me with an opportunity to point out once again how rich our public collections of ukiyo-e are. The 257 prints shown here have been chosen from a total of about 5,400, of which half are Hiroshiges. The Museum of Fine Arts in Boston owns a total of more than 54,000 marvelous prints. For example, Utamaro once issued a set of six portraits of women against gray grounds, superbly designed and looking much like Print 163, but better. Certainly, they are among Utamaro's masterworks and became quite popular, because later he reissued the series with new titles and minor changes. There are thus twelve different prints in this memorable series, and for the past ten years I have been hoping to find one. None has ever come my way, but Boston has eight excellent copies. It is probable that only a very few of the prints shown here would be needed by Boston to fill holes in its collection. For example, this book has nine Utamaros. Boston has over seven hundred.

A good way to judge any collection is by the number of big sumizuri-e and tan-e prints it has, because these are the ultimate rarities in ukiyo-e. I have managed to acquire four: one tan-e, the Kiyomasu, Print 16; and three sumizuri-e, the Kaigetsudo, Print 15 and the two Kiyomasus, Prints 21 and 23. But the Art Institute in Chicago has a total of thirty-seven, including eight sumizuri-e and twenty-nine tan-e. In general, it has a magnificent collection, as does the Metropolitan in New York.

A cautious assessment of the condition of each print will be found in the notes, but certain of the prints are in such exceptional condition as to merit special notice. The big Masanobu uki-e, Print 43, was kept in a traditional Japanese scroll box, apparently from an early date, and is breath-takingly beautiful. The Buncho portrait of Osen, Print 127, is in handsome condition, while the Kitao Masanobu book on the Yoshiwara, of which Print 141 forms the middle pages, is in an unusually good state of preservation.

Like most collectors, I find much pleasure in identifying prints once owned by illustrious predecessors. For example, the notable Japanese pioneers Wakai and Hayashi once held many of these prints, and their seals are seen, respectively, on Prints 21 and 226; Kobayashi, Kuki, and Mihara are also represented. Most of the distinguished French connoisseurs, who in Europe launched both the love of ukiyo-e and its scholarship are here: Gonse, Manzi, Haviland, Jacquin, Bing, Rouart, Vignier, and Koechlin. The finest German of them all, Straus-Negbaur, is represented in strength; Jaeckel, Von Heymel, and Tikotin also appear, as do Bateson, Kington Baker, and Hillier of England.

Most of the Americans are here, of course, from Fenollosa, the dean of all ukiyo-e collectors, to Happer, Morse, Wright, Chandler, Ficke, Gookin, Field, Ainsworth, Metzgar, Mansfield, Ford, May, Schraubstadter, Ledoux, Grabhorn, Packard, Lane, and the two pioneering collectors of moderns, William Hartnett and Oliver Statler. Present in the collection, but not represented in this book is one extremely distinguished name: De Goncourt, with several fine Harunobus and others. Four distinguished collections are missing, and I regret their absence; Vever, Morrison, Swettenham, and the Spaulding brothers.

The reader will find, running through the collection, recurrent portraits of three famous actors: Sanokawa Ichimatsu, with his mon, or crest, in the form of a stylized Chinese character, well shown in Prints 41 and 44, appears twelve times; Segawa Kikunojo, with his mon of a sheaf-like bale of cotton padding, as seen in Print 27, is shown seven times, always in female roles; while the various Ichikawa Danjuros, with their memorable mon of concentric squares representing nested rice measures, as seen in Print 71, appear eighteen times. These same mon also appear often as decorations, as in Prints 43, 53, and 60, and such thematic repetitions are one of the peculiar pleasures of ukiyo-e.

The reader will also spot for himself the many deliberate cross-references presented in these prints. It is interesting to compare how Masanobu and Kuniyoshi, many years apart, handled the same incident in Prints 46 and 215; and how Kiyomasu borrowed from himself in Prints 19 and 20.

At present these prints find their home in the Honolulu Academy of Arts, where they may be seen and where I hope they may remain permanently. I am not unmindful of the glowing passage written by De Goncourt, one of the most perceptive comments ever made about collecting: "My wish is that my drawings, my prints, my curios, my books – in a word those things of art which have been the joy of my life – shall not be consigned to the cold tomb of a museum, and subjected to the stupid glance of the careless passer-by; but I require that they shall all be dispersed under the hammer of the auctioneer, so that the pleasure which the acquiring of each one of them has given me shall be given again, in each case, to some inheritor of my own taste."

It was this passage that inspired Louis Ledoux to direct that his fine collection be broadcast upon his death, so that men new to collecting could enjoy what he had once treasured. In fact, Prints 126, 177–78, and 183 appear in this book only because Ledoux shared De Goncourt's view. But I like museums and consider them one of the major adornments of our civilization, and the Academy in Honolulu is one of the best.

I am indebted to many experts for help in preparing this book, but mostly to Richard Lane, who with his meticulous knowledge of Japanese and his love for ukiyo-e seems certain to become America's equivalent of the great German scholar Fritz Rumpf. Dr. Lane is responsible for the captions and the critical notes and has enriched the text at many points. Miss Marion Morse, of the Honolulu Academy of Arts, tracked down the provenance of each print and in consultation with the Academy staff determined its condition. Raymond Sato, also of the Academy, took the photographs, while those genial friends Marvell Hart and Robert P. Griffing kept all moving forward. Tseng Yu-ho, distinguished Chinese artist, expertly checked the colors of the plates.

In Japan three notable experts, Ishizawa Masao and Kondo Ichitaro of the Ueno Museum staff, and Adachi Toyohisa of the printing firm, inspected many of the prints shown here for authenticity and helped me weed out certain fakes whose inclusion would have been embarrassing. I thank them. Finally, I want to express my appreciation of the way in which Ogimi Kaoru and Kuwata Masakazu have designed and laid out this book and the patience with which Meredith Weatherby has edited it, by air mail, across many miles of ocean.

9. MASANOBU: *Lady Murasaki.*
See note, page 257

Section
I:
THE EARLY PRINTS

THE AESTHETIC heart of any ukiyo-e collection must be found among prints like those presented in this section, for here the basic spirit of ukiyo-e asserts itself, and without an appreciation of these early prints one can never savor the essence of this enchanting art form. Fortunately, a fair number of these are in circulation today, and some of the finest are not prohibitively expensive, being within the reach of any collector.

Technically, ukiyo-e developed from book illustrations printed by means of carved wood blocks, and it was from such a page that Print 257 was taken. As the artists' skill grew, it was easy to drop the text from the book and offer albums composed solely of black-and-white prints. These were the sumizuri-e which were discussed earlier, and four of the most pleasing are shown as Prints 17–20. Some of the finest ukiyo-e appeared originally in such albums, and many sheets are still available at reasonable prices. Print 18 was among the first ukiyo-e I purchased, and it remains one of my favorites, a storybook thing whose joyous, saucy line catches the spirit of this art. If I were interested in the essence of ukiyo-e and could afford only one print, I would not select either a Harunobu or a Sharaku, for I might study such a color print without ever discovering what it was that made ukiyo-e great; unquestionably I would choose a sumizuri-e, say Moronobu's masterwork, Print 11, for then I would see constantly before me the essence of the art: its singing line.

From album sheets bound together to summarize a popular story or erotic incident it was an easy jump to single sheets which stood forth as their own justification, and it is these towering sheets that are the glory of ukiyo-e. Print 15 is a classic example and one of the high points of this collection. The two Kiyomasus, Prints 21 and 23, show what vigor could be obtained. Such sheets are excessively rare; fortunately, they are not essential to a basic understanding of ukiyo-e, for one can also learn the lessons they teach through the lesser album sheets. But as artistic units, the swirling Kaigetsudo women, standing aloof and solemn against their white and formless background, are wonderfully pleasing. Furthermore, they epitomize the early period, during which the ukiyo-e artists did their strongest work.

The next step in the development of ukiyo-e was inevitable. Print 16 shows what gratifying results were achieved when one of the massive sumizuri-e was turned over to a worker who daubed it with primitive colors; legend says that the original artist rarely bothered with this brushwork, leaving it to someone else, preferably elderly women. The red lead, called *tan,* was especially effective, and prints which featured it were popularly called tan-e. Prints 16, 22, and 25 feature *tan.*

The next development was a multiple one, consisting of three distinct parts, and which came first is difficult to say, but Print 28 is an example of what occurred. First, the color palette was broadened; *tan* was dropped and the artist was free to choose from more than a dozen different colors. In this case Kiyomasu used red, pink, yellow, khaki, and smoky gray. Second, gold dust was sprinkled over selected areas, here the foremost boat, in order to heighten visual appeal. Third, urushi, a lacquer-like substance often made of black ink and cheap glue, was daubed over areas that were required to stand out, in this

小刺乱れ肌や筆の二輪咲

10. TOYONOBU:
Girl after Bath.
Page 262

case the woman's coat, lending them a scintillating brilliance. Adding these three innovations together, one gets the famous urushi-e, "lacquer print." Sometimes, as in Print 24, the urushi was not mixed with black but appeared as a thin, glistening, translucent fixative. The collector who loves urushi-e is fortunate, for many of these prints are in circulation at modest prices. I find them delightful, small in size, sometimes gaudy in execution, but always evocative of the beginning days of the art. In many ways they resemble primitive Italian paintings depicting the lives of lesser saints: they are awkward, flamboyant, and tenderly reverent. Urushi-e depict not saints but actors, as in the case of Prints 24, 26, and 27, and I commend these affectionate little prints most warmly, for one can often derive from them a personal pleasure that larger, more polished prints do not generate. As we saw in the case of tan-e, the three components – the colors, the gold dust, and the urushi – were applied by hand and pretty surely not by the artist himself.

The next development was a crucial one, and from it grew the later perfections of ukiyo-e. Print 73 was not colored by hand. It was printed exclusively from blocks, the black outline having been obtained from the key block, the rose-red from a second and completely separate block, and the apple-green from a third. This innovation of printing colors from blocks rather than applying them by hand produced startling results. At first, however, its use was restricted to two colors only, rose-red and apple-green, and since the former is known as beni, the two-color prints are called benizuri-e, "red-printed pictures." Why these particular colors were chosen no one knows, nor are we sure what artist first used them, although there is a suspicion that Masanobu in some work like Print 51 may have done so. It is an extraordinary fact, possibly unmatched in art history, that for more than a decade a group of vivid, experimental, and strong-minded artists were willing to confine their palette largely to these two apparently haphazardly selected colors. On the other hand, some of the choicest ukiyo-e resulted from this discipline, for when one's eye becomes accustomed to rose-red and apple-green one derives from their skillful juxtaposition an entire range of color values. In this book Prints 73 and 81, among others, illustrate what was accomplished in this form, but since the beni used fades rapidly when exposed to light, their original impact is today somewhat diminished.

I should now like to make one simple recommendation to anyone wishing to start an ukiyo-e collection: acquire an album sheet, an urushi-e, and a benizuri-e. This can be done at no great expense, although it may take several years to find appropriate bargains. With good examples of these three beginning types, the collector can add what he will, or avoid what he does not like, yet always be sure of having a selection founded upon the artistic principles that made ukiyo-e originally popular in the streets of Edo and later treasured in the art galleries of the world.

More tardily than one might have expected, ukiyo-e artists mastered the technique of keeping three different colors in register, as demonstrated in the print on this page where blue joins red and green. In Print 85 gray was the third color, and in others yellow was added with great effectiveness. Obviously, at this point the ukiyo-e artists were aesthetically ready to make prints utilizing the full color spectrum; but they had to wait a while for the perfection of some device that would insure perfect registry of their blocks through eight or ten different printings, for this simple trick of printing with many colors was not yet forthcoming.

For the time being the artists experimented with a technique that proved to be somewhat less than successful. In Print 98 the artist has used three basic colors; red, green, and blue. But for the actor's outer robe he has also experimented with this new technical development: he has printed blue over red in an attempt to produce purple. But the result is rather muddy, for the two components have remained separated and have not blended. Similarly, in Print 85 red has been overprinted by gray in a most unsatisfactory attempt to achieve purple. The collection contains several dozen prints showing the basic failure of this particular experiment. Blue and yellow should yield green, but only when mixed; when one is merely superimposed upon the other the colors remain blue and yellow and the result is muddy. But these prints do prove that the buying public was hungry for more color and that the artists were eager to produce it; in this technical impasse the era of the early prints ended.

These prints are also interesting for other technical reasons. Print 43 has been reproduced as large as possible to show how the early ukiyo-e artists were fond of experimenting with European perspective, which they studied in pictures introduced by the Dutch at Nagasaki. Such perspective prints are called uki-e, loosely "bird's-eye pictures," and it is noteworthy that Japanese artists rejected what we think of as accurate perspective because they preferred the tilting Asiatic convention, as shown in Prints 9 and 52, which produced pictures that were much more pleasing to them.

Print 50 shows how Japanese artists used wood blocks to achieve the same effect the Chinese had obtained from stone rubbings, and the Japanese name for such prints, ishizuri-e, "stone-printed pictures," indicates this derivation. Print 36, of which more later, shows how pleasing such prints can be.

When the smaller prints known as hoso-e, "narrow pictures," became popular, publishers found it convenient and no doubt profitable to carve onto one large block three related pictures, with each one separately titled and signed. To rich patrons they sold the entire unsevered triptych, as shown in Prints 86–91. A few such complete triptychs have come down to us, and they are rare and treasured. More often, the canny publisher cut his big sheets into three separate items for quicker sale to his poorer customers; but in later years collectors were occasionally able to reassemble these cut triptychs. Thus the three perfectly matched single sheets, Prints 93–95, must have come from the same original big sheet; but more often collectors have stumbled upon three different prints from three different original sources, as seems to have been the case with Prints 68–70.

At the same time, publishers occasionally provided their artists with choice large pieces of wood upon which single designs rather than triptychs were cut, and these again are treasured items. Prints 81 and 92 were carved upon such oversized blocks, the latter being instructive in that it shows how poorly the artists usually designed such large areas, being more at home in smaller compositions.

On the other hand, these artists exhibited the most extraordinary skill in designing tall, narrow prints. They varied from fairly wide prints like 33, through standard sizes like Prints 76 and 83, and on to the culmination of this branch of the art, the extremely narrow print shown on the facing page. The wider prints were known as kakemono-e, "hanging-thing pictures," and the narrowest as hashira-e, "pillar pictures."

In leaving these early prints one must not forget that when ukiyo-e reached Europe to dazzle and instruct the impressionists and to startle the general art world, it was not these early prints that did the work; the international fame of ukiyo-e has always rested on the later color prints. Nevertheless, many collectors find their greatest joy in these earlier prints, a choice that is neither affectation nor antiquarianism. These early prints are bold, vigorous in design, excellently drawn. They are authentic Japanese art from one of the great periods of Japanese history and as such are treasured.

The Beginnings :

FIVE OF the handsome sumizuri-e which mark the beginnings of ukiyo-e are shown in this first group. Print 12, one of the most interesting, had small areas of hand-applied color, and is thus disqualified as a pure sumizuri-e, but since the color was probably added later and has been deleted from the present reproduction, it is not altogether inappropriate to include the print here.

The basic characteristic of these early prints, a flowing line which is used in varied ways to express emotion on the one hand and to enclose interesting spatial areas on the other, is nowhere better exemplified than in Print 11, where the bold, black line fairly sings. The movement of the drapery of the mosquito net from lower left to upper right, repeated in the two female figures, is Moronobu at his best, and although the print is florid in design and therefore not typically Japanese, wherever the line goes it is of itself interesting.

In the original print the blacks are of an intensity that is difficult to reproduce by means of printer's ink. They create such powerful contrasts that the addition of what we commonly call color – red or green, for example – would merely detract from the dynamic quality of the print. Its color, as in the case of all really fine sumizuri-e, already exists in its blacks, and no other is needed.

Print 12 is one of the most joyous works in this book. It shows a typical highway scene of a two-sworded samurai hiking to the right, having just passed a group of five chattering ladies who, with their two servants, are walking to the left. There is the customary Moronobu interplay between the groups, while in the background appear the fragments of landscape, artistically positioned and artfully drawn, that set the stage. There are eight or ten such Moronobu sheets that combine rural travel and impressionistic landscape, and they have always seemed to me almost the essence of the Genroku period. They are intensely Japanese: simple, poetic, handsomely achieved, and evocative of nature. I enjoy them enormously and wish I had others besides this one.

The artist who did Print 13 is a fascinating person; for nearly three centuries he had no artistic existence, his prints having been assigned totally to Moronobu. Then the Japanese expert on erotic prints, Shibui Kiyoshi, noticed that on many prints hitherto ascribed to Moronobu appeared the character Mura or the inconspicuous word Jihei, and working upon this clue he began to resurrect the artistic personality of Sugimura Jihei and to take from Moronobu many prints that were once ascribed to him. This collection contains two additional Sugimura prints of high quality, the black line being especially good, but they are too erotic in content to be reproduced. I regret this, for they demonstrate what artistic effects can be achieved by this singing line.

Single-page prints by Sukenobu are excessively rare. I know of less than a dozen subjects and it is only by accident that one happens to appear in this collection. I stumbled upon it one day in a folio in London, and although a more appropriate subject for this most successful early portrayer of young women would have been one of his traditional beauties, the print shown here is a fine Sukenobu and one of the rarities of the collection.

As for Print 15, I have already discussed the problem of finding a Kaigetsudo, and here I should like merely to stress again that the powerful blacks of this early period provide their own color. A fair portion of the great Kaigetsudo prints are handcolored, but like most collectors, I much prefer those that are not, and this print, somewhat more florid in design than I should have liked, demonstrates why color is not required. If one seeks a single print by which to summarize the impact of ukiyo-e, he customarily selects one of these large black-and-white figures of standing women. It is an appropriate choice and one with which I would not wish to argue.

II. MORONOBU: *Lovers with Attendant. Page 254*

12. MORONOBU: *Groups of Travelers.* Page 254

13. SUGIMURA: *Lovers by a Screen.* Page 254

大和繪師
西川祐信筆

14. SUKENOBU: *Hairdressing.* Page 255

15. KAIGETSUDO DOHAN: *Courtesan.* Page 255

Kiyonobu
Kiyomasu :

ALL BOOKS on ukiyo-e face the perplexing problem of how to explain the relationships between the two or three different men who called themselves Kiyonobu and the two different men who used the name Kiyomasu. I have argued the problem elsewhere, and here I should like merely to point out some of the major types of prints produced by these excellent artists of the Torii school. They did sumizuri-e albums, some of whose pages are shown in Prints 2 and 17–20. They did marvelous big prints, both as sumizuri-e, Prints 21 and 23, and as tan-e, shown opposite. They did hundreds of hoso-e, some in tan-e form, like Prints 22 and 25, but most in urushi-e, like Prints 27 and 28. And at the end of their careers they issued many benizuri-e, of which this collection has numerous examples; none are reproduced because it was thought that readers would prefer to see the rarer urushi-e.

Were an informed collector given his choice of all the prints contained in this book, he would probably select, in this order: first, the print opposite; second, the Kaigetsudo woman, Print 15; third, the Kiyonaga night diptych, Prints 145–46; and fourth, the rare Choki snow scene, Print 174. Certainly, the big tan-e facing this page is one of the finest prints of its kind; when the Japanese publishers of the *Ukiyo-e taisei,* which reproduces over five thousand prints for quick reference, sought a distinctive cover for their series, one which would remind the public of the power of ukiyo-e, they chose this Kiyomasu, and as a result it has become the most widely known of all tan-e. It is also a glowing indication of why collectors have always prized Torii art. The artistic merits of this print are great: the position of the actor, his balance, the counter-poising of the umbrella, and the harsh modeling of the drapery combine to produce a most striking design.

If Print 16 is a gem among the larger sized prints, Print 24 is a no less noble example of what can be achieved within the narrower measure of the hoso-e. This print seems to me extraordinarily winning in its design — perfect even in the placement of the title and signature — color and general effect.

Prints 29 and 31 are of importance in the study of ukiyo-e because they effectively illustrate the two basic characteristics of Torii art. The first is known as hyotan-ashi, "gourd legs," a convention of drawing legs in the shape of gourds to produce an illusion of strength, which before long was also applied to arms. And the second was mimizu-gaki, "worm drawing," whereby the design was achieved through using lines that looked like wiggling worms, thereby lending a sense of frenzy and dramatic chaos to the print. These two conventions help explain why Torii prints caught so effectively the spirit of the Kabuki theater, which in many of its plays specializes in frenzy and rude power.

Prints 28, 30, and 32 are by Kiyomasu II, and their presence in this book requires something of an apology. Earlier I wrote of this strange artist: "Kiyomasu II is responsible for some of the most boring art in ukiyo-e, disasters consisting of one actor standing and one seated." I still think the bulk of his work boring, but Print 28 shows what he could accomplish when he avoided stock design; so far as I know this is his masterpiece. Print 30 is one of the best of his standard subjects. And as for Print 32, I have actually grown fond of it, for it epitomizes the wiggling-worm school of art and I believe the casual reader will also discover a certain frenzied joy in its lively design. One of the pleasures of art is constant re-evaluation of what constitutes merit, and ukiyo-e provides fascinating subject matter for such review. The possessor of a print is forced to decide what he thinks about it, and in arriving at conclusions his artistic sensibilities are sharpened, which is a very good thing.

16. KIYOMASU I: *Nakamura Senya in the Role of Tokonatsu.* Page 256

17. KIYOMASU I: *Goro, Shosho, and Asahina.* Page 256

18. KIYOMASU I: *Saint Narukami and Princess Taema.* Page 256

19. KIYOMASU I: *Agemaki and Sukeroku.* Page 256

20. KIYOMASU I: *Fuwa and Okuni.* Page 256

21. KIYOMASU I: *Warriors in Combat.* Page 256

りくう母新蔵
市川ゑん十郎
ふり源氏に

22. KIYOMASU I: *Takie, Shingoro, and Danjuro.* Page 256

23. KIYOMASU I: *Heikuro and Takesaburo*. Page 256

24. KIYONOBU I: *Fujimura Handayu.* Page 255

25. KIYOMASU I: *Courtesan*. Page 256

26. KIYONOBU II: *Fujimura Handayu.* Page 257

27. KIYONOBU II: *Segawa Kikunojo.* Page 257

44

28. KIYOMASU II: *The Maiden Tamamushi*. Page 257

30. KIYOMASU II: *Danjuro and Hiroji.* Page 257

29. KIYONOBU I: *Kantaro and Takenojo.* Page 255

32. KIYOMASU II: *Segawa Kikujiro.* Page 257

31. KIYONOBU I: *Ichikawa Kuzo.* Page 255

Masanobu :

MY FAVORITE ukiyo-e artist is Masanobu, which accounts for the fact that I have here allotted more prints to him than to any other. He is important because he arrived on the scene when ukiyo-e was in danger of petrifaction. Men like Moronobu, Kiyonobu, the Kaigetsudo artists, and Sukenobu had given the art a vigorous initial impulse, but as their fires died down, prints fell into ritualistic patterns of color, design, and content. It was mainly Masanobu who blasted the art loose from such conventionalism and launched it upon vigorous new paths.

The six hoso-e shown together, Prints 46–51, fairly well summarize his art experience. Starting with Prints 48 and 49, he issues urushi-e that are as muscle-bound as anything done by the Torii school. The design is formal, the drawing harsh, and the coloring heavy. But in Print 46 he gives us a handsomely designed little print in black and gray; while in Print 47 he offers one of the loveliest urushi-e that was ever issued. I am sorry that it could not be shown in color, for it is a gem. In Print 50 he experiments with ishizuri-e, and late in life he comes up with many perfect benizuri-e, as for example, Print 51.

He is supposed to have initiated the following new ideas that revitalized ukiyo-e: urushi-e; gold dust; mica grounds; European perspective; the triptych form; the tall upright print, narrower than the size used by the Kaigetsudo and Torii masters; the narrow pillar print; the ishizuri-e; the landscape print; the embossing which Harunobu later used with such success; the selection of rose-red and apple-green as basic colors for benizuri-e; and the printing of all colors from blocks. Most of these supposed Masanobu inventions are illustrated in the nineteen prints shown here.

It is appropriate that the emotional highpoint of this collection is found in the sadly worn pair of Masanobu prints appearing as 39–40. They show the nonpareil Sukeroku and, possibly, his love Agemaki. I do not feel capable of describing what Sukeroku means to a Japanese theater audience when he swaggers down the hanamichi, defying the authorities by wearing about his head a knotted scarf of purple, a color forbidden to commoners. I have heard Japanese men whistle and shout when he appeared; women have wept. These prints are in such wasted condition that normally I would not have kept them; but they are more than prints: they are the finest extant portrayals of the Robin Hood of Japan and his love and they symbolize the spirit of Masanobu. Other recollections of the Sukeroku drama are found in Prints 81, 123, and 133–35.

The famous design which appears here as Print 36 presents a difficult problem. Most European and American critics have always accepted it as a brilliant example of Masanobu's skill, and in Hillier's book on ukiyo-e it is accorded a place of honor. Japanese critics and Dr. Lane, however, condemn it as a much later issue, an opinion in which I concur. It is reproduced to show fellow collectors that sooner or later every collector makes major mistakes.

Print 38 is one of the most distinguished in this book insofar as history is concerned. The print occurs in four distinct versions: as a much wider kake-mono-e showing the full body of the actor; in the same form but with a marked split running from the left heel of the actor up to his left shoulder; the form shown here, which was made from the original block after it had been neatly sawed down the split; and in a completely recut version. The first and last versions can be seen in the Chicago catalogue, Masanobu 95 and 96. The second can be seen at Boston. The present copy, which has been widely reproduced, is the best extant of the third version and is well known for that reason. Finally, to show what a canny publisher and artist Masanobu was, he redid the whole print with all new blocks and made it into a benizuri-e, as shown in the *Ukiyo-e taisei,* III, 106.

33. MASANOBU: *Young Samurai on Horseback.* Page 257

34. MASANOBU: *Cutting up the Flute for Firewood.* Page 257

35. MASANOBU: *Lovers Playing Checkers.* Page 258

36. "MASANOBU" (19th–century imitation): *Courtesan Walking.* Page 258

37. MASANOBU: *Girl with Mirror*. Page 258

38. MASANOBU: *Onoe Kikugoro*.
Page 258

39. MASANOBU: *Ichikawa Ebizo*. Page 258   40. MASANOBU: *Courtesan Walking*. Page 258

41. MASANOBU: *Sanokawa Ichimatsu with Puppet.* Page 258

42. MASANOBU: *Courtesan with Love Letter.* Page 258

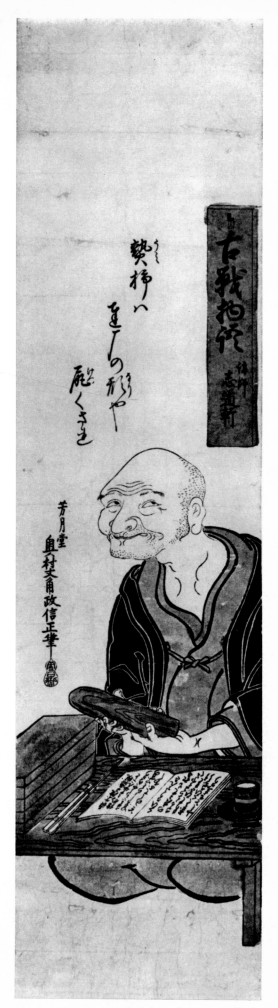

44. MASANOBU: *Sanokawa Ichimatsu.*

Page 258

45. MASANOBU: *Shidoken the Storyteller.*

Page 259

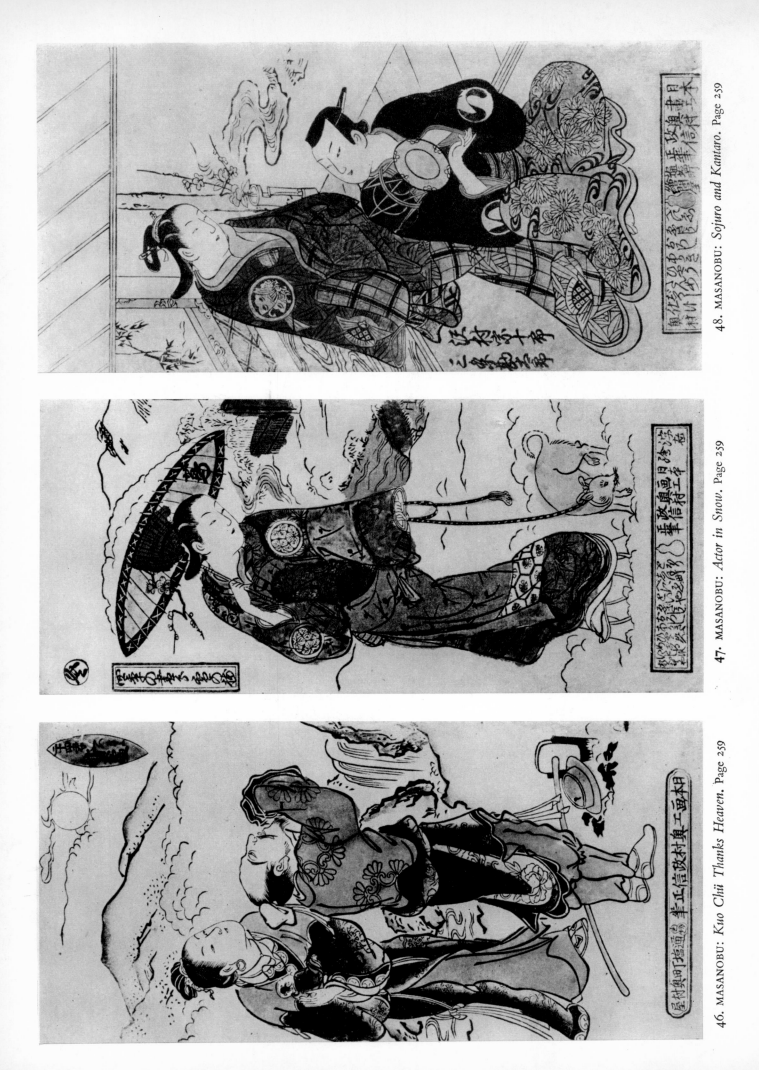

48. MASANOBU: *Sojuro and Kantaro*. Page 259

47. MASANOBU: *Actor in Snow*. Page 259

46. MASANOBU: *Kuo Chü Thanks Heaven*. Page 259

51. MASANOBU: *Sanokawa Ichimatsu.* Page 259

50. MASANOBU: *Hsü and Ch'ao Resist Temptation.*
Page 259

49. MASANOBU: *Ichikawa Monnosuke.* Page 259

Minor
Masters:

IN EVERY period of ukiyo-e, side by side with the acknowledged masters there flourished a small, lively group of capable workmen who turned out minor prints of persuasive charm. In the early period, among the more commendable were those who appear in this next group, and a collector who could gather together one or two good examples of the work of these men could well forgo the most expensive prints, for here he will find most of the beauties of ukiyo-e capably exemplified.

The print reproduced in color on the opposite page is an appropriate opening to such a section, for its author is not known. Up to now it has always been catalogued as a Masanobu, and it compares favorably with his best urushi-e; but Japanese critics doubt that it was done by that master. Some think it might be by Toshinobu; others question that attribution. I feel that it is close to Masanobu; Dr. Lane suggests that it may be the work of another, unknown master, working after the manner of Toshinobu. At any rate, it is a perfect little gem of a print, colorful, musical, flecked with gold and sparkling with urushi. The reader is invited to make his own attribution.

As a result of some happy accident, the collection is unusually strong in urushi-e by Toshinobu, and the four designs chosen here to fill two pages, Prints 57–60, were selected purposely to show as many characteristics of this fine print-maker as possible. He loves strong color, clashing designs, and movement. For many years he was supposed to have been the son of Masanobu, but firm dates recently established for some of his prints require Masanobu to have been ten when he sired him, after which Toshinobu began designing polished work at the age of nine months, both of which events seem unlikely. Whoever he was, he is most congenial and his prints are minor lyrics.

Shigenaga, represented here by Prints 61–64, is a focal figure in ukiyo-e because, with his harsh angular style, he produced many prints that strike us with their power; furthermore, he taught a host of successors on whom much of the subsequent glory of ukiyo-e rests: Toyonobu, Harunobu, Koryusai, Shigemasa, and Toyoharu, the latter of whom taught Toyohiro, who taught Hiroshige. The two prints of Shoki the Demon Queller present an interesting problem in that in the Western world such prints have always commanded high prices; in Japan they sell for little, for they were originally painted as good-luck charms to ward off evil and are thus not counted true art objects.

Academically, the highlight of this section is the pair of Mangetsudo triptychs, Prints 65–70. They were once a part of the Hayashi collection, became separated, and are here published together for the first time. They are important because they provide a summary of this little-known man's work. In their *Japanese Colour Prints*, Binyon and Sexton use as the first color plate a handsome benizuri-e by Mangetsudo; otherwise we do not know much of his accomplishment. Prints 65–67 show him to have been weak in design, fond of clutter, and unable to achieve a unified effect. Prints 68–70 show just the opposite, for the gothic-style design is unusually effective, and the black line by which it was achieved is both strong and rhythmic. But this very excellence raises serious suspicions, for this print exists in the Stoclet collection in Brussels, with marked variations in design, fully signed by Masanobu. It can be seen in the Happer catalogue. Other versions have been found signed Hogetsudo and Kogetsudo, so that Dr. Lane raises the interesting query: "Is it not possible that Mangetsudo might be only a name used by a pirate publisher when reissuing Masanobu's work, and not an artist at all?"

52. STYLE OF TOSHINOBU: *Girl Playing Samisen.* Page 260

54. KIYOTOMO: *Yamamoto Koheiji with Puppet.* Page 259

53. WAGEN: *Yamashita Kinsaku.* Page 259

55. TERUSHIGE: *Mangiku and Danjuro.* Page 260

56. KIYOTADA: *Osome and Hisamatsu.* Page 260

58. TOSHINOBU: *Sanjo Kantaro*. Page 260

57. TOSHINOBU: *Ichikawa Gennosuke*. Page 260

60. TOSHINOBU: *Sanjo Kantaro.* Page 260

59. TOSHINOBU: *Monnosuke and Wakano.* Page 260

峯あまた
さえて
観賢よ
まれ
雲田里
なびき
たつる
うすび孫

あくま
悪魔
もらふて
家治
春

61. SHIGENAGA: *Descending Geese at Katata.* Page 260

62. SHIGENAGA: *Shoki the Demon-queller.* Page 261

63. SHIGENAGA: *Shoki the Demon-queller.* Page 261

64. SHIGENAGA: *Sanokawa Ichimatsu.*
Page 261

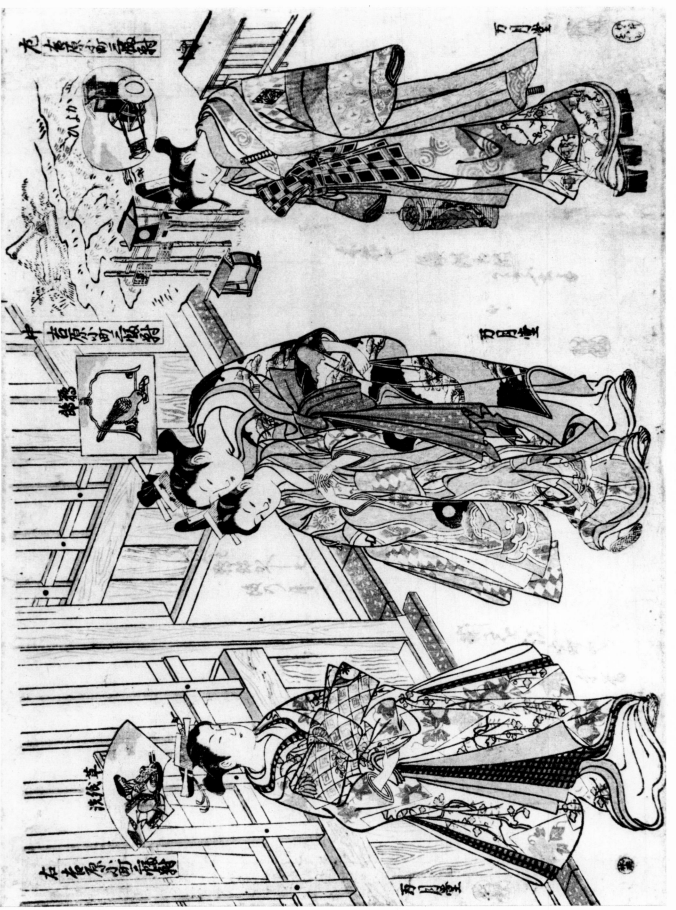

65–67. MANGETSUDO: *Yoshiwara Komachi*. Page 261

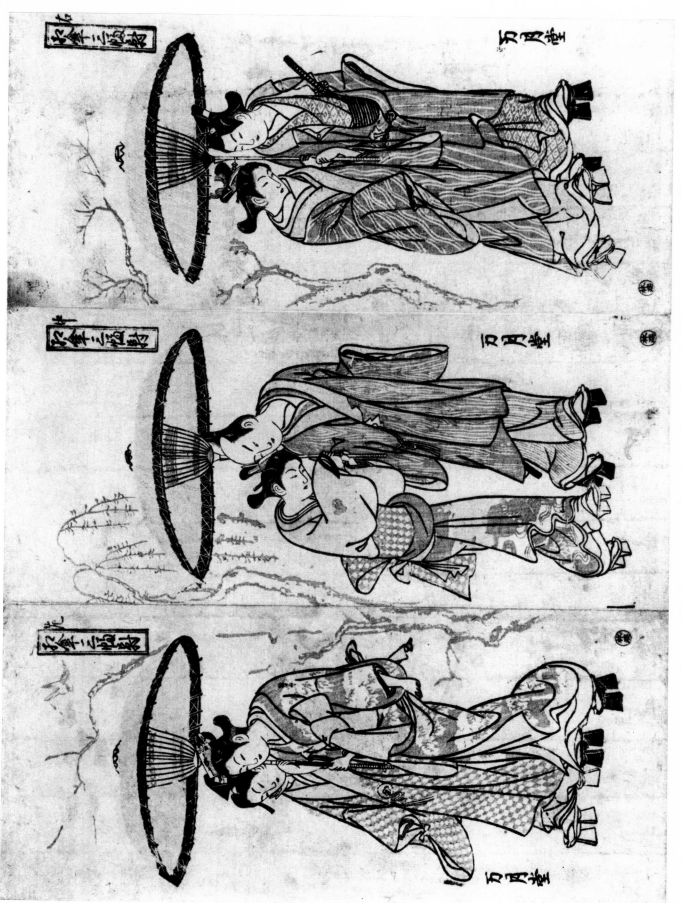

68–70. MANGETSUDO: *Lovers under Umbrellas.* Page 261

72. SHIGENOBU: *Girl Selling Flowers*. Page 261

71. SHIGENOBU: *Ichikawa Ebizo*. Page 261

The End of an Epoch :

ONE OF the more interesting problems of ukiyo-e concerns the authorship of the two prints on the facing page. They are clearly signed as having been done by Shigenobu, and a fairly large number of other prints similarly signed exhibit identical characteristics, so that there can be little doubt that we are dealing with one man who issued a consistent body of work. Some of his awkward and angular compositions are pleasing and demonstrate that Shigenobu, whoever he was, had an interesting artistic personality. He worked only a brief time, then vanished, and it has always irritated critics that one so important should have no secure place in the history of ukiyo-e.

At the same time another mystery perplexed the critics: Why did Toyonobu, the artist whose highly skilled work follows, leave no early prints showing his apprenticeship? By a process of logic a clever scholar decided that both of these irritating gaps could be filled by one simple theory: Shigenobu was the name used by Toyonobu when the latter was beginning; and elsewhere I confidently reported this rather clever deduction, as did most catalogues and auction lists.

Now we are not so sure. There seem to be pretty substantial stylistic differences between the work of the two men, enough at least to counsel hesitancy; the reader is invited to compare the Shigenobus with the Toyonobus. At the same time he should make his own estimate as to which of two very popular prints borrowed from the other: Prints 60 and 72.

Print 73 is one of historic importance, and when Frank Lloyd Wright owned it he described it in the following terms, not conspicuous for their temperance: "The noblest design of the primitive period in flawless state and one of the noblest Japanese prints of any kind in existence. A triumph over the limitations of the two-color print. . . . Certainly one of the most important things that has appeared." This print was among the first to show American collectors how brilliant a benizuri-e could be when its original colors were preserved, and it is reproduced here in color to reiterate that fact.

Print 81 is perhaps even more treasured, faded though it is, for it is a handsome design, and no other copy is known to the author, although others probably exist without having been published. Print 82 is being published with a special purpose in mind. In the early 1900's the American market was flooded with adroit counterfeits of benizuri-hoso-e, and they were so well done that many of them got into museum collections. The present collection appears to contain several. For some years Print 82, which also reached America via Frank Lloyd Wright, was suspected of belonging to this notorious group of forgeries, and some critics challenged it. About thirty years ago the print was sent to Japan for authentication, and critics there not only accepted it but proudly reproduced it in *Ukiyo-e taika shusei* as an example of Toyonobu at his best. Even so, I had doubts about its validity and took the print with me to Japan in 1957, where a new generation of scholars studied it and found it identical with the great Toyonobus now housed in the Ueno Museum.

The last two color plates, Prints 93–95 and 98, show the excellent work being done on the eve of full-color printing. The first is a standard-type benizuri-e to which a striking blue has been added, yielding a curious color harmony indeed, but one not inappropriate to the subject matter. Print 98 merits careful study, for as noted earlier, it utilizes three basic colors and achieves a fourth by overprinting. Technically, it marks the end of the early-print epoch.

73. TOYONOBU: *Ichimatsu and Kikugoro.* Page 262

74. TOYONOBU: *Ichimatsu and Kikunojo.* Page 262

75. TOYONOBU: *Maiden.* Page 262

76. TOYONOBU: *Girl Holding Umbrella.* Page 262

77. TOYONOBU: *Girl with Flowers.*
Page 262

78. TOYONOBU: *Girl with Umbrella.*
Page 262

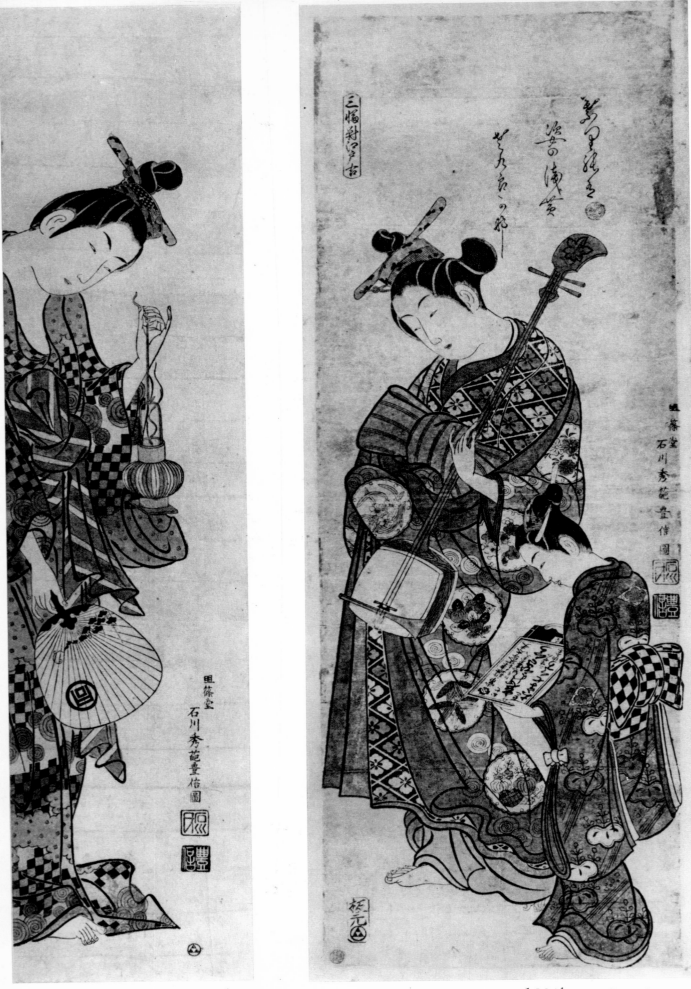

79. TOYONOBU: *Girl with Lantern and Fan.*
Page 262

80. TOYONOBU: *Courtesan and Maidservant.* Page 262

82. TOYONOBU: *Young Man with Flower-cart.* Page 262

眠篠堂

石川秀葩豊信圖

81. TOYONOBU: *Ichimatsu and Kikugoro with Puppets.* Page 262

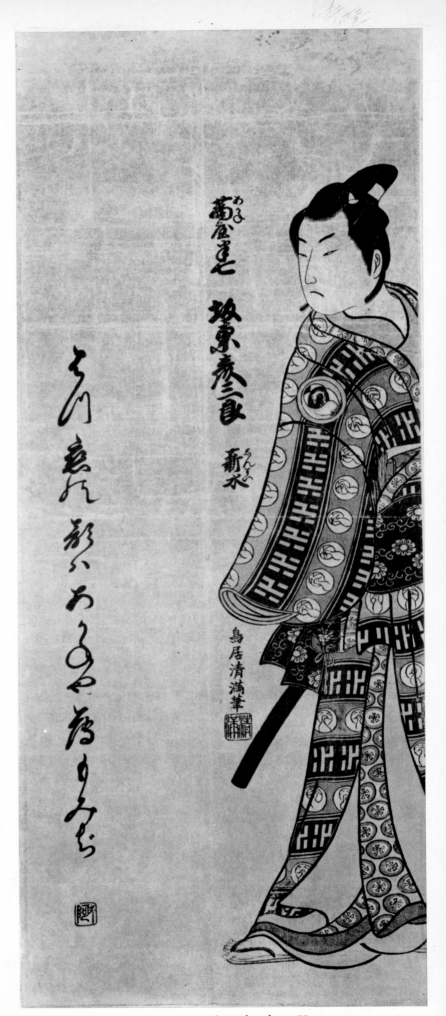

83. KIYOSHIGE: *Sanokawa Ichimatsu.*
Page 262

84. KIYOMITSU: *Bando Hikosaburo II.* Page 263

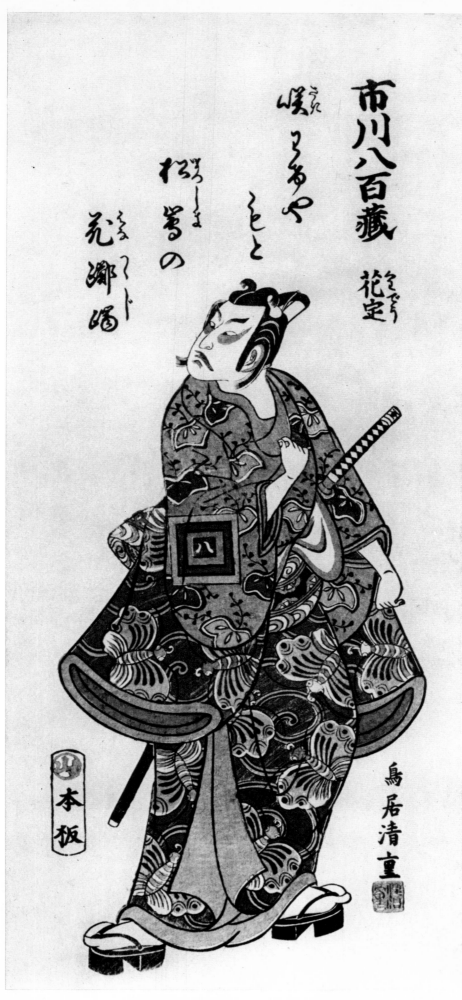

85. KIYOSHIGE: *Ichikawa Yaozo.* Page 263

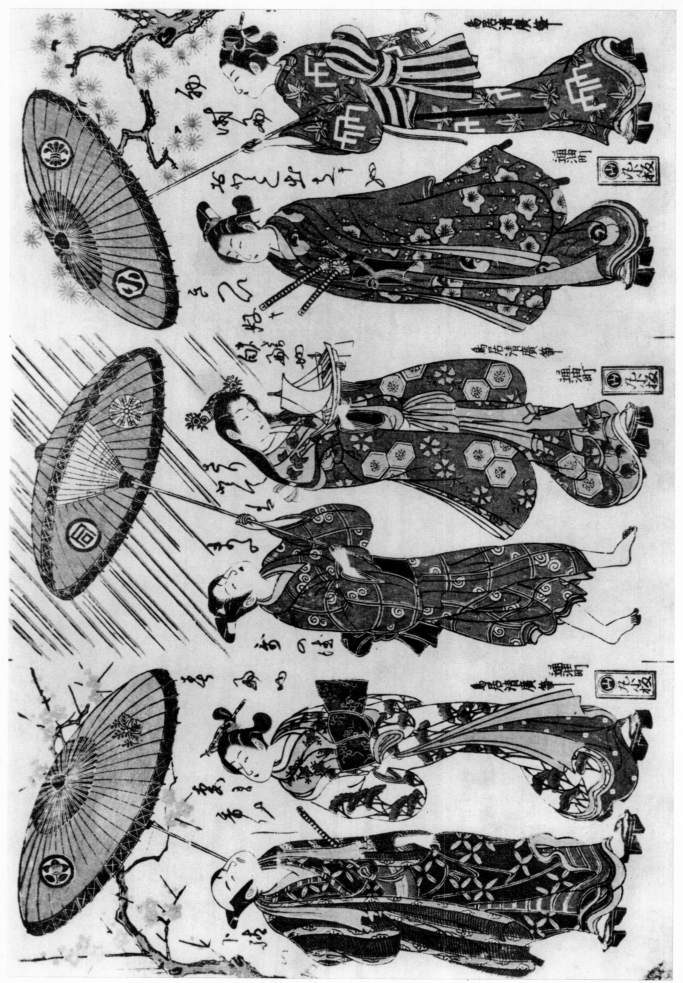

86–88. KIYOHIRO: *Couples under Umbrellas.* Page 263

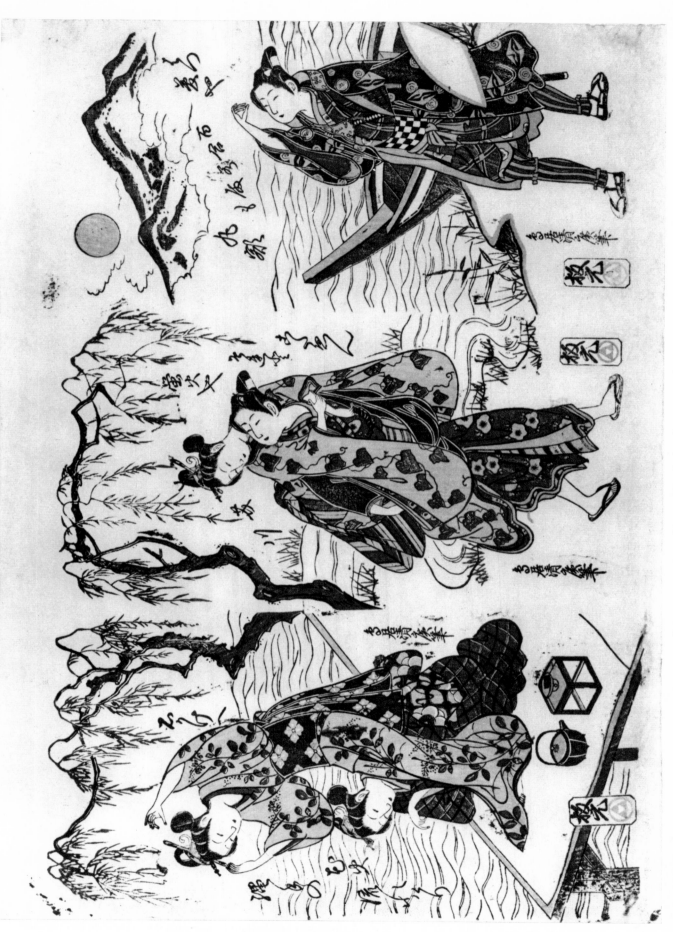

89–91. KIYOHIRO: *Young People by the Waterside*. Page 263

92. KIYOMITSU: *Maiden Dreaming.* Page 263

93–95. KIYOMITSU: *Dancers*. Page 263

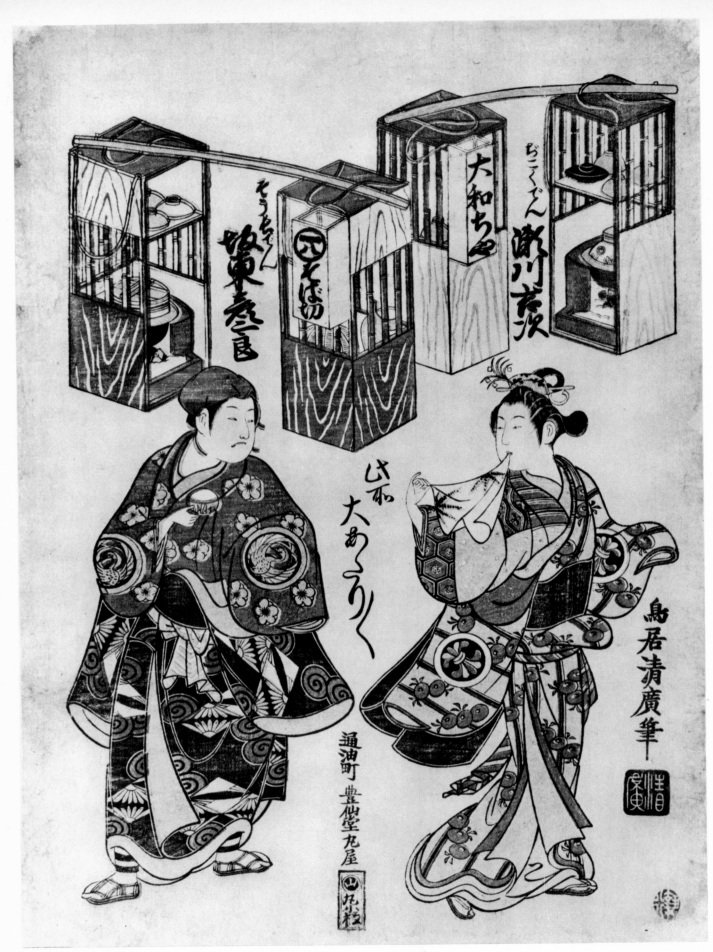

そうどん　坂東彦三郎

元そばきり

ごくびん　瀬川吉次

大和ちや

此所　大あくりく

島居清廣筆

通油町　豊仙堂丸屋

96. KIYOHIRO: *Hikosaburo and Kichiji.* Page 263

86

97. KIYOMITSU: *Ichikawa Ebizo.* Page 263

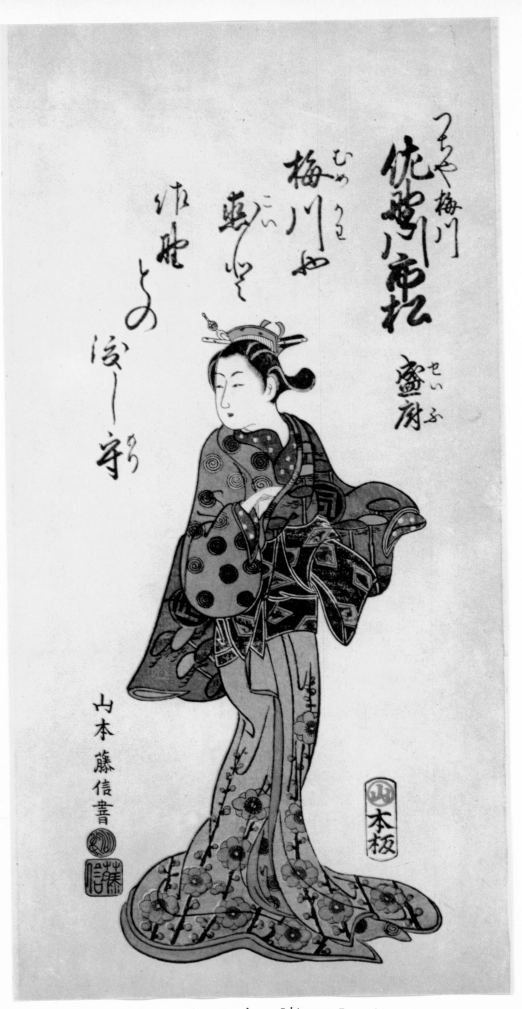

98. FUJINOBU: *Sanokawa Ichimatsu.* Page 263

Section 2:

THE FULL-COLOR PRINTS

THE FLOWERING of ukiyo-e was made possible by the invention and perfection of the kento, "aiming mark." At the lower right-hand corner of the wood block on which the basic design had been cut, the carver cut away the block to leave standing a right-angle stop, each leg being about one inch long. Obviously, if the corner of a sheet of paper to be printed were snugly jammed into that right angle, a rough kind of registry would be assured, and the exquisite color prints that began to be issued in 1765 were so printed.

But a moment's reflection will show that this right angle alone would not insure general registry. The paper could be snug in that corner but could still slip noticeably in other areas. To correct this, the carver next added, at the bottom edge of his wood block, an additional kento, this time a straight-line stop about an inch long. Now, if the corner of the paper is snug in the angle, and if the bottom edge is secure against the guide line, perfect register throughout the entire length and breadth of the paper is automatically insured. This method is clearly shown in Print 249, where the rough-edged paper was trimmed away smoothly at two points so that it would fit into the kento; so far as I can recall, this is the only print in the collection still showing such kento trimmings, for which reason they have been retained in our reproduction even at the risk of some injustice to the print itself.

To cite but one example of the remarkable effects the kento made possible, Print 141 is probably the most intricately designed work in this book. The paper is oversize and was printed about twenty times, yet the colors were kept in exact registry. And in exhibitionistic prints of a later date more than forty different colors were applied in sequence, yet thanks to the kento, all appeared in perfect registry. The shimmering beauty of the Japanese color print was thus assured.

We do not know who invented the kento. Four rather widely varied persons have been given credit: a fan manufacturer; a bookseller who was trying to force his way into the fan business; the publisher of a street guide who wanted to show routes in yellow; and that genial experimenter Okumura Masanobu. At any rate, by 1764 several technicians in Edo were technically prepared to experiment with the system, and artists were eager to see what could be accomplished with it.

In 1765, Harunobu began issuing prints utilizing up to a dozen different colors, with each in registry, and his work was so instantly appreciated that the further issuance of older-style prints such as hand-colored urushi-e and two-colored benizuri-e was unprofitable. In each of the remaining prints shown in this book the color was applied exclusively by means of wood blocks, except for certain experimental work in the 1950's, where paper blocks and sometimes glass were used instead of wood. Handcoloring was not to be seen again until its occasional use by present-day experimenters.

The prints that appear in this section represent the classic accomplishment of ukiyo-e. These are the subjects that have become most popular throughout the world, and critics have usually felt that upon this body of work will ultimately rest the artistic reputation of ukiyo-e. Certainly, these lovely scraps of paper present a kaleidoscope of color judiciously arranged insofar as the inter-

99. KORYUSAI: *Young Man with Hawk.* Page 266

relations of color harmonies are concerned; and from these prints the observer can deduce the second and third artistic lessons to be derived from ukiyo-e, the first having been the use of line.

Japanese prints demonstrate how adroitly the flat space represented by a sheet of paper can be broken up into pleasing patterns. The placement of figures, the allocation of color, the addition of significant details, and the location of the artist's signature are apt to be harmonious, in good aesthetic taste, and pleasing to the eye. In austere, uncomplicated form Prints 101 and 140 are held to be masterpieces of design, each component being exactly in place. For more complicated patterns Prints 114 and 160 show typical Japanese dispositions of space, with some elements of the design off-balance, but all handsomely interrelated. As for the placement of heads within a portrait, it would be difficult to excel the examples provided by Prints 137 and 168. If the prints of this great era of ukiyo-e demonstrate anything, it is that in the design of flat spaces the Japanese woodblock artists were supreme.

The third artistic lesson of ukiyo-e is the artist's skill in using flat masses of color. Those of us brought up in the West have been trained to prize color which modulates form, as in the work of Michelangelo, or expresses plane relationships, as in the paintings of Cezanne. We are apt to forget that there was an earlier use for color: the application of flat areas across a solid design, so distributed as to yield pleasing results and so interrelated as to produce satisfying color harmonies. Duccio and Fra Angelico knew how to use flat areas of color in this manner, but the experiments of the High Renaissance outmoded their technique in favor of modulated colors which suggested the weight of the subjects to which the color was being applied. Today the earlier use of color has again become popular, and there are few art forms in which this style is more easily studied than ukiyo-e; for here flat areas of color are utilized to perfection. Print 173 is a color masterpiece; in more involved style, Print 177–78 shows how effective the use of flat color can be. The color plates of this section have been chosen with special attention to the wide variety of effects that can be achieved by the Japanese method.

The prints of this classical period fall into several distinct forms, and each has its own ingratiating charm. Easily identified are the chuban, "medium size" prints, which are small and almost square, by Harunobu, like Prints 101 and 102. Their restricted size invited the artist to keep his design simple and his use of color harmonious, for if he failed in either respect, his chuban was apt to be a disappointment. Kiyonaga also did a masterful group of chuban, but space could not be found for any of them, his larger prints being so much more effective.

The hashira-e, "pillar picture," flourished in this period, and the nine presented here, Prints 116–24, have been chosen from nearly a hundred in order to show different artists at work on representative themes. This is not an art form that I enjoy, but I do admire the adroitness with which artists contrived to fill the exacting dimensions, the example shown on this page being especially poetic.

Most of the artists represented in this classical period designed hoso-e, the short, narrow prints like the three Bunchos, Prints 125–27. Prints 128–29 demonstrate how pairs of hoso-e were sometimes combined to make a diptych, while Prints 133–35 demonstrate their effectiveness in triptych form. Hoso-e are not expensive and inch for inch undoubtedly represent the simplest and most rewarding way of augmenting a collection.

But the characteristic print-format of the classical period was the oban, "large size," and the first two offered in this book, Prints 114–15, are splendid examples. The paper is solid, with a life of its own; it is handsome to see and exciting to touch; it is a much more vital background for a work of art than either canvas or wood, which accounts for the fact that in the greatest prints it was so often left bare to sing its own song. I find the paper of an early oban one of the most lyric materials in art; in later stages of the classical period the paper grows thinner and loses some of its appeal, but in a print like 115 it is a magnificent substance and from its heavy, resilient body both color and line stand forth brilliantly. The oban size is particularly appropriate to the best Japanese papers; it is also of a proportion pleasing to most eyes; and it accommodates itself well to a wide variety of subject matter, being especially well adapted to portraiture. In fact, an oban on fine early paper is about as harmonious an art form as the world has produced; and in this book we are fortunate to be able to present some excellent examples. As in the case of hoso-e, pages have been set aside to demonstrate how effectively two oban unite to form a diptych, Prints 177–78 and 180–81, and how impressive they are when three are strung together in triptych form, Prints 153–55.

In subject matter the classical period continued several established types and developed others of its own, and it is the latter which give it character. For example, the three Bunchos already referred to, Prints 125–27, are in content nothing but an extension of the actor prints popular in the earlier urushi-e period. True, they are refined and the color is expertly block-printed rather than hand-applied, but spiritually the Bunchos are little different from the Kiyomasu II actor prints. Nor is there much change in content of the hashira-e. But in three areas, the classic oban did make significant new contributions. First, the two prints that combine to make the striking diptych of Prints 177–78 seem to me to present an idea of content that is radically different from what one finds in the early period. Six women and a boy, each differentiated and with her own personality, rest in a specific and developed landscape with living trees, atmosphere, and the smell of flowers. This is quite an advance over Print 92; the picture is more complete; the psychological content is more interesting; and the sense of the world is much more impressive.

The second major innovation of the oban in this period was the portrait of a big head that fairly filled the print. It has not yet been ascertained who initiated this striking new manner, but Prints 137–38 were among the earliest, just as the four Sharakus of Prints 167–70 were among the greatest. In the market today the so-called "big heads" command top attention after the Kaigetsudo women.

The third innovation was the portraiture of beautiful professional women, the bijin-e, "beautiful-woman pictures," Prints 183–86 being typical examples, although Prints 162 and 164 are perhaps the more pleasing.

Finally, the prints of this period are marked by two unusual technical experiments. When certain prints, such as 160 and 170, were finished, with all colors in place, a stencil was cut masking everything but the background. To the parts thus left exposed a workman applied, by brush and not by block, a mixture of glue and powdered mica. When dried, the mica ground scintillated with an iridescent quality, and today such prints are unusually attractive to collectors. Such use of mica was known in the early period, but we have come to think of it as one of the marks of the classical period. A second type of background, the vivid yellow seen in Print 182, was achieved by blocks used in the normal manner; such prints are also eagerly sought today, for not many were issued.

But despite the many technical advances in this period, the wealth of variation resulting from earlier experiments was now no more; after Print 98 and until we reach the moderns, all the succeeding prints are nishiki-e, "brocade pictures." All are polychrome prints.

Harunobu :

WITH THE prints of Harunobu, that sweet singer of youth and innocence, we enter the full-color period. Study of the frontispiece along with Prints 5, 100, 103–4, and 116 will show what Harunobu was able to accomplish when his printers had perfected their kento marks to permit the use of many different color blocks in succession. The diptych of Prints 103–4 was apparently printed from eight different blocks, including one which caused subtle ripples on the water to be raised in delicate gaufrage, embossing achieved by means of blind printing. Print 5, as we have seen, seems to have utilized about seven different color blocks. From now on there will be no return to earlier styles of print-making, so that Harunobu constitutes one of the great watersheds of the movement. After him, nothing could be the same.

Prints 101, 103–4, and 109 have special charm in that they remind us of one of the most exciting artistic finds of this century. In 1873 a British civil servant named A.M. Litchfield served in the city of Yokohama as crown prosecutor. When it came time for him to return to England, a Japanese admirer gave him as a going-away present a small album into which forty prints of no great apparent value had been pasted. Because the unknown donor had loved the work of Harunobu, all the prints were by that artist and in nearly flawless condition. They were kept in England largely unappreciated for thirty-seven years, by which time a craze for Japanese prints had been generated by exhibitions in Paris, and someone recalled the collection, which was to become famous as the Litchfield Album. It went on sale in 1910, where it was bid in by the London dealer Tregaskis for the sum of $1,500. Today it would unquestionably bring at least $25,000.

Tregaskis broke up the album, soaked off the near-perfect Harunobus, and began quietly to sell them singly at fairly high prices. Whenever one appeared at auction it was labeled "From the Litchfield Album," and this became one of the prized cachets of ukiyo-e history. The present collection has five of the Litchfield prints, and possibly a sixth; they are magnificent specimens of Harunobu at his best.

Print 107, while not in Harunobu's classic style, is important in that it stems from the Hayashi and Straus-Negbaur collections and is apparently the only copy known to critics who wrote on this artist, for it has been widely reproduced. A slightly different version exists, less appealing in execution, and other copies of this are known.

Print 112 presents a fascinating question in attribution. It is signed Harunobu and has always been attributed to him in catalogues and auction lists. The fine artist Shiba Kokan, famous later for his studies in Western art, worked for some years with Harunobu under the name Harushige. Later he confessed that many late Harunobus were actually his forgeries. For various stylistic reasons, both Dr. Lane and I attribute this delightful subject to Shiba Kokan.

Print 113 is not reproduced in color here because it has been done so often before; this must surely be one of the best-known ukiyo-e subjects, and in recent years its notoriety has been increased by the fact that it has become one of the most popular Christmas cards, the subdued coloring being especially attractive in juxtaposition to the snow. Of course, two versions of the print are known, and the variations between them are so substantial – different branches at the top, a black line outlining the snow on the umbrella, and a different obi pattern – that they must have been printed at least in part from different blocks. It is impossible to say which appeared first, but this has not affected adversely the acceptance of either version.

100. HARUNOBU: *Girl by Veranda.* Page 264

101. HARUNOBU: *Shoki Carrying Girl.* Page 264

102. HARUNOBU: *Princess Nyosan.* Page 264

103–4. HARUNOBU: *Two Girls by Stream.* Page 264

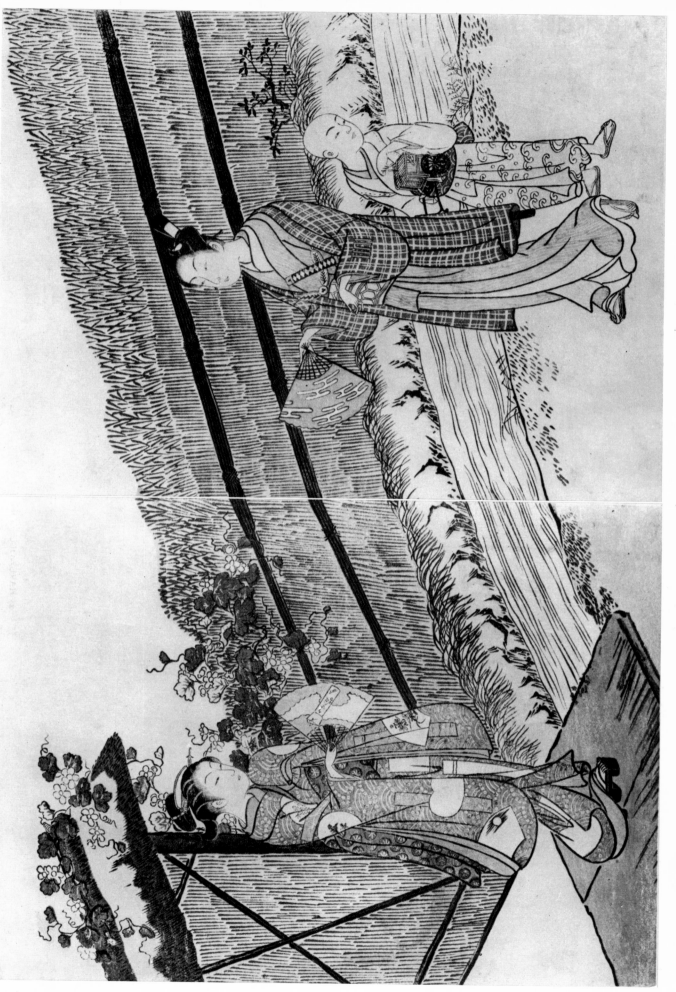

105–6. HARUNOBU: *Girl Greeting Lover*. Page 264

107. HARUNOBU: *The Emperor's Ladies at Backgammon.* Page 264

109. HARUNOBU: *Lovers Reading Letter*. Page 265

108. HARUNOBU: *Lovers Reading Letter*. Page 265

110. HARUNOBU: *Chinese Scholar and Japanese Geisha.* Page 265

III. HARUNOBU: *Lovers and Plum Tree.* Page 265

112. STYLE OF HARUSHIGE: *Girls with Snowball*. Page 265

113. HARUNOBU: *Lovers in the Snow.* Page 265

Koryusai:

FOR THE beginning collector who must budget his funds severely, there is probably no ukiyo-e artist on whom it would be more sensible to specialize than Koryusai. Because he is less popular than either Harunobu, who preceded him, or Kiyonaga, who followed, his prints are usually marked below their real value and offer real bargains to the discerning. But what makes him especially appropriate is the wide range of his types.

His early chuban can sometimes not be distinguished from Harunobu's, and I regret that space precludes the offering of some of his lovely prints in this form. His later chuban are as good as Kiyonaga's, and if one could together six or eight of these, they would provide a fine understanding of this period.

It has usually been claimed that Koryusai pioneered the fifteen-by-ten-inch oban size, which became standard for ukiyo-e, and some of his works in this dimension, like the two shown here, are superb. In design they are apt to be unhackneyed, and in color, vivid. Their printing is technically excellent, as if the workmen wished to show off their newly acquired skills. But I especially appreciate the balance between the garish colors of the prints, particularly the Koryusai brick-orange, and the heavy texture of the paper. To get a good Koryusai from this middle period is to acquire a print which tells one a great deal about this art. The trail-blazing series of about four dozen prints from which Prints 114 and 115 were taken, *First Designs of Model Young Leaves,* was started by Koryusai and finished by Kiyonaga; there is always a good chance of picking up some of the earlier prints and they are well worth having. After Koryusai, literally thousands of advertising prints were issued showing famous courtesans attended by their child-servants, but never again did they attain the fresh, startling quality they enjoyed when Koryusai launched the type. The collection contains half a dozen good prints from this series, but lacks the masterpiece: a manservant holding an umbrella over a courtesan while her two girls huddle under their own, which they carry at a different angle. I have never known of a copy's coming onto the market.

The specialist in Koryusai can also obtain fine bird prints of high quality and, above all, the hashira-e which are the special mark of this artist. Print 118 is a good example of his work in this field. Some of the finest hashira-e issued were designed by Koryusai, for he had an aptitude for filling the awkward space presented by a piece of paper twenty-eight by five inches, and each year some of his pillar prints come on the market.

But it is probably a waste of effort to accumulate too many hashira-e. Usually they are not in good condition; by their very nature they were intended to be tacked to pillars, there to accumulate grease, thumb marks, tears, and bleaching. In time even the best are apt to become tedious, but the ones shown here are of interest because of their good condition and general high quality and because they demonstrate how nine different artists adapted themselves to this peculiar strait jacket. Prints 121 and 124 provide two variations on the most popular single theme for hashira-e, and it would not be difficult, in our larger collections, to uncover two or three dozen fine hashira-e depicting this mitate-e, "parody," of the seventh act of Japan's dramatic masterpiece, *Chushingura,* or *The Forty-seven Loyal Ronin.* One of the highlights of the play occurs when the geisha Okaru from a balcony reads with her mirror a secret letter held by the hero Yuranosuke, while the villain Kudayu reads the tag end of the letter from his hiding place beneath the porch. Masunobu's and Choki's versions of the scene exemplify the lightheartedness of ukiyo-e, as also do Harunobu's earlier parodies, Prints 108–9.

114. KORYUSAI: *The Courtesan Michinoku with Attendants.* Page 266

115. KORYUSAI: *The Courtesan Michiharu with Attendants.* Page 266

116

117

118

116. HARUNOBU:
Young Man Playing Kick-ball.
Page 265

117. KUNINOBU:
Lovers Walking at Night.
Page 266

118. KORYUSAI:
Girl with Mouse.
Page 266

119. TOYOHARU:

Lovers with Kite.

Page 268

120. SHUNKO:

Ichikawa Danjuro V.

Page 267

121. MASUNOBU:

Chushingura Parody.

Page 266

122. KIYONAGA:

Maiden Watching a Young Man. Page 268

123. UTAMARO:

Agemaki and Sukeroku.

Page 270

124. CHOKI:

Chushingura Parody.

Page 272

Buncho :

IN MANY respects Buncho is the most difficult ukiyo-e artist about whom to formulate a secure artistic evaluation, for in studying him one is constantly faced by anomalies. His reputation is excellent and he is always referred to as a superior artist, but the average collector would find it difficult to list offhand six top-notch Buncho prints. It is an obligatory cliché for sales catalogues to state of any Buncho print: "A fine example of this rare artist"; yet year after year so many of his prints come onto the market that he does not begin to be as rare as men like Shigemasa, Toyoharu, and Yoshinobu, to name only three of his contemporaries. The individual collector usually says, "I was lucky to find this rare Buncho," whereas what would be remarkable would be to collect for any period of time without coming across half a dozen "rare" Bunchos. Further to restrict one's judgment, Buncho's output is extremely limited in form: some delightful fairy-tale chuban, and a good many hoso-e of actors and lovely women. And finally, his style is not easily appreciated; it is angular, harsh, powerfully colored, and rarely completely satisfying.

Yet his reputation remains toward the top of any list, for he is what might be called the artist's artist. The superior quality of his work is instinctively felt, even though when analyzed its various components may not support that first feeling. His prints carry distinction and seem more intellectual than those of either Harunobu, whose chuban excel Buncho's, or Shunsho, whose hoso-e are superficially more appealing. He is a tight, well-disciplined artist and is always fresh in his approach. Collectors grow to love his work, for it speaks to them in much sharper accents than that of other artists more widely known. Yet the myth that his prints are excessively rare, whereas in fact they are fairly common, has kept their price up and many beginning collectors forgo acquiring a Buncho, when actually they would derive more ultimate pleasure from a good example of his work than from the prints they do buy.

Prints 126–27 show the phenomenally popular teahouse waitress Osen, whose fame and beauty preoccupied Edo in the 1770's and whom we have met in the Introduction and seen in Print 5. She worked at the Inari Shrine, dedicated to the fox god, located at Kasamori in the outskirts of the city. It was the custom for visitors to the shrine to stop at Osen's teahouse to buy dumplings, and there are many prints of that day showing Osen standing beside the shrine's red torii bearing in her hand a trayful of dumplings, and for some curious reason which I do not understand but to which I am a prey, these prints have always been eagerly sought after by collectors. Perhaps the reader will share with me the suspicion that the girl shown on the kakemono held by the Japanese geisha in Print 110 also depicts the divine waitress.

The most famous portraits of Osen are those by Harunobu, but I have never seen any more exquisite than Print 127, which seems to me an almost perfect print. If we could see Osen, I think she would look something like this.

Print 127 is also of interest in light of my earlier remarks concerning Japanese mastery in using flat masses of color, because the oxidation of time has here given flat color the effect of Western shading. Is this print more interesting because of the oxidation? Is this escape from flat color the reason Japanese connoisseurs especially prize oxidized prints? And note in Prints 145–46 how the blacks representing night have been shaded upwards for more powerful effect. Do Westerners, including myself, particularly praise these because they do, in effect, reject the Japanese system of flat color and pay lip service to our standards of modulated and more plastic color values? These are tantalizing problems, but they serve principally to underline the basic fact: ukiyo-e artists used flat masses of color with maximum effectiveness.

125. BUNCHO: *Otani Hiroji III.* Page 266

126. BUNCHO: *Osen.* Page 266

127. BUNCHO: *Osen.* Page 266

Shunsho
Shunko
Shun'ei :

THE THREE artists presented here were members of the same school, along with thirty-five others at least, all bearing names beginning with Shun and all to greater or less degree stemming from the influence of Shunsho, a prolific, long-lived, and persuasive teacher. Shunsho's actor prints are one of the high-lights of ukiyo-e. For the most part they are hoso-e marked by cluttered back-grounds and a monotony of treatment that would disqualify them from serious consideration except that in spite of their monotony they charm us with a sense of time past. They are distinctive art and taken in large lots remind one of a Bach fugue, playing back and forth upon the same theme yet somehow send-ing the intellectual content forward. From a large number of Shunsho prints, some in fine condition, I have selected five rather unusual types. The diptych facing shows actors about to do the duck dance and is one of his finest, yet each print taken separately is both typical and satisfying. The early print reproduced in color as Print 130 is unusual both in size and composition and comes to us in such a fine state of preservation as to be useful in reminding us of what ukiyo-e looked like when issued. Print 131, facing the color page, is quite the opposite. It is famous historically, having been used in several studies of Shunsho, but its basic colors have faded to the patina so often seen in exposed ukiyo-e. Print 132 is a joyous thing, one of Shunsho's best, but I would rather have included here one of the famous red Danjuros, for they are marvelous prints indeed. But alas I have never found one.

The Shunko triptych, Prints 133–35, is a strange group. In previous instances of its publication these central characters from one of Kabuki's strongest plays have been disposed in various ways, but never as shown here. Originally there may have been two additional prints, and Tomita Kojiro of Boston be-lieves that the print which appeared as item 102 in the Frank Lloyd Wright catalogue of 1927 was intended to stand left of Print 133, while a print now lost must have stood between Prints 134 and 135.

The big heads that appear in Prints 137 and 138 have already been com-mented upon, but it is important to observe that they appeared rather earlier than we once thought; and the design was not invented by Sharaku.

The placement of the artist Shun'ei in a book like this presents a major prob-lem. Originally I had him far back in this section, just before Sharaku and Toyokuni, where stylistically he belongs, and the reader is invited to see for himself how well this greatly gifted, restrained, and somewhat acidulous artist fits in there. I notice that Ledoux puts him between Sharaku and Toyokuni. But when a group of Japanese experts in this field saw such an arrangement they protested that it gave quite a false impression of Shun'ei; he stands close to Shunko in his big heads and to Shunsho in his fine hoso-e. I am not entirely satisfied with the impression this book now gives; certainly Shun'ei, whom I like increasingly, is later in spirit than Shigemasa, Kitao Masanobu, Toyoharu, and Kiyonaga, and the reader will see that this is true. Apparently he is an artist who fits in nowhere exactly, which is the reputation he has always had. But is there a more distinct, underivative work of art in this book than the hesitant dancer seen in Print 140? Who cares where such a gem is placed in history? It stands as its own self-justification.

128–29. SHUNSHO: *Kikunojo and Sangoro.* Page 266

130. SHUNSHO: *Kojuro, Tsuneyo, and Sojuro.* Page 267

131. SHUNSHO: *Sukegoro and Nakazo.* Page 267

132. SHUNSHO: *Nakazo as Hotei.* Page 267

136. SHUNKO: *Mokuemon, Yamauba, and Kintoki.* Page 267

133-35. SHUNKO: *Sukeroku, Agemaki, and Ikyu.* Page 267

137. SHUNKO: *Ichikawa Monnosuke.* Page 267

138. SHUN'EI: *Ichikawa Ebizo.* Page 267

139. SHUN'EI: *Ichikawa Ebizo.* Page 267

140. SHUN'EI: *Nakayama Tomisaburo*. Page 267

K. Masanobu
Shigemasa
Toyoharu :

THE FOUR prints grouped together here are of unusual interest in that each is a typical masterwork of its artist. In 1784, Kitao Masanobu, no relative of the greater artist of this name, who had died in 1764, issued an oversize picture book consisting of seven huge plates in full and intricate color, bound in accordion style. It was a book of stunning impact, frequently termed the most beautiful book of its kind ever issued. As the print opposite shows, it was rather garishly colored; the collection contains two complete copies of the work, the one not shown having the more subdued coloration. A surprising characteristic is the size of the cherry boards from which the prints were printed; there could not have been many such trees in Japan, so that these boards must have been special treasures. The subject matter of the print facing is accurately described by the curious title of the book: *Autographs of Famous Beauties of the Greenhouses*. The poems which appear attached to the two courtesans thus being introduced were presumably composed by them and written in their handwriting, a delicate Japanese conceit.

Prints 142–43 form one of the most pleasing pairs to appear in this book, for prints showing the industrious little women of Shigemasa are sufficiently rare to merit attention, and they are so designed that almost any two or three, placed together, constitute an attractive frieze. This collection is fortunate in having six of these subjects, two with duplicates showing variations, but it lacks the choicest design of the lot, which can be seen in Ledoux as No. 12. There is something perpetually winning about these Shigemasa studies of women; the designs are simplified and the colors are subdued; great attention is paid to the rendering of fabric and to the precise fall of draperies. But what endears them to me is that within the whole range of classic ukiyo-e, it is only Shigemasa's women that look like Japanese women as the Westerner sees them. For example, Prints 161–62 offer full-length portraits of beautiful women, but I have never seen Japanese women who resemble them; I am afraid they are carefully idealized depictions, taller, slimmer, more ethereal than reality. But if I were to stroll along the banks of the Sumida tonight, nearly two hundred years after Shigemasa worked, and if I reached the geisha quarter, I could see the determined little women from his prints, hurrying along to their night's entertainments. And they would look exactly like the women in Prints 142–43. The world tends to cherish artists who epitomize an age. This is why we accord such praise to men like the Kaigetsudo and Toulouse-Lautrec. That is also why we love Shigemasa and his unpretentious little women. They look like Japan.

Print 144 demonstrates ukiyo-e mastery of European perspective when desired, plus the general up-tilting of rear planes as required by Oriental convention. Here the mixture is applied to a depiction on one contrived landscape of the classic Omi Hakkei, or Eight Views of Lake Biwa. These eight most charming sights in the world were originally identified in tenth-century China by a local painter and applied to scenes of his homeland; six centuries later a scholarly Japanese transferred the subjects to Lake Biwa, near Kyoto. Starting at the extreme upper right and moving counter-clockwise, they are: wild geese descending at Katata; night rain on the Karasaki pine; lingering snow on Mount Hira; evening bell at Mii-dera; autumn moon at Ishiyama; evening glow at the Chinese-style bridge at Seta; returning sails at Yabase; and, almost lost in the center of the print, clear sky at Awazu.

143. SHIGEMASA: *Geisha with Maidservant.* Page 268

144. TOYOHARU: *Eight Views of Lake Biwa.* Page 268

Kiyonaga :

IT IS ALWAYS a pleasure to leaf through the prints of Kiyonaga, for no matter what this sweet, reasonable man attempted, he stamped it with his stately concept of human beings moving with dignity against largely static backgrounds. He invests humanity with a grandeur that is good to see, and his men are just as interesting as his women. I would think that in this respect the two unimportant hoso-e Prints 156–57 were almost perfect examples of his art. The three men stand with dignity, their robes falling in heavy, Grecian lines. Their faces are alive but not exceptional. The backgrounds against which they stand are effective but not obtrusive. And the general air of the pictures is one of competence. They form a handsome pair of prints, and although as an admirer of Kiyonaga I had half a dozen more representative prints vying for this space, I preferred these two as an ideal summary of the man. The reader will find that they will live in his memory for a long time, just because they are so unpretentious and right.

Kiyonaga is, par excellence, the artist of the diptych, and in this form he has created nearly a dozen masterpieces. They are so spacious, so filled with light and majesty as to exact praise from almost any viewer. Print 151 is the left half of one of the best and a rare gem even by itself. Prints 147–50 show two of Kiyonaga's good diptychs, the upper one having been selected over several other more famous subjects because it was the only copy known to Hirano Chie when she did her definitive study of Kiyonaga, and therefore may have the accidental merit of uniqueness; and it is interesting that the collection also contains an extra version of the left-hand sheet in different coloring, also the only copy known to Miss Hirano.

Why Kiyonaga should have been so adept in designing diptychs remains a mystery, for other ukiyo-e artists found themselves cramped in this format and preferred the triptych. Possibly Kiyonaga's superb sense of balance and space permitted him to adjust his compositions most easily to the symmetry of a two-sheet format. I have never thought much of his triptychs, for they seem to lack the stately balance of the diptychs, and usually one sheet of the three is either lacking in distinction or unnecessary to the over-all design. The triptych shown here, Prints 153–55, is one of the best, but as always in Kiyonaga's work, the left-hand sheet is a thing by itself and is usually so presented.

As for the diptych that appears in color on the following pages, long before there was any chance that I might one day be its custodian, I wrote: "This is my favorite, a diptych of such subtle yet simple beauty as to epitomize the best of ukiyo-e. . . . There is nothing unusual about the coloring of the kimono except that each subdued color is right for its position. There is no striking design except that the potentially monotonous heads are subtly varied in position so as to produce a satisfying pattern. . . . There is no striking background, only a rough black reaching up to the shoulders and topped by a pale gray. And neither half of this triptych amounts to much when taken alone, for the left is a little crowded, the right a bit empty. But taken together, weighing both mood and technique, this passage of noble human figures constitutes a diptych which makes the frequent comparison of Kiyonaga to the best of Greek sculpture not only reasonable but a way of expressing praise for the Greeks." Today I would phrase this more simply and say: "All in all, this is the most satisfying Japanese print I have ever known." I am delighted to own it temporarily.

145

145–46. KIYONAGA: *Evening Scene at Shinagawa.* Page 268

147–48. KIYONAGA: *Snowy Morning in the Yoshiwara.* Page 269

149–50. KIYONAGA: *New Year's Scene at Nihombashi*. Page 269

135

151. KIYONAGA: *River Cool at Dusk.* Page 269

152. KIYONAGA: *Komazo and Monnosuke.* Page 269

153–55. KIYONAGA: *Sudden Shower at the Mimeguri Shrine.* Page 269

157. KIYONAGA: *Matsumoto Koshiro IV with Geisha.*
Page 269

156. KIYONAGA: *Iwai Hanshiro IV with Manservant.*
Page 269

Utamaro:

IT IS GENERALLY agreed that ukiyo-e reached its climax in the classic period. Some critics hold that Kiyonaga represented the apex, and the author has shared with many other ukiyo-e students the experience of first underestimating Kiyonaga and then awakening to the fact that he was one of the supreme artists. His proficiency, if not always his psychological warmth, was astonishing, and I would not object if one were to claim that he represented the high-water mark of the Japanese print. What I *do* object to is exalting Kiyonaga at the expense of Utamaro, for the latter seems to me a very fine artist indeed and I am afraid that those who denigrate his art are blind to its accomplishments. Since the two men were born within a year of each other, I see no reason why one should not conclude that ukiyo-e reached its highest point in the combined work of these two men. It is the good fortune of collectors that many of their lesser works are available at bargain prices – indeed, Kiyonaga's chuban represent one of the real bargains in ukiyo-e – and no collector need deprive himself of a good Kiyonaga and a good Utamaro.

Appropriately, all the prints shown in the following group portray women, for Utamaro excelled in their depiction. And the twelve women shown, plus the little girl, relay to us the charm he constantly saw in the women he so lovingly drew. These are exquisite prints, alluring, delightful, and evocative. I am particularly fond of the two pairs of tall women who face each other, Prints 161–62, even if I said earlier that the figures were too elongated. Print 161 shows two examples of sedate, well-trained women from the upper class – in this series of three he also did the middle- and lower-class types – engaged in the genteel occupations of playing the koto and listening to the chirping of insects; while across the page stands one of the Yoshiwara's leading prostitutes, to whom her kneeling maid presents a cup of tea. It is the Hour of the Snake, nine to eleven in the morning, and the lassitude that pervades this print is skillfully suggested by line, placement, and coloring.

Print 163, of course, has a special responsibility in this collection, for it presents the famous eighteenth-century courtesan Hanaogi, and I have reported elsewhere on my preoccupation with the dozens of prints recording her fame and beauty. This is the only one that has ever been offered to me, and it is, I am afraid, somewhat battered and worn with time, but glowing withal. It was from my account of this haunting woman that I was able to afford most of the prints shown here, so in a very real sense she can be called the patron saint of this collection, except that the word saint is one which hardly applies to this remarkable woman.

Print 164 is an almost perfect Utamaro, for it is not only one of his most handsomely designed and executed prints, but it portrays one of those scenes which the artist so deeply loved: a group of beautiful professional women ready to parade through the Yoshiwara, made up to represent monks from a Buddhist temple.

Prints 165–66 are interesting as demonstrating the high degree of skill attained by the professional woodcarvers and printers at the apex of ukiyo-e production. These two pictures appear on the front and back of a single sheet of nearly translucent paper, but the dual registry is so nearly perfect that no line on one side shows through to betray its existence on the other. Of course, the print would have to be classed as mere exhibitionism except for the fact that it is also a most handsome portrait of one of the popular waitresses of the day and has an artistic merit of its own.

相見 歌麿筆画 婦人相學十體

158. UTAMARO: *Girl with Glass Pipe.* Page 270

159. UTAMARO: *Okita Carrying Teacup.* Page 270

160. UTAMARO: *The Courtesan Wakaume with Maidservant.* Page 270

風俗三段娘 上品圖

161. UTAMARO: *A Maiden of the Upper Classes.* Page 270

162. UTAMARO: *Courtesan after Bath*. Page 270

163. UTAMARO (II?): *The Courtesan Hanogi.* Page 270

164. UTAMARO: *Festival Trio*. Page 270

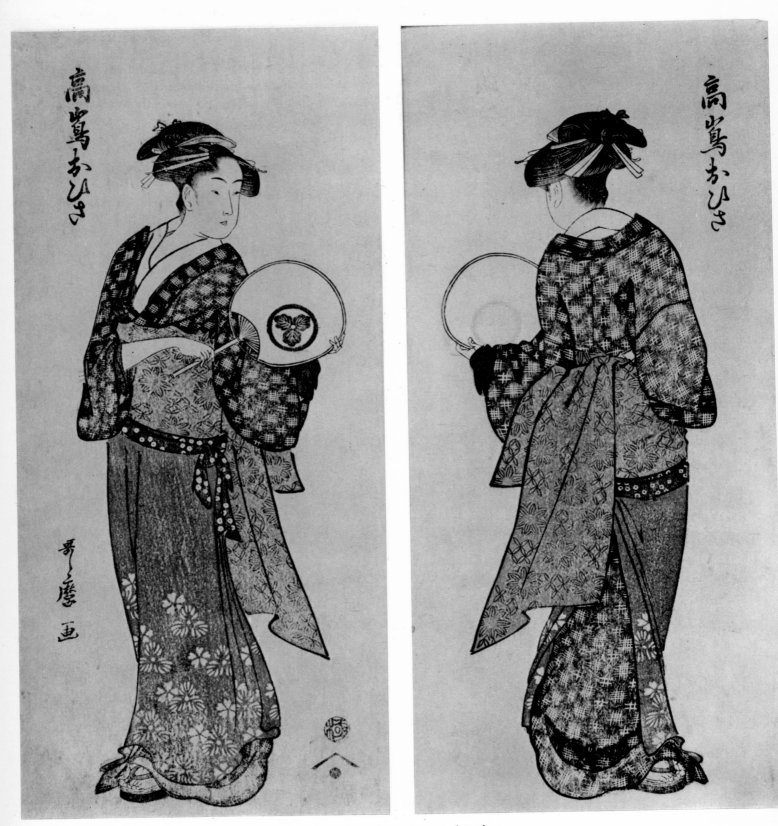

165–66. UTAMARO: *Ohisa, Front and Back.* Page 271

Sharaku:

ANYONE who loves prints approaches Sharaku with awe, for his powerful works stand apart in history. They are psychologically profound, spiritually tortured, and mysterious. Issued more than a century and a half ago, they are nevertheless as modern as El Greco, and they are among the most eagerly sought-after prints in all the world.

Their mysteriousness has always impressed me. In the fourth month of 1794 a Japanese Noh actor of whom we know nothing – neither his antecedents, nor his training, nor his personality, nor his subsequent history – came to a publisher in Edo and volunteered to prepare for him a series of prints depicting actors in the popular Kabuki theater, of which he was not only not a part, but to which, as a classic Noh actor, he would normally have been professionally opposed.

In a burst of energy unparalleled in art history, this strange, nebulous man, produced about 145 prints that are known plus perhaps another 45 that have been lost but whose presence can be logically deduced. He issued his sketches in four series: large heads containing dark-mica grounds, like Prints 167–70; large prints containing two full-length actors posed against white-mica grounds, like Print 172; smaller heads on smaller-sized paper with a yellow ground; and hoso-e showing individual actors without mica grounds, like Print 171. His prints were so violent in character that they shocked contemporary Edo and were not a success. A critic at the time wrote: "He drew portraits of actors but exaggerated the truth and his pictures lacked form. Therefore he was not well received and after a year or so he ceased to work."

It is a fact difficult to comprehend that Sharaku issued all his prints within a period of only nine months: at least 190 prints finished within a space of 300 days. Legend says that he left Edo a disappointed man, but today, of course, his works have become prime treasures.

Print 171 is of special interest in that it was once owned by the Danjuro family and was treasured by them, which helps disprove the once-accepted theory that Sharaku was run out of Edo because actors despised his portraits of them. Actually, his portraits seem to have been rather lifelike; it was their psychological probing which doomed them in their day – and made them immortal in ours.

In recent years an unhealthy emphasis has been placed upon buying art as a financial investment, which introduces totally extraneous factors into appreciation. I am glad to report that Japanese prints are poor material for such speculation, as the history of a series of sales of Print 168 testifies:

Year	Sale	Price	Value of $	Value of Print
1903	Bing	$850	1.000	$850
1911	Paris	715	.917	651
1917	Hirakawa	170	.507	85
1918	Metzgar	880	.454	400
1920	Ficke	1050	.386	406
1921	Jacquin	490	.610	299
1928	Straus-Negbaur	600	.615	369
1935	Private	400	.744	297
1945	Private	250	.563	141
1957	Japan	1050	.327	344

Investment in almost anything else would have done better, which is consoling. It should caution those who might be thinking of buying prints for irrelevant reasons to leave them for those who appreciate them for their artistic content.

167. SHARAKU: *Tanimura Torazo.* Page 271

168. SHARAKU: *Ichikawa Ebizo.* Page 271

153

169. SHARAKU: *Arashi Ryuzo*. Page 271

170. SHARAKU: *Sawamura Sojuro III.* Page 271

171. SHARAKU: *Ichikawa Danjuro VI.* Page 271

172. SHARAKU: *Oniji and Omezo.* Page 271

Choki :

CHOKI is remarkable in that he designed only a limited number of prints, but all with great distinction, and the three shown here comprise one of the highlights of the collection. Of Choki's output, I prefer the mysterious moon-lit landscape with two women smoking pipes, which is handsomely reproduced in color in Ledoux, No. 29. It is now in the collection of the Chicago Art Institute and can be seen there. This has always seemed to me one of the perfect prints.

In all that he does, Choki exhibits delicate judgment. His drawing is elfin; his color harmonies are exquisite; his figures are pinched together at the shoulders in Modigliani-style; and his backgrounds are apt to be stunning. He was a fine artist gifted with a personal vision that dominates his prints. After even a brief acquaintance with his work, it is impossible to attribute his prints to anyone else. Besides the pinched shoulders, his artistic signature includes a woman whose draperies fall in a severely straight line down one margin of the print, as exemplified in Print 173, and to a lesser degree in Print 175. But an even better touchstone is an ineffable quality which is not easily analyzed. One feels instinctively: "Only Choki could have done this print."

Print 174, one of his greatest, falls somewhat outside his general pattern, except for the pinched shoulders of the woman, and in unsigned versions has sometimes been accorded to Utamaro. The signed copy shown here was one of the highlights of the Straus-Negbaur collection in Germany, but critics suggest that the red of the old man's robe must have been touched up by newly-cut blocks sometime in the late nineteenth century, a process at which Japanese dealers proved most skillful and which is technically known as revamping.

Print 175 has always been the subject of argument, feud, and delightful discussion among experts and owners, and a full-length essay could be written about this copy and another which always competed with it. Briefly, the story is this: In Paris in the early years of this century two distinguished and competing collectors, Louis Gonse and Raymond Koechlin, both owned copies of this rare and beautiful print. Koechlin's copy, marred by a cigarette burn in the face of the woman, went ultimately to Ledoux. Gonse's copy was sold for one of the highest prices ever paid for a single sheet to Chandler, whereupon Ledoux stated that he had never liked the Gonse copy, while Chandler let it be known that he did not particularly care for the cigarette-scarred Koechlin version. In time the Koechlin-Ledoux copy passed into the hands of the Art Institute, Chicago, whose curators naturally sustained Ledoux's preferences, while the Gonse-Chandler copy came to me, and I hope that I may be excused for having adopted the Chandler attitude. But it is important to remember that when Louis Gonse sold the copy shown here, his friend Raymond Koechlin himself sponsored Charles Vignier's catalogue, which contained this expert appraisal of the Gonse print: "A faultless proof of this sumptuous and rare print." Edwin Grabhorn, of San Francisco, owns a third copy, which came from the Morse collection and which has remained outside the amicable Koechlin-Ledoux-Chicago *versus* Gonse-Chandler-Honolulu feud.

173. CHOKI: *The Courtesan Tsukasa-dayu.* Page 272

174. CHOKI: *Girl in Snow.* Page 272

175. CHOKI: *Firefly-catching.* Page 272

Shuncho:

ONE OF the finest prints in this book is the diptych which appears in color as Prints 177–78. It is Shuncho's masterwork and in the case of this example has a distinguished history, but it has always created argument because it has sometimes been put together reverse to the way shown here; and there are many who remain convinced that these are but two sheets of a triptych, the extreme right-hand sheet having vanished. Various facts are cited to support this belief: (1) since the signature of the right-hand sheet is in the center, symmetry would require a third sheet to balance it; (2) the woman with the pipe is obviously looking off toward friends; (3) the bench would fit the picture better if it were continued; (4) there is something odd about the relationship of the various parts of the tree.

One of the most enchanting little prints in the collection appears below. The gap down its middle makes it look like an uncut diptych, but the fact that it is all in one piece on a standard-size sheet, with signature at one edge and title at the other, would suggest it was meant to be folded, perhaps in an album. A moment's study of this print will show that insofar as the tree and the backward-looking woman are concerned, these are Shuncho trademarks. And a glimpse at the powerful, awkward diptych Prints 180–81, here joined together for the first time, proves further that the angular design and the odd placement of signatures were Shuncho characteristics. This diptych also exhibits once more the backward-looking women. So it may well be that the conjectured third panel to accompany Prints 177–78 never existed.

Print 179 is interesting in that it was the work of two artists. Shuncho did the women in his accepted style; Shun'ei did the men in his. There were many such collaborations in ukiyo-e and the resulting prints were sometimes very fine. This is not one of the best, but these two artists did another in what may have been the same series in which two unusually graceful Shuncho women stand with one fine Shun'ei man, probably the actor Danjuro V, and since the design is less crowded, the result is more pleasing.

Shuncho is a continually fascinating artist. Trained by Shunsho, he broke away from that artist's confining style, but quickly fell under the influence of Kiyonaga, of whom he often seems a flagrant copyist. Yet in his finest pieces, he shows strong draftsmanship and a rugged, inarticulate design which anyone acquainted with his work grows to appreciate.

176. SHUNCHO: *Picnic Procession.*
Page 272

春潮画

春英画

179. SHUNCHO and SHUN'EI: *Street Scene.* Page 272

180–81. SHUNCHO: *Riverside Scene.* Page 272

Eishi
Eisho
Shucho :

THESE six delightful prints are good ones with which to end this classical period of the full-color print. Each is attractive, feminine, highly stylized, and subdued in both color and effect. The yellow ground of the print opposite is not garish, and the mica grounds of Prints 183–86 add to the subjects the touch of luxury they deserve.

Prints 183–84, which show the courtesan Misayama preparing to retire, are famous in ukiyo-e circles in that they have been the subject of much argument. The left-hand print, from the Ledoux collection, shows what is presumed to be the original issue, with flaked mica above a brown background, with a harsh line cutting the background into two parts. This subject has always been a favorite with collectors, and when Ledoux owned this copy he said of it: "This impression of one of the great masterpieces among Japanese prints is in wretched condition – like Komachi at the end of her career. It is worn, faded, repaired and the original luster of the upper part of the ground is gone. It remains, however, a thing of such elegance and beauty that it outranks many a subject in excellent condition and one turns from it always with regret, turns to it always with recognition of its supremacy."

The right-hand print appears to have been issued sometime later than the original brown version and probably from different blocks. Where the first version had translucent mica above brown, this has mica mixed with white. This famous copy was owned by Hayashi, whose seal is seen lower left, but went from Paris back to Japan, where it was widely exhibited and where I finally found it, matching it with the earlier version. The arguments of which I spoke concern the authenticity of Print 184. All surviving copies are in suspiciously good condition; but the print is a glorious thing, and if it is indeed a modern forgery, it is nevertheless a masterpiece in its own right.

There is presumed to have been a third state of this print – since such third states exist of the other two prints in the series – in which the harsh line between the two parts of the background was eliminated, leaving only a handsome pale-brown ground covered with shimmering mica. Artistically, this third state must have been particularly handsome on the print shown here, because when seen on the other two it is most effective, but apparently none has survived. There seems also to have been a fourth state, lacking mica, signature, and publisher's mark; it was probably run off to sell at reduced rates.

As prints, these portraits of Misayama on her way to bed are unforgettable. I find them awkward, off-balance, and curiously colored. But I suspect that this is pretty much the way a courtesan looked at the end of the night, with her butterfly hair-do and wearing the costly garments which her owner forced upon her so that she would remain perpetually in his debt.

The Eisho big heads are merely two, and not by any means the best, of a distinguished series issued by this artist. Any print from this set is worth having and some are almost the equal of the best that Utamaro did in this style, but they are difficult to find in good condition.

The Shucho big head, Print 187, is interesting in that prints by this attractive artist often appear without signature, and Dr. Lane has suggested that the publisher was responsible for this, hoping to fob off as original Utamaros work by this lesser-known man. There are several handsome Shuchos extant, and the best contain an animal or a bird held in the hands of an attractive woman. The one shown here is among the finest.

182. EISHI: *The Doll Festival.* Page 273

183. EISHI: *Courtesan Preparing for Bed.* Page 273

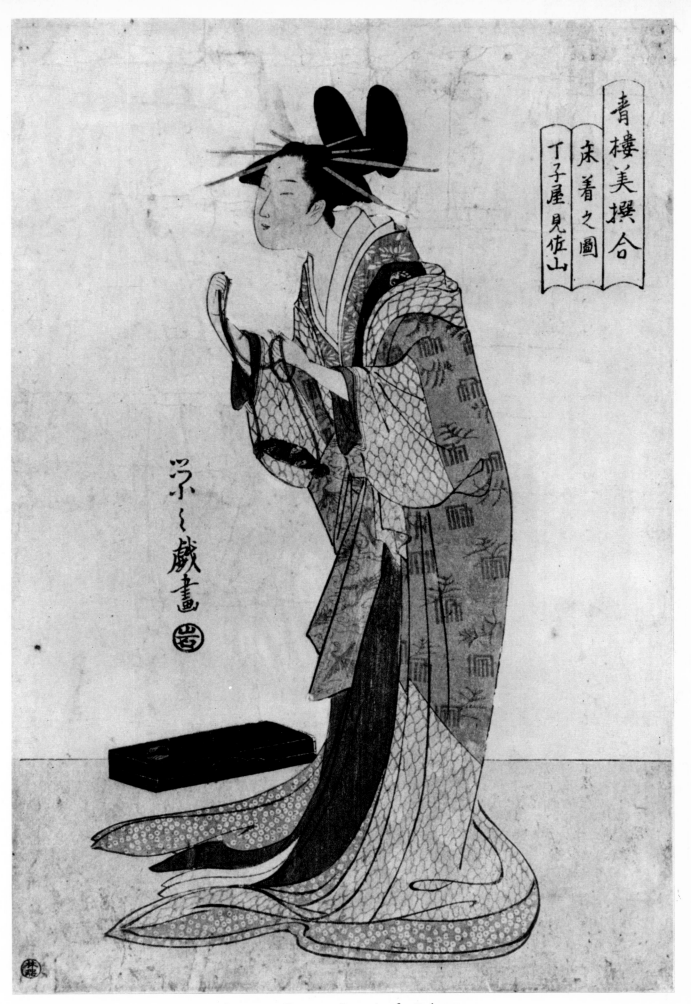

184. EISHI: *Courtesan Preparing for Bed.* Page 273

185. EISHO: *The Courtesan Shinowara.* Page 273

郭中美人競
松葉屋染山

鳥高斎栄昌画

186. EISHO: *The Courtesan Someyama.* Page 273

187. SHUCHO: *Girl with White Mouse.* Page 273

Section
3:
LANDSCAPE AND FIGURE PRINTS

REGARDLESS of how one defines the rise and fall of ukiyo-e, pinpointing the apex at Kiyonaga or at Utamaro, any acceptable theory must take into account the belated flowering of the two landscape artists Hokusai and Hiroshige, and the following pages present some of their finest works. It is erroneous to think that these two great masters, who have been so loved in the Western world, invented Japanese woodblock landscapes, for the art had an ancient beginning and an honorable life long before these two men issued their famous series.

Moronobu Print 12 shows how landscape was used sparingly and with fine effect in the earliest prints; while Kiyomasu Print 18 makes a lilting poem out of the formalized waterfall background. Masanobu frequently used similar landscape effects to good purpose, as in his evocation of Lady Murasaki, author of the *Tale of Genji*, Print 9, and I find such works most pleasing.

One of the first artists to use landscape as a major component of a print, with the human figures subordinated, was Shigenaga, whose Print 61 is a good example of this early, highly symbolized style. Kiyomasu and Masanobu also issued prints in this manner, and they provide tender little glimpses of an idealized nature, similar in effect to the landscapes being done in Italy at the time of Lorenzetti. For an example of this type of landscape art at its most ineffective, see Kiyohiro Prints 89–91, where there is much formalism and little charm.

With Kiyonaga, landscape attains an important role in a series of superlative prints, 149–50 being typical. I have always thought that the diptych of which Print 151 forms a part had a Vermeer quality; but the triptych Prints 153–55 shows our first example of what is to become, with Hokusai and Hiroshige, almost the touchstone of ukiyo-e landscape art. The human beings are kept small in size and toward the front of the picture. The landscape is conventionalized, both as to form and color, in this case with rain represented by carefully drawn parallel lines, another hallmark of the Japanese print. The gods aloft are atypical, but the wind that ruffles dresses but not trees is often seen. It is difficult to believe that the people under the gate who are repairing damage caused by the rain are really wet, but the landscape as a whole is highly satisfactory.

Shuncho's masterpiece, offered in full color in Prints 177–78, seems to me to be landscape of a different sort. It is imaginary in color and form, the fine yellows forming a conventionalized background for the human figures. The tree branches are formalized and the flowers on the far bank are much too large, but this is a dream landscape and objects are not required to appear in proper color or proportion. Nevertheless, these two prints form one of the finest landscape pairs in ukiyo-e, and the eye never tires of seeing these stately women in their imaginary world.

It was from such a formalized heritage that Hokusai sprang with his startling visions of contemporary Japan, and it was his landscape prints that helped awaken French impressionists to problems of color, the rendering of atmosphere, and the organization of a landscape painting. But it seems to me that if one looks carefully at the Hokusais shown here, they are as formal in manner as their predecessors, as arbitrary in coloring, and as idealized in subject matter.

I want to stress this lest anyone think, erroneously, that in some mysterious way Hokusai sprang to birth full-blooded without having had numerous predecessors. But having made the point, I must hasten to express my keen delight in these poetic, evocative landscapes of the mind. They are really one of the most impressive accomplishments in ukiyo-e. They are static, unreal, monumental, and contrived; but they sing of nature.

The eight works by followers of Hokusai, Prints 197–204, illustrate how this formalism degenerated into merely reporting the patterns of nature, but several of the prints are minor masterpieces of design and are widely treasured as such.

With the advent of Hiroshige, landscape prints of quite a different type appeared, for Hiroshige, a hard-drinking, roistering man, loved nature. He studied her moods, reveled in storms, sang with birds, sketched the effect of night shadows upon a scene, and spent a lifetime reporting what he saw. He designed a prodigious number of prints, one every other day for thirty-three years, and in them he showed the world a different vision of nature from that which Hokusai had created. His best prints are spontaneous rather than formal. They smell of the earth rather than of the mind. There is humor in them rather than austere impressions. And there is constant evidence of a personal affection for nature.

Eventually each collector of ukiyo-e finds himself comparing the two leading landscape masters, and I have come to think of Hokusai's vision of nature as epic, of Hiroshige's as lyric. One of the best ways to get at the differences between the two is to compare their bird-and-flower prints. Two of Hokusai's are shown, Prints 188 and 193, and they are characterized by careful architectural design, bold use of color to achieve effect rather than to report on the actualities of nature, heaviness in handling, and marked ineptness in drawing birds or butterflies. Nature is seen in a hard, harsh, brightly-lighted reality. Yet the resulting pictures are striking; as art they are fine; it is only as nature that they are inadequate.

Now compare the three Hiroshige Prints 226–28, and one finds that the selection of color is appropriate to the aspect of nature being shown, the birds are lively creatures, there is great movement in each print, and the observation of nature is both keen and accurate. Over each subject there is diffused a tender, but not sticky, romanticism, and it is obvious that the man who created these three prints actually loved nature and with a certain joy reported what he saw. Not one of the Hiroshiges is as fine a print as Hokusai's masterful arrangement in blue; but any one of them is more lyric and honest in its reflection of nature.

The more one studies ukiyo-e landscapes, the more he becomes convinced that these Japanese works must not be compared to those created in the West. Hokusai and Hiroshige did not see nature in the way that Lorraine, Turner, Constable, and Cezanne saw it. The Japanese artists entertained a special vision, and from it built a major contribution to world art. It derives from Chinese and Japanese antecedents and cannot be confused with any other. That was one of the reasons why ukiyo-e landscapes were able to speak so strongly to men like Van Gogh, Degas, and Manet; their shock value was undiminished, and remains so today. One of the reasons why I like Japanese landscape prints so much is that they show me a world which by myself I would never have discovered. From Hokusai I learn the monumental grandeur of nature and the way in which various components combine to form architectural designs of lasting beauty. Under his guidance, the majesty of nature becomes an intellectual thing to be appreciated, studied, comprehended, and filed in memory. From Hiroshige I learn the poetic gentleness of rain, and mist, and snow, and evening, and birds across the moon. I see for the first time the effects of atmosphere upon different natural settings and I catch something of the harmony of everyday life. Particularly, since I have always loved birds and in my own way have studied them since childhood, I am grateful to Hiroshige for capturing the deft, winging quality of birds. In this he is incomparable. It is for such reasons that men in all parts of the world have grown to like Japanese landscape prints.

The second major type of print appearing in this section is the full-length figure standing against a solid background, and this art form is so impressive that I have given all of the Toyokuni pages, Prints 205–11, to this type alone, even though this master was one of the most versatile in ukiyo-e history. In no sense did Toyokuni invent this form, for solitary figures of great power have always flourished in ukiyo-e. Starting with the Kaigetsudo Print 15 and continuing with the Kiyomasu actor, Print 16, these striking creations have served as the symbol of the art. Both Masanobu and Toyonobu created masterful works in this form, several of which are reproduced in this book. In smaller size, as in Kiyonobu's dramatic figure, Print 31, the tradition continued until in the work of Shunsho and Shunko the hoso-e actor print with a simplified background became standard.

But starting with Shunei, Prints 139–40, a new type evolved showing human figures standing against solid-color backgrounds, and these are powerful prints. The Eishi Print 183 is in this tradition, as are certain Kiyonagas, but the form reaches its apex with the works of Toyokuni. The prints shown here are masterpieces of the type and their appeal is instantaneous. This stems partly from the fact that one instinctively feels them to be a culmination of an art form that started back at the beginnings of ukiyo-e, and one can see in the Toyokunis an honored inheritance; but it stems also from the controlled dramatic power of these stately figures. They do not gesticulate unnecessarily, nor do they engage in heroics. They simply stand, coiled and tensed, like ominous forces poised against impersonal, timeless backgrounds. They evoke a very powerful sense of awe and are art of high quality. The skill with which these figures are posed, the appropriate use of subdued color, and the effective utilization of drapery combine to make these figure prints a major achievement of ukiyo-e.

With these stately figures, and with the landscapes of Hiroshige, the great period of traditional ukiyo-e ends. Technically, the art had developed its ultimate resources. In the graphic art of no other country was it possible to print the intricate lines shown in the hair-do of the girl in Print 187. The subtle gradations utilized with such striking effect in Hiroshige's "Sudden Rain at Ohashi," Print 221, represented the ultimate in ukiyo-e techniques.

In the dying days of the art, yellow backgrounds enjoyed a brief popularity, then mica grounds, then solitary figures against bleak backdrops, but finally the various vogues spent themselves and a poverty of invention provided no new ones. Without new styles to tempt the public taste, the market for prints diminished. Then from the West came the box camera and the newspaper engraving, and the destruction of ukiyo-e was completed. By the 1880's the art was apparently moribund.

Of course, as it fell toward desuetude, along with the major artists we have been discussing there flourished the usual group of minor men, and in this particular period they were artists capable of beautiful work. If one were to collect the best big heads of the period, such as Prints 212–14, and the finest landscapes of the minor men, such as Prints 216–17, he would have a respectable body of art. In fact, any collector who applied himself to these artists should in time be able to compile a group of prints that would help us all to appreciate better the causes of the decline of ukiyo-e, but such work has not yet been done.

Hokusai
and
Followers :

FROM THE wealth of Hokusai prints available, it is difficult to select nine that do justice to this powerful old man. Obviously, one ought to represent the major series, but this cannot be done in brief space, so let me point out what series and types of prints have had to be eliminated.

The *Waterfall* series is missing, primarily because its prints are vertical in form and thus cannot be used facing the typical horizontal landscape. This is a most handsome series and one that I especially like, but it has been reproduced many times, and its absence here is not grievous. *The Hundred Poems Explained by the Nurse* is absent, and this is a loss, because even though I do not appreciate the typical beauty of this series, the prints do represent both Hokusai's capacity as a humorist and the type of work he was doing in the last years of his life. However, it did not seem to me worth while to devote a full page to this amusing, silly series, enchanting though some of its prints are. I do regret very much the absence of Hokusai's horror series, in which ghosts and snakes are featured, for this is powerful art, executed in some of the finest printing and coloring to be seen in Hokusai; but I have never come upon a print from this series in good condition. Also missing, although they were available, are his great surimono (special prints for New Year's gifts) and the best sheets from his second series on *Chushingura.* It was difficult to eliminate his famous study of cranes, his fan prints, and what is reputed to be the last print he made, his oversize study of surveyors using European transits to lay out a road; somehow this awkward and unlovely print summarizes Hokusai's questing spirit and would not have been out of place.

Now a word as to how certain of the prints shown here were selected, for Hokusai holds a special place in my affection, and I carry the memory of his prints in my mind wherever I go. Obviously, the print that appears opposite is a happy combination of design and color and probably the masterpiece of this series of small-sized bird-and-flower prints.

Two prints were chosen from his best-known series, *Thirty-six Views of Fuji,* to allow the reader to compare Hokusai's concept of trees along a road with Hiroshige's version of the same subject, as seen in Print 220.

The pair of prints that face each other as 191 and 192 form one of the most handsome spreads in this book. The former comes from Hokusai's imaginary studies of the Ryukyus. It seems highly doubtful that he ever got to Okinawa, but his prints depicting the Chinese-type life and architecture there are among his most poetic. Print 192 is, of course, a glowing classic and comes from a series which contains others equally fine. Even when one recalls the greatest of Hiroshige's snow scenes, this Hokusai remains majestic in the eye.

Two prints were also chosen from his greatest series, the *Imagery of the Poets,* and the Li Po gazing at the waterfall was printed in color in order to point out certain perplexing problems relating to this print. If one studies the present version minutely and with the aid of a magnifying glass, he will find that it differs in slight details from the version also printed in color in Ledoux. The version shown here is identical with those contained in two major American collections, but if I remember correctly, the Ledoux version is also duplicated in other collections. One is therefore tempted to conclude either that this magnificent series was at one time skillfully forged (we know that there were many incompetent forgeries), or that enough copies were originally struck off so as to require a slight recutting of the key block.

188. HOKUSAI: *Bullfinch and Drooping-cherry.* Page 274

189. HOKUSAI: *Fuji from Kajikazawa.* Page 274

190. HOKUSAI: *Fuji from Hodogaya.* Page 274

191. HOKUSAI: *Ryukyu Seascape*, Page 274

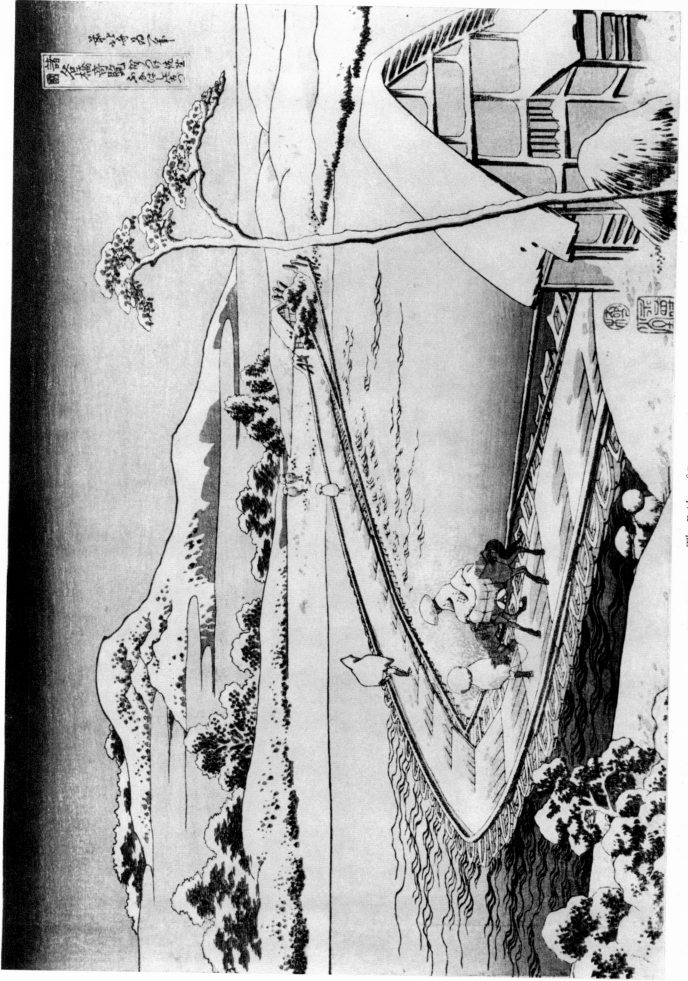

192. HOKUSAI: *The Bridge of Boats at Sano.* Page 274

193. HOKUSAI: *Butterfly and Tree-peony*. Page 274

194. HOKUSAI: *Winter Landscape by the Sumida River.* Page 274

195. HOKUSAI: *The Poet Li Po Admiring a Waterfall.* Page 274

196. HOKUSAI: *Traveler in the Snow*. Page 274

187

197

197. HOKUJU: *Monkey Bridge.* Page 275

198. GAKUTEI: *Squall at Tempozan*, Page 275

189

199. HOKKEI: *Foreign Warship Saluting.* Page 275

200. HOKKEI: *Ferryboat in Rain.* Page 275

201. HOKKEI: *Travelers at Fudo Pass.* Page 275

202. HOKKEI: *Sumiyoshi Shrine.* Page 275

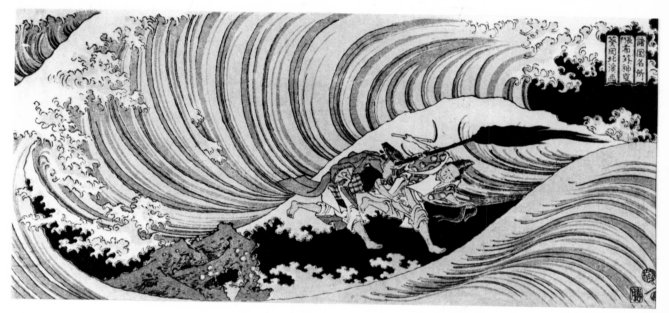

203. HOKKEI: *Night Festival at the Seashore.* Page 275

204. HOKKEI: *Waterfall at Nikko.* Page 275

Toyokuni:

THE WAY the seven pages reserved for Toyokuni turned out presents something of a surprise, even to the author. I doubt if any other ukiyo-e artist tried so many distinctive styles as Toyokuni, and this collection is fortunate in having fairly good examples of most of them; so that at one time these seven pages provided a moderately satisfactory cross-section. There were yellow-ground prints copied from Shuncho, big heads done in the style of Sharaku, a beautiful girl that looked as if Utamaro might have done her, some fine hoso-e that looked like Shunsho, and that rhythmic masterpiece, the triptych of princesses tying poems onto the branches of wind-whipped cherry trees, which exists in this collection in excellent condition.

But the more I studied these pages the more convinced I became that the essential Toyokuni resides in his powerful series of single figures standing stark against bare backgrounds, and one by one the other subjects disappeared until at last there stood these seven majestic prints. They represent Toyokuni at his best. Experienced collectors around the world seek these subjects, and they form a fitting capstone to ukiyo-e's honorable tradition of actor prints.

Six of them come from Toyokuni's masterwork, *Yakusha butai no sugata-e,* "Views of Actors in Role." This series, which has never been catalogued in full, may contain as many as fifty separate subjects, some of which are positively dazzling. The actors are strikingly posed, well drawn, excellently colored, and sometimes graced with mica backgrounds. Each critic has his own preferences as to finest subjects in the series, but Print 209 appears on almost everyone's list. Of his copy, Louis Ledoux wrote: "This print, uniting as it does distinction of composition with fineness of impression and the partly accidental beauty of color and condition brought by time, represents Toyokuni at the highest reach of his achievement in actor prints." By a fortunate accident, Ledoux's copy is now in the Honolulu collection, where it can be compared with the one shown here. At the extreme bottom of the actor's robe, the two prints vary minutely, in that Print 209 has an added ripple, whereas the Ledoux print does not. The series was apparently very popular and probably some of the blocks had to be retouched. The collection also has two fine copies of Print 206, and these show similar minor retouchings of the master block.

Unfortunately, in later years, when the *Yakusha butai* series became popular with European and American buyers, unscrupulous Japanese dealers bought up as many of Toyokuni's untitled actor prints as possible. It was then a simple matter to carve on a new woodblock the *Yakusha butai* cartouche and stamp it upon such prints. The collection has a very enticing example of such a forgery. In that respect Print 208 raises special problems, for it is known in another version without the cartouche and with noticeable differences in the background; but it is believed that Toyokuni himself ordered these changes in order to bring a popular single print into a more popular series.

Of Print 211, its former owner J. Hillier, England's leading expert on ukiyo-e, has written that it is "the finest mica-ground Toyokuni in existence," a judgment with which I am not inclined to argue, but some Japanese critics have wondered if the mica dates from Toyokuni's time, a question I am not competent to judge.

Long before I ever thought to own the print which appears opposite in color, I wrote that to me it seemed even better than any of the *Yakusha butai* series. I still think so.

205. TOYOKUNI: *Sawamura Sojuro*. Page 276

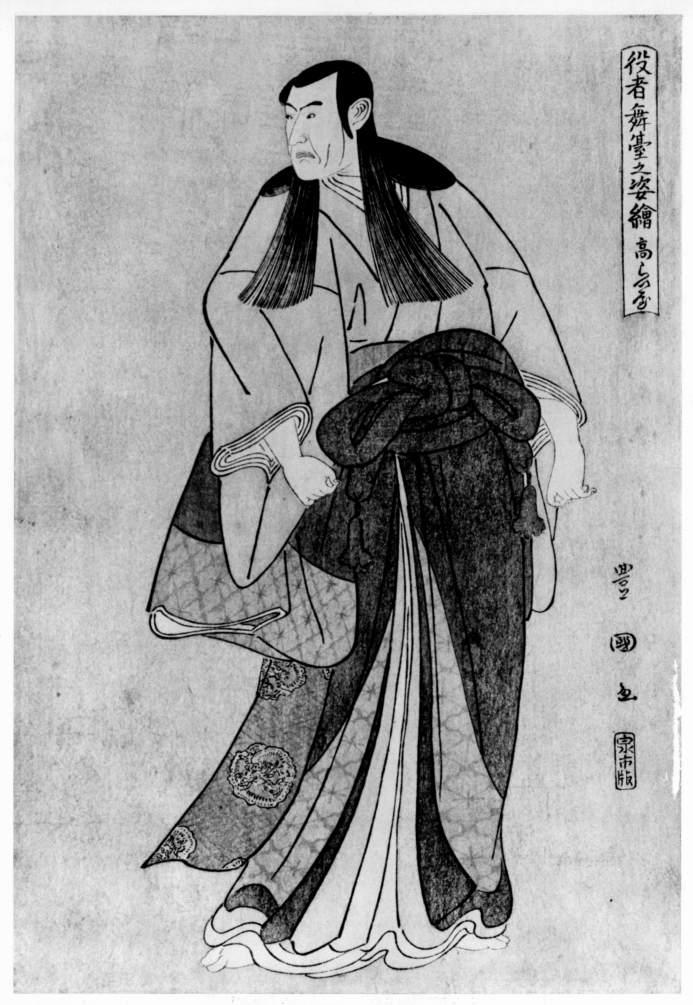

役者舞臺之姿繪 高らいや

豊國画 東市版

206. TOYOKUNI: *Matsumoto Koshiro.* Page 276

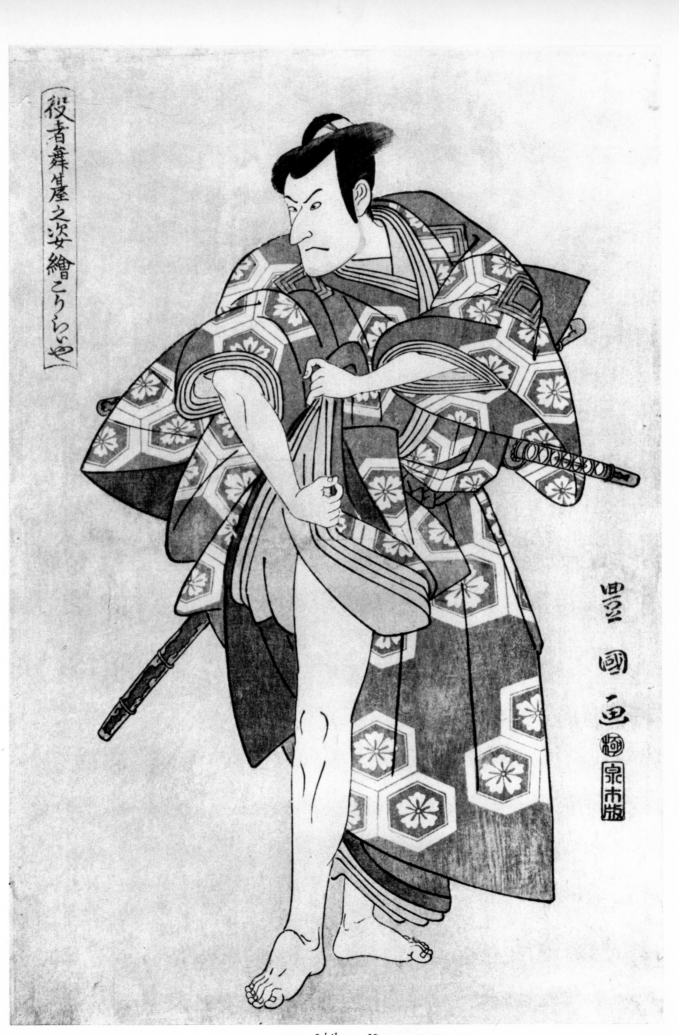

役者舞台之姿繪こりちいや

207. TOYOKUNI: *Ichikawa Komazo.* Page 276

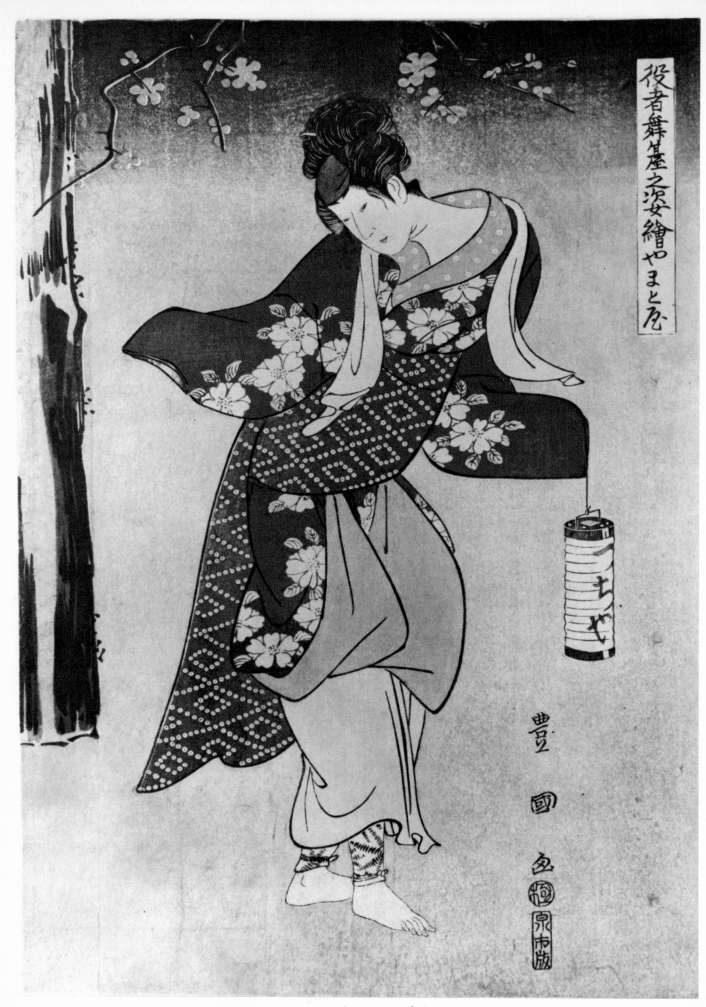

208. TOYOKUNI: *Nakamura Noshio.* Page 276

209. TOYOKUNI: *Iwai Hanshiro.* Page 276

210. TOYOKUNI: *Ichikawa Yaozo.* Page 276

211. TOYOKUNI: *Onoe Shosuke.* Page 276

Minor Masters:

AT THE end of ukiyo-e's vital period, when only the longevity of the last of the great masters, Hokusai and Hiroshige, was delaying the day when the art was to pass into its moribund period, a group of minor artists appeared to produce a handful of prints that were surprisingly good. These men are often ignored both in collections and in literature on ukiyo-e. It would be folly to pretend that they were great artists, for their limitations were so obvious that an assembly of their worst prints – and ninety-five percent of their output falls into that classification – could be used as an example of why ukiyo-e died. But interspersed with their horrors – poorly designed, poorly drawn, and wretchedly colored – one comes upon occasional prints that are exciting, seven of which are here presented.

Kunimasa was born a little early to qualify as a typical member of this group, and the general quality of his output was higher than that of the others here mentioned, but he was such a minor artist that he fits in here. One does not expect him to do fine prints, yet the three portraits shown here have always commanded attention, while the one reproduced in color has become almost the symbol of the prints of this period. It has been widely reproduced in Japan, is the subject of numerous copies, and has recently been transformed, by a series of nine large ceramic tiles, into a huge and striking wall decoration. It is a most appealing print and if it were not known to be by Kunimasa, I would judge it to be one of the better Shun'eis. Print 214 has also enjoyed a favorable reputation in Japan and is a fitting subject with which to end our series of big heads: the hero tugs at the ends of his towel lest, as I have been told, he fall backward in disgrace after having had the courage to disembowel himself.

Kuniyoshi has always been a minor favorite of mine, for working alone he discovered many of the principles of contemporary art and applied them to a marvelous series of prints, not well received at the time of issue but later recognized for the pioneering work they were. Print 216 is a good example of this style, for here in some strange way Kuniyoshi anticipates many of the devices that were to come later in Europe. Only the fact that I have reproduced elsewhere his masterpiece in this form, the night raid of the ronin, prevents me from using it here, for it is an excellent print and a landmark in Japanese art history. Print 215 shows another unexpected aspect of Kuniyoshi's work, his experiments in European-style draftsmanship; the woman to the left is almost the same as that drawn repeatedly by the minor Italian master Beccafumi.

Print 217 is a unique gem, Kunisada's futuristic study of the planes created in nature by a heavy mist falling capriciously across a ravine. It is an extraordinary print, difficult to reproduce but startling in effect. Like earlier critics, I find it difficult to believe that Kunisada was capable of such work, but he signed it.

I found Print 218 at the bottom of a pile. I know nothing about it, except that Eisen, a man of little taste, designed it, and I have never seen it reproduced or discussed, but all who see it agree that the mottled background, the perfect placement of the bamboo, and the severe Chinese lettering combine to make a haunting work. Anyone who looks constantly among the odds and ends of ukiyo-e usually comes up with some unexpected pleasure, like the seven prints shown in this group, and this is one of the rewards of Japanese prints: the field is far from exhausted. In Paris, in London, or in San Francisco tomorrow, one may come upon some unheralded print which he will always regard as highly as I regard this superb Eisen. And the joy of such discovery is that no critic has ever said that the print is meritorious. This is a decision that each discoverer must make for himself, and in the major historical fields of art only in ukiyo-e is this intellectual adventure available almost daily.

212. KUNIMASA: *Ichikawa Ebizo*. Page 276

213. KUNIMASA: *Nakamura Noshio*. Page 276

214. KUNIMASA: *Ichikawa Danjuro.* Page 276

215. KUNIYOSHI: *Kuo Chü Finds the Pot of Gold.* Page 276

216. KUNIYOSHI: *Tile-kilns at Imado.* Page 276

217. KUNISADA: *Landscape in Mist. Page 277*

218. EISEN: *Bamboos and Moon.* Page 277

Hiroshige:

IT IS IRONIC that a man who once wrote, "Hiroshige's work has never charmed me as it does most collectors," should wind up, as I have done, the chance custodian of what Judson Metzgar called: "America's finest private collection of Hiroshige. Schraubstadter's was larger but lacking in the wonderful quality that marks these Chandler prints." From this wealth it has not been easy to select a mere eleven that will do justice to the man.

Others think more highly of the long letter-sheets than I, but I do recognize them as free, flowing statements of nature, more poetic in concept than some of his other work, and it has here been possible to give them the full sweep they deserve. "Sudden Rain at Ohashi" well exemplifies Hiroshige's famous rain and is the print that moved Van Gogh to paint his own glowing copy of it. The snow scene from *Wakan roei shu* is the masterpiece from one of Hiroshige's finest series, while the two panels facing it are choice items from his narrow views of Edo. Print 224 has always been avidly sought by collectors, and with reason, for it is a happy composition in fine color and marked with Hiroshige's best style. Print 228 has been termed ukiyo-e's greatest nature print, a judgment I find no difficulty in accepting; note how extraordinarily Japanese it is, how exactly right the three elements of nature – bird, rain and tree – are handled, how flawless the design and coloring.

But so far as this collector is concerned, the most important print in the book is 229, not because it is undoubtedly one of the sublest works ever produced in print form, and not because it was chosen by Robert Treat Paine, Jr., to illustrate his essay on ukiyo-e, but because it was the first Japanese print I ever saw. It was shown to me many years ago by a tenderhearted woman in Buffalo, Mrs. Georgia Forman, and I believe I sensed then all I was one day to discover in ukiyo-e. Years later, in Afghanistan, I received a most improbable letter from Mrs. Forman's son. He said that on the morning of his mother's death she had unexpectedly thought of the afternoon she had shown me her best Hiroshige: "And she said, 'Why should I leave my prints to a museum that may appreciate them . . . or may not? Why not leave them to Michener?'" She had neither seen me nor written to me for twenty-five years, and yet she remembered that I had shared her enthusiasm for this Hiroshige; upon her gift of prints my collection has been built.

In 1896, Ernest Fenollosa concluded the first important American essay on ukiyo-e with an obiter dictum that was to become famous: a list of the more important artists classified into three groups of descending excellence. In 1915 Arthur Davison Ficke updated the list. Today I would classify the major artists roughly as follows. In each group the artists appear in the same order as in this book. The first number shows Fenollosa's judgment in 1896; the second, Ficke's in 1915; an asterisk means that the artist in question did not appear on that list. Observe that neither critic had yet heard of Sugimura Jihei and that neither thought much of Kuniyoshi, whose work I heartily admire.

First Group			Second Group			Third Group		
Moronobu	2	1	Sugimura	*	*	Shigenaga	3	2
Kiyonobu	2	2	Kaigetsudo	2	2	Kiyohiro	3	*
Masanobu	1	1	Kiyomasu	2	2	Kiyomitsu	3	2
Harunobu	1	1	Toyonobu	3	2	Shunko	*	3
Kiyonaga	1	1	Koryusai	2	1	Shun'ei	*	3
Utamaro	2	1	Buncho	3	2	Shigemasa	2	2
Sharaku	*	1	Shunsho	3	1	Shuncho	2	2
Hokusai	1	1	Choki	*	2	Eishi	3	2
			Toyokuni	3	2	Kuniyoshi	*	*
			Hiroshige	3	1			

221. HIROSHIGE: *Sudden Shower at Ohashi.* Page 277

219. HIROSHIGE: *The Salt-beach at Gyotoku.* Page 277

220. HIROSHIGE: *Cherry Blossoms at Koganei.* Page 277

雪似鵝毛
飛散乱
人被鶴氅
立徘徊

和漢朗詠集

222. HIROSHIGE: *Mountain Village.* Page 277

223. HIROSHIGE: *By Ryogoku Bridge.* Page 277

224. HIROSHIGE: *Autumn Moon over the Yoshiwara.* Page 277

225. HIROSHIGE: *Moon through Leaves.* Page 278

226. HIROSHIGE: *Plovers in Flight.* Page 278

214

227. HIROSHIGE: *Wild Geese in Flight*. Page 278

228. HIROSHIGE: *Cuckoo in Flight*. Page 278

229. HIROSHIGE: *Evening Bell at Mii Temple. Page 278*

Section 4:
THE MODERNS

MOST COLLECTIONS of Japanese prints and most works dealing with them end with Hiroshige; and this is not illogical, for following the death of that great master in 1858 there can be no question but that the art of traditional ukiyo-e declined sharply. A dreary sequence of hacks, known as the Kuni's and the Yoshi's – a recent work lists eighty undistinguished artists whose names begin with the former character and fifty-seven beginning with the latter – poured forth an endless series of prints marked by cluttered design, boring historical content, and some of the most garish coloring ever seen in serious art. Because most of those later prints were abominable, it became fashionable for critics to ridicule all work done after 1858, and some extremely sweeping condemnations have been made by otherwise perceptive critics. I prefer not to embarrass anyone by digging up a series of such judgments; but I must point out that if one were to accept such criticism blindly, no print that appears in this last section would be worth collecting. My contention is otherwise: after the dreadful flood of garish color prints, a good many artists went seriously to work to see what could be done to rescue the art from extinction, and the first five prints offered here show what was accomplished.

The five have these attributes in common: They appeared after the high tide of ukiyo-e. They were definite attempts to revive a dying art. Each was produced in the old way; that is, the artist drew his sketch, the woodcarver carved it on a block of cherry wood, the printer applied the colors to the finished block and struck off the copies. And except in the case of Print 233, the finished copies were peddled to the public by a professional publisher. In other words, Print 234, which so far as I am concerned is the last great print produced in the classic tradition, is technically not a bit different from Print 1, which appeared about 156 years earlier.

I am very fond of these five prints and consider them markedly underpriced in present markets, for they are of fine quality, have a content which appeals to me, and are worthy echoes of a great past. I cannot understand any theory of art which would condemn them to oblivion; for if one is eager to be in at the birth of an art, and if he wants to own an album sheet so that he can remember what happened in those far-off days, he ought also to be interested in the decline; and it is with Kiyochika, Goyo, and Shinsui that we witness the actual end of ukiyo-e.

Why were these five prints, excellent as they are, not sufficiently strong to keep the traditional print-making process alive? Four explanations come to mind: the subject matter was circumscribed and old-fashioned, so that modern taste could not take it seriously; the color harmonies were muted at a time when color in Western art was becoming increasingly bold; the precise and refined techniques of carving and printing were more appropriate to the age of Harunobu than to the age of Picasso; and there was nothing in the art that allied it with the great movements that were sweeping the rest of the world, where techniques were rough, colors vibrant, and content psychological. Traditional print-making, even in these marvelous final examples, had lost itself in a cul-de-sac, and it is with a feeling of mournful affection, rather than of vital participation, that I revere these last prints.

But with Print 235 I enter a joyous new world, and one in which I feel at home. Take a moment to leaf through the twenty-two prints shown in these last pages. Try to determine which betray the fact that they were done by Japanese artists. I find thirteen that give no evidence at all that they were of Oriental derivation. They stand forth as competent examples of the best in international art. The men who did them have obviously shaken themselves free of antique preconceptions and exist as blood-brothers to Picasso, Mondrian, Marin, and Gauguin. This is the great accomplishment of the modern Japanese print: it has set free both the artist and his technique.

At the same time, look at Prints 237 and 254. These are as Japanese as a Harunobu or an Utamaro. They revive the loveliest traditions of an ancient subject matter, and reveal that some of the most eloquent Japanese content in the history of print-making is being utilized today. This is the second outstanding accomplishment of the modern print: it has provided the artist with techniques for preserving what is essentially Japanese in his tradition. Thus the modern artist can utilize subject matter that is either international or intensely national, and he can accomplish fine work with either. This is one of the earmarks of a mature art.

The technical development which differentiates these later prints from all that precede is the fact that each has been drawn, carved, printed and published by the artist himself, a difference the artists have emphasized by calling their works sosaku hanga, "creative prints," not ukiyo-e. Thus, when you look at the glowing Onchi 242, you are seeing only his handiwork. Where possible, he even ground his own colors, and if he had been able to lay the paper himself, he would have done that too. Because the formal techniques used in the classic period of print-making had led to formalized art, the modern artists felt obligated to perform all functions themselves. Thus, when Yamamoto, the artist responsible for Print 235, saw what vigorous work European artists were accomplishing by cutting their own blocks, he established the principle that Japanese must do the same; and much of the wild power of the modern Japanese print stems from this precept of Yamamoto's. For example, Print 243 shows an insolent disregard for precise cutting, perfect registry, and exact handling of color. In seeking new freedoms the artists who made these prints were taking a step essential to the revitalization of Japanese print-making.

From what I said in the Introduction, it is obvious that I do not place much emphasis on the specific technique whereby a work of art is created. I feel reasonably sure that Yamamoto and his followers could have achieved with old-style block-cutters and old-style printers the fine work they ultimately accomplished, and I give none of the credit whatever to the fact that they elected to carve their own blocks; but the significant factor is that they thought they had to do so, and anything that will help the individual artist attain the freedom to do singing, soaring work is to be treasured. If these men thought they had to cast aside the old carvers and printers, then they were entitled to do so, even if in reality the step was not so essential as they thought. With that qualification, this is the third significant accomplishment of the modern print: it allows the artist himself to control each step of its creation.

Other characteristics are self-evident. The prints are much bigger than before; previously their size was determined by the size of board that could be cut from a cherry tree, but modern artists often forswear solid cherry in favor of plywood. Colors are much bolder; the muted harmonies so loved by Harunobu and Kiyonaga are not often seen, for the bright international palette has triumphed. Abstract designs are becoming common; and contrary to sentimental taste which would require the Japanese artist to restrict himself to antique themes, this is an appropriate development, for the Japanese have always been strongly inclined toward abstraction, as indicated in their ceramic and kimono patterns. Finally, the modern print is apt to have a profounder psychological content than those of the classical period; it is true that Sekino's fine study of Lafcadio Hearn, Print 236, stems directly from Sharaku, but Onchi's vision, Print 243, and Hatsuyama's, Print 253, derive from no Japanese antecedents; they are new and part of the total international art movement.

There is one point about these modern prints that rises frequently to plague me. Well-intentioned people, looking at them, often exclaim: "Isn't it a pity that the artists no longer do Japanese scenes like Hokusai and Hiroshige." I am afraid this is what must be termed "the tourist approach to art criticism." One wants a Dutchman to paint windmills and wooden shoes, an Italian to do madonnas in red shawls, and a Mexican to create sleeping Indians in big hats. This type of criticism demands that if an artist is Japanese he is obligated to paint geisha girls, cherry blossoms, and Mount Fuji. Carried to logical absurdity, what such critics contend is that it is all right for a Spaniard like Picasso or an American like Pollock or a Russian like Chagall to paint in an international style, but it is forbidden for a Japanese to do so. I find no logic in this whatever. There surely can be no categorical imperative for unborn generations of artists to keep on turning out pale copies of Hokusai and Hiroshige, just to titillate tourist appetites. Let the modern artist work as his will dictates, and the tourists of a later age will mysteriously grow to recognize his work as the essence of things Japanese. It is unthinkable that an artist should be arbitrarily confined to any one subject matter, or denied full membership in the international society of creative minds. In Japan, the modern print artist has labored diligently to prove this point.

But perhaps I am not an unprejudiced critic, for I confess a special affection for these modern prints. I have known most of the artists represented here and for some years have followed their work. By a fortunate accident I helped bring Onchi and Hiratsuka to the attention of an international audience; and before most of these men were as well known as they now are, I experienced the joy of discovering for myself what I thought of their work. It is their prints that I keep on my walls at home. It is their work that speaks to me in contemporary accents. For each classical print that I study, I find myself reviewing two or three of these strong, vibrant moderns. I am excited by them, and I love them. I am convinced that in years to come the artists shown here will be increasingly recognized as worthy revivers of an art form that in its classical manifestation had died; and to revitalize an art, even if one has to modify the techniques that helped make it strong originally, is no mean accomplishment.

My respect for these men transcends their artistic successes, for I well know with what dedication they have labored through lean years. Men like Onchi, Hiratsuka, and Yamaguchi are more courageous men than I, and now that one international jury after another is awarding them first prizes for the best print work being done in the world today, I am most happy. If a collection of art must inescapably be a portrait of the man who assembled it, I would be content to be represented by Prints 244 and 245. They are of my spirit.

The book closes with two panels, Prints 255–56, from one of the most profound works of art produced in Japan in this century, and certainly one which has received more international acclaim than most. In 1939, Munakata Shiko, one of Japan's most distinguished print artists and a man of abounding vitality, issued a series of towering sumizuri-e titled *The Ten Great Disciples of Buddha*, including the ten disciples and two bodhisattvas. These twelve dynamic prints have won numerous awards in exhibitions throughout the world. They form a fitting conclusion to a vivid journey.

Transition :

OF ALL the prints represented in this book, those in this next group have been most ignored by scholars, if not by the general public, for in spite of the fact that they have been widely bought, so that in many parts of the world there are numerous respectable collections covering this period, there is no satisfactory treatise dealing with these artists and no critical account of their work. This is a regrettable omission, and one that should be corrected, for it was by means of these ingratiating, if not great, works that hundreds of collectors came to know Japanese prints, and a careful review of what these men accomplished will go far toward correcting the easy assumption that after Hiroshige the Japanese print was completely dead. It was moribund, and the fire infused into it by men like Sharaku and Hokusai was no more, but it continued underground, as it were, as a respectable minor art, and when this period has been summarized by some careful scholar with a critical eye and a discerning appreciation, we will close a painful gap in our knowledge.

The five artists whom I have chosen as typical of this attractive, quiescent period are varied. No pages in this book give me more personal pleasure than the next three. From the first day I planned this work I intended using these three prints, exactly as they appear here, but I was six years in finding them, for they turned out to be extremely rare. The Kiyochika reminds me of Ryder and shows what Japanese artists, working alone, were accomplishing. It is a moody, evocative masterpiece. The Ryuson stands apart in my affections, for it seems to me to summarize the end of an epoch. The moon is rising on this night over a Tokyo that will soon be no more; as ukiyo-e dies, so dies the ancient life. There are many Japanese who feel the same way about this print, which is why I feared I would never find a copy. Then on the last day in which I was to be in Japan, Adachi Toyohisa, the famous publisher of ukiyo-e reproductions, came with the news that he had found a copy of this night scene and that a friend had uncovered the Kiyochika "Hiki-fune." They were the last prints I acquired in Japan and among the most meaningful.

I left resigned to the fact that I would have to publish without the Yasuji, for copies were simply not available; but a year later and only days before the plate-maker reached this section of the book, Shobisha, the Tokyo dealer, sent word that a copy had been found. If the Ryuson signalizes the end of one age, this famous, impressionistic Yasuji heralds the beginning of another: Western-style canned goods and gas lights have arrived on the Ginza!

I especially commend these two pages, Prints 231 and 232, for they summarize the meaning of this book: the old passes in a moment of positively haunting beauty, the garish new is inevitable and it is the artist's job to hammer it into some semblance of beauty. These are prints at their best: reportorial, widely disseminated, artistic, compelling to the eye. I truly love these two pages.

Goyo's delicate portraits of women are justly famous, their reputation being somewhat tarnished by the fact that most examples available today are post-humous copies issued by men who got hold of the original blocks. And the Shinsui serenader is a flawless print made by a painter still living in Tokyo. It is not inappropriate to place it at the very end of a great tradition.

If more pages had been available for these dying days of ukiyo-e, I would have included representative prints by these artists Kyosai, who did inky-black crows, and Zeshin, whose studies of mice are delectable; Yoshida Hiroshi, who almost alone kept the antique art alive with a prodigious output; Yamamura Koka, whose modern portraits of actors are held by Japanese to rival Sharaku's; and Hasui, the best known of the group. But it was a period with which I myself am not particularly attuned, and I must leave its description to others.

NIGHTLY VIEW OF HIKI-FUNE AT KO-OOME IN TO-KEI.
A BOAT IS GUIDED BY THE ROPES.

230. KIYOCHIKA: *Pulling the Canal-boat.* Page 278

231. RYUSON: *Moonlight at Yushima.* Page 278

232. YASUJI: *Shop on the Ginza.* Page 278

233. GOYO: *Woman at Toilette.* Page 279

234. SHINSUI: *Samisen Minstrel at Ikenohata.* Page 279

First Group:

NO PRINT in this book is more important than the one which appears opposite this page. Its effect upon Japanese print-making was cyclonic, and much of today's accomplishment stems from this print, and from others which Yamamoto sent back to Japan from his artistic explorations in Paris in the years 1912–14. It is the first print in this book which in no way betrays its Japanese ancestry. It was conceived, drawn, carved, colored, and printed in European style, but of course the superb paper had to be Japanese; no other would do.

It is a revolutionary print and almost by itself thrust the entire world of Japanese print-makers into the orbit of men like Van Gogh, Kandinsky, Munch, and Kokoshcka. From this time on the precise, meticulously carved blocks of ukiyo-e are gone. The new artists will carve with bold strokes, and they will use the wood as a major component of their designs. Areas will be modeled, shadows used, and forms carefully built up. Bright new color combinations will become popular and a bold impressionism featuring European characteristics will predominate. That is why Yamamoto Kanae's portrait of the Breton girl is one of the most revolutionary prints ever issued. After it flashed through Tokyo, no serious artist could go back to the classical style.

Yamamoto's greatest prints are those showing European subjects, especially his Russian landscapes. This collection is fortunate in owning eight fine examples, but the one shown here most strikingly illustrates Yamamoto's effect upon his contemporaries: it is so modern, so un-Japanese, so much within the sophisticated international tradition that it merits our special attention. That it reached me from the hands of Oliver Statler, a young American from Chicago who worked in Tokyo with the Army of Occupation and who in his book *Modern Japanese Prints* launched the serious study of Yamamoto and contemporary prints, adds to its attractiveness for me.

The Sekino, Print 236, is especially noteworthy in that it represents the American who did the most to explain Japan to the West, Lafcadio Hearn. His portrait well illustrates the way in which Yamamoto's successors adapted his lessons, but for me the print has an unusual personal importance. A few days before his death, Judson Metzgar, last of the original group of American ukiyo-e connoisseurs, entertained me in his Los Angeles home, and when we had finished studying his collection of classical ukiyo-e, he showed me a print which he had come especially to love, and it was this modern Sekino. It thus became the last print that the great classicist Metzgar sold and testifies that even he was converted to modern work.

The output of Saito Kiyoshi, represented here by Print 238, which I especially treasure because it came to me from William Hartnett, another American who served with the Occupation and who first drew the world's attention to what was happening in Japanese print circles, is widely known in America. Saito is amazingly skilled as a craftsman, a fine designer, and a man imbued with a sense of things Japanese.

The Hashimoto, Print 241, is of value to students in that the copy shown here is accompanied, at Honolulu, by ten preliminary pencil sketches, five trial paintings in rough oil, two proof sheets of the key block, and a complete set of the six printing stages required to produce the finished print. With such a wealth of material, it thus becomes an encyclopedia of modern print-making.

235

235. YAMAMOTO KANAE: *Woman of Brittany.* Page 279

Lafcadio Hearn in Japanese Costume by Sekino

236. SEKINO JUN'ICHIRO: *Lafcadio Hearn in Japanese Costume.* Page 279

237. MAEKAWA SEMPAN: *Akita Dancer*. Page 279

238. SAITO KIYOSHI: *Winter in Aizu.* Page 279

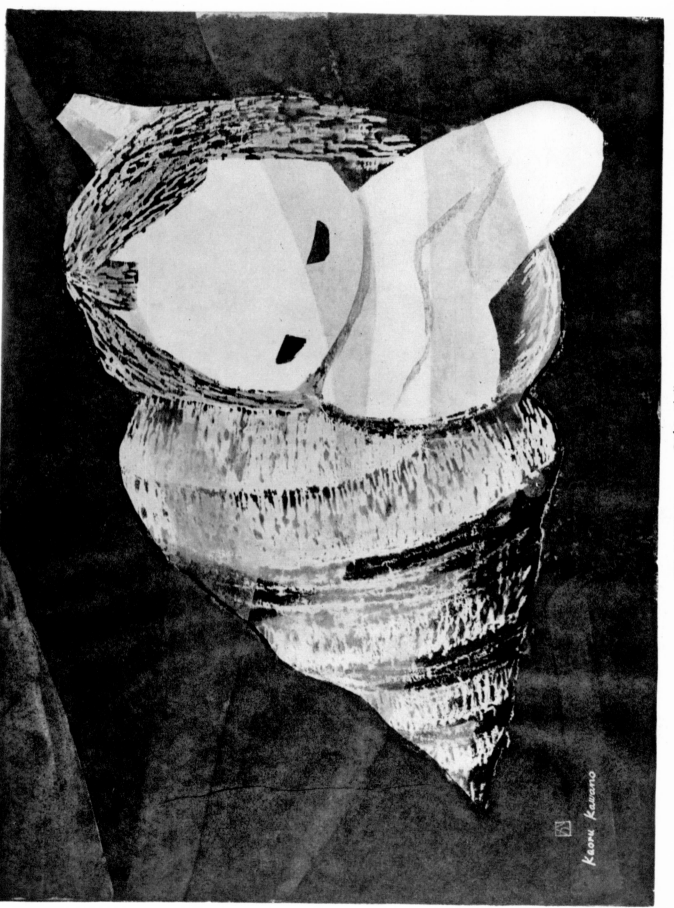

239. KAWANO KAORU: *Girl in Shell*. Page 280

240. MABUCHI THORU: *Afternoon Sun.* Page 280

橋本奥衣作

241. HASHIMOTO OKIIE: *Gate and Retainer's Hall, Nijo Castle.* Page 280

Onchi : THE COLLECTION represented in this book will never be remembered for

its 45 Masanobus, because any attentive collector ought to be able to acquire equivalent prints over the next ten years; surely they will come on the market. Nor will it be remembered for its 108 rather handsome Harunobus, for these prints appear regularly in major sales and in much less than a decade a collector could well surpass what this collection has to show. In the past the collection has been favorably known for its wealth of Hiroshige prints, but with a little care any collector could duplicate these, for Hiroshiges are quite easy to acquire.

But I believe that the 44 Onchis in this collection will be long remembered, for I am convinced that this powerful, gifted man will ultimately be recognized as the genius of this period of print-making. His prints were few in number, with rarely more than half a dozen to an edition. But they were highly prized both by his contemporary artists and by a discerning group of collectors. Few are now coming on the market, and it was only because others associated with the production of this book counseled restraint that I forswore presenting here eight or ten of his finest works. Certainly, my taste inclined me toward doing so.

Onchi Koshiro died in 1955, a tall, gray-haired, lively poet with a fine acid sense of humor. He was a wonderful man to know, for he laughed most of the time and his ready wit played upon many subjects. He was a brave man and during World War II had the fortitude to combat the military nonsense then rife in Japan. Above all, he was an international spirit, roaming the entire world. He felt himself a brother to Munch of Norway and Kandinsky of Russia. He signed his name in European characters and used French and German titles for his work. Above all, he was a magnetic, vital human being, absorbed in aviation, in the study of nature, and like so many Japanese intellectuals, in the symphonic music of Beethoven, Brahms, and Bruckner. As a man he was an adornment to his society.

As a print artist his ultimate effect was even greater than that of Yamamoto Kanae, for he produced more work, at a time when numbers of young men could come into contact with him. Also, since he came from samurai stock, he had entree to circles denied most of his fellow artists. He was therefore a towering influence, and his cavalier attitude toward materials, using anything so long as it helped him create a vibrant, poetic print, was instrumental in setting his contemporaries free from their servitude to wood, its professional carvers, and its professional printers. With splash and abandon, Onchi used glass, waxed paper, string, glued leaves, and charcoal. His printing was apt to be impressionistic rather than meticulous, and his results were scintillating rather than controlled.

It has been especially difficult for me to select the three best Onchis, for I ruled out his superlative portrait of the poet Hagiwara, which I have published elsewhere, and one of my prime favorites, "Object Number 2," which is handsomely reproduced in color by Statler, who also uses up two other choice subjects, "Poem Number 8" and "Poem Number 22." Thinking it important that we see as much as possible of Onchi's work, I have avoided the foregoing. By far the best Onchi I know is Print 244, but I have been advised that it might not reproduce well in color, since it stresses muted blues. The principal omission both in this book and in Statler's is that series of great final prints where Onchi, who knew death was near, utilized phallic symbols with astonishing power. It was appropriate that this wild, free spirit should end with such thoughts.

242. ONCHI KOSHIRO: *Loneliness.* Page 280

243. ONCHI KOSHIRO: *Caricature No. 8.* Page 280

244. ONCHI KOSHIRO: *Poem Number Nineteen: The Sea*. Page 280

Second Group :

WHEN YAMAGUCHI GEN was in the midst of making the print which appears opposite, he wrote me a letter that summarizes the problems which have always beset Japanese print artists: "For many years I have been working at my art and at times I have not had the courage to go ahead. I have had to watch the work done by men like me ignored, abused, and left unsold. Some critics avoid us because we do not work in the old style, and others say harsh things because we do not copy old Japanese themes. It has been a very hard life indeed to bear such indifference and recently I have often thought about stopping. But the great interest you and Mr. Statler have shown in my work makes me believe that I am doing right. So I keep working."

As anyone can see, the print that came out of the spirit of that letter, which reached me almost a year late while I was working in northern Burma, is a marvelous, poetic thing, and I would be gratified beyond expression if I thought that anything I had said had encouraged a man to stay at such work. But Yamaguchi is a tough-minded man, and the next print after this one went to the international exhibition in Lucerne, where it won the world's number one award. It was very good to be with Yamaguchi when he got word and to see him win belatedly the accolades he had so long deserved.

Almost every print in this section reminds me of the circumstances under which I got it from its creator. For example, I did not want to publish this book without at least one example from the remarkable Yoshida family, worthy successors of Yoshida Hiroshi, yet out of all their work I could not find a print that fitted my page requirements, until late one wintry afternoon I was looking through a stack with Yoshida Hodaka and came upon Print 249. How striking its Mexican motifs seemed then, and now!

It is a special pleasure to be able to reproduce one of Uchima Ansei's prints, 251, for he is a young American-born Japanese who was trapped in Japan during the war and who applied his time to the study of painting. In 1955 Uchima turned to print-making with striking success. And Shinagawa Takumi's abstraction, Print 252, is a joy, with its emphasis on textures and vivid color; the day I got it, Shinagawa said: "I'm so glad you are willing to buy an abstraction. For weeks everyone has been taking only formal prints."

The Hatsuyama Shigeru, Print 253, has a story of its own. This fine artist, who illustrates children's books with wildly imaginative charm, is so popular as a print-maker that the few he produces are instantly sold. I therefore had little chance of acquiring any good copies, but when I visited him on the edge of Tokyo he said: "I work in books and you work in books. I will not sell you any prints, but I will give you all you want, and when you return to America, you will send me a crate of children's books, because I want to see how your illustrations compare with mine." For that reason, this collection has about two dozen of the choicest Hatsuyamas, of which the one shown here is a fine example.

I have written elsewhere of my dear friend Hiratsuka Un'ichi. I see him now in his cluttered study, wearing a Russian-type smock close-buttoned at the neck, a little wisp of a man, with a goatee and the kind of childish wonder in all things that anyone who works with words wishes he could preserve in his own life. That Hiratsuka also did the print which appears on the back jacket-flap of this book is a particular satisfaction.

And if the reader can visualize a wall bearing a frieze of tall, black figures like Prints 255–56, he will understand why the work of Munakata has been so highly praised and why today, as at the beginnings of ukiyo-e, the sumizuri-e technique still produces the most powerful prints.

245. YAMAGUCHI GEN: *Deep Attachment.* Page 280

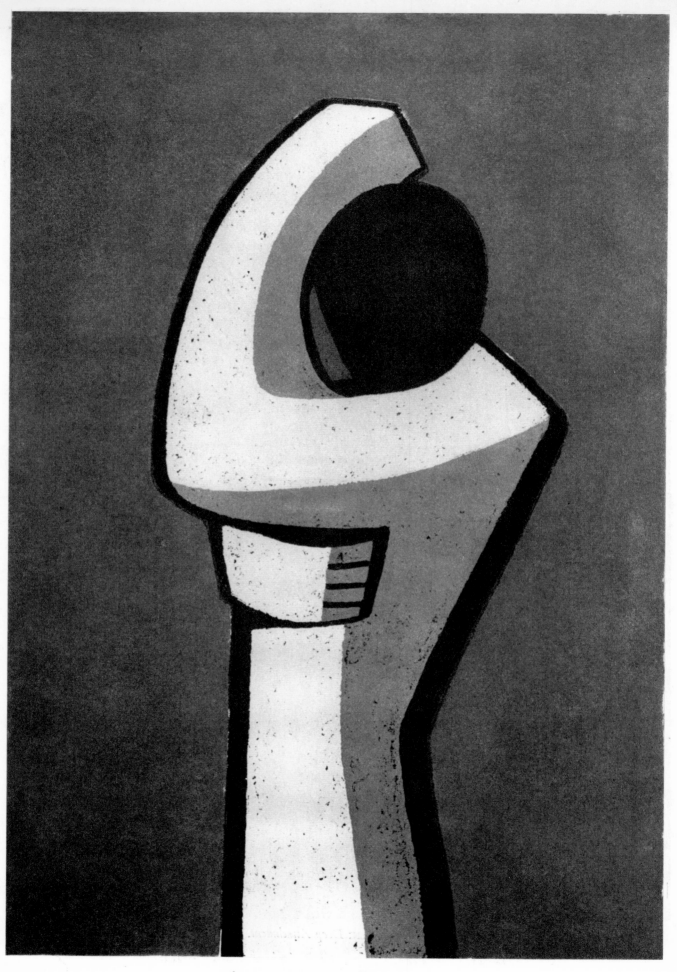

246. NAKAO YOSHITAKA: *Figure.* Page 280

247. AZECHI UMETARO: *Bird in Safe Hands.* Page 280

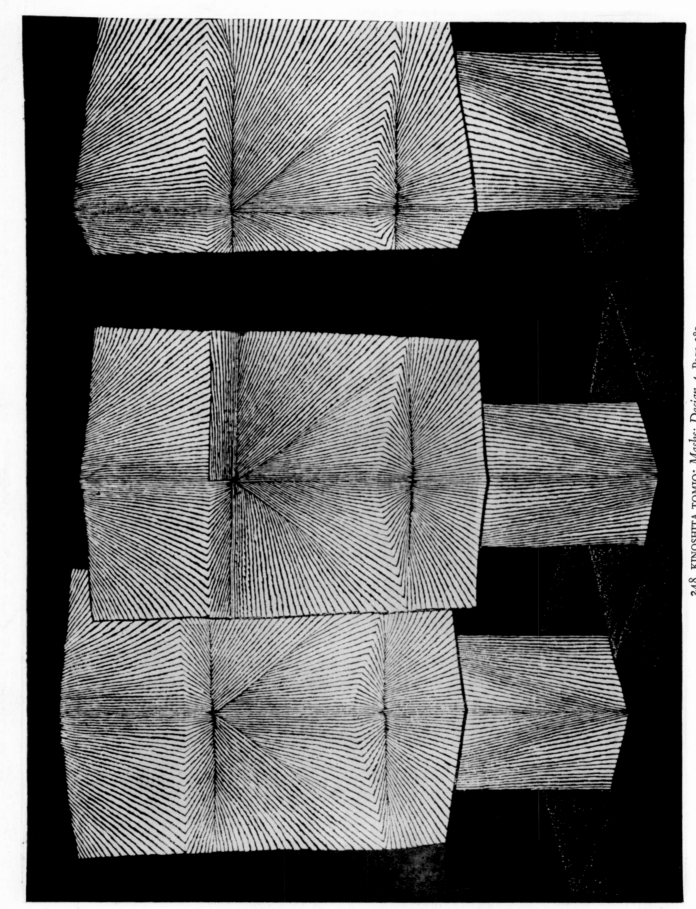

248. KINOSHITA TOMIO: *Masks: Design 4.* Page 280

249. YOSHIDA HODAKA: *Ancient People.* Page 281

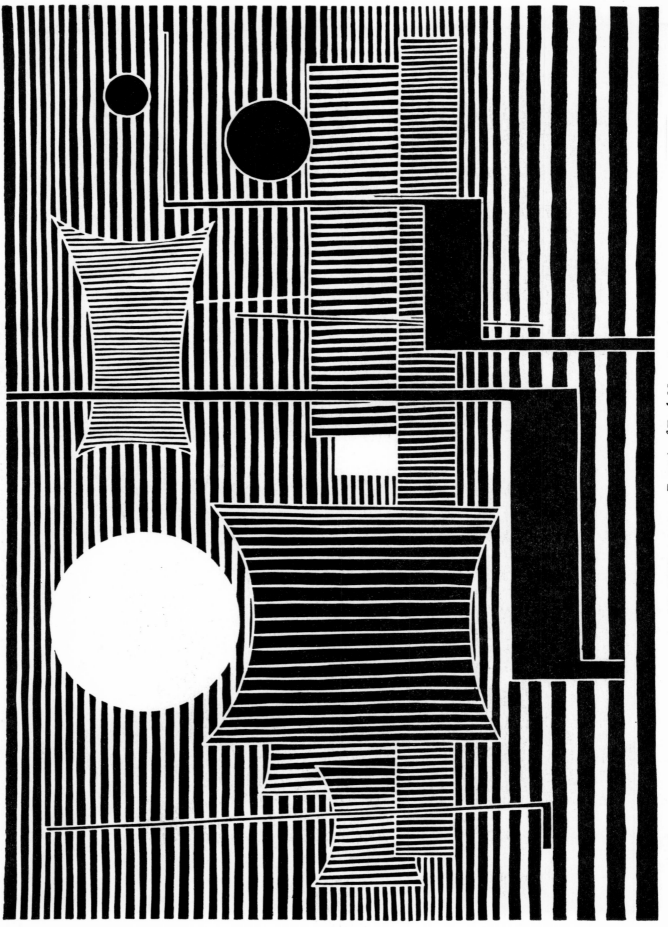

250. YOSHIDA MASAJI: *Fountain of Earth No. 1. Page 281*

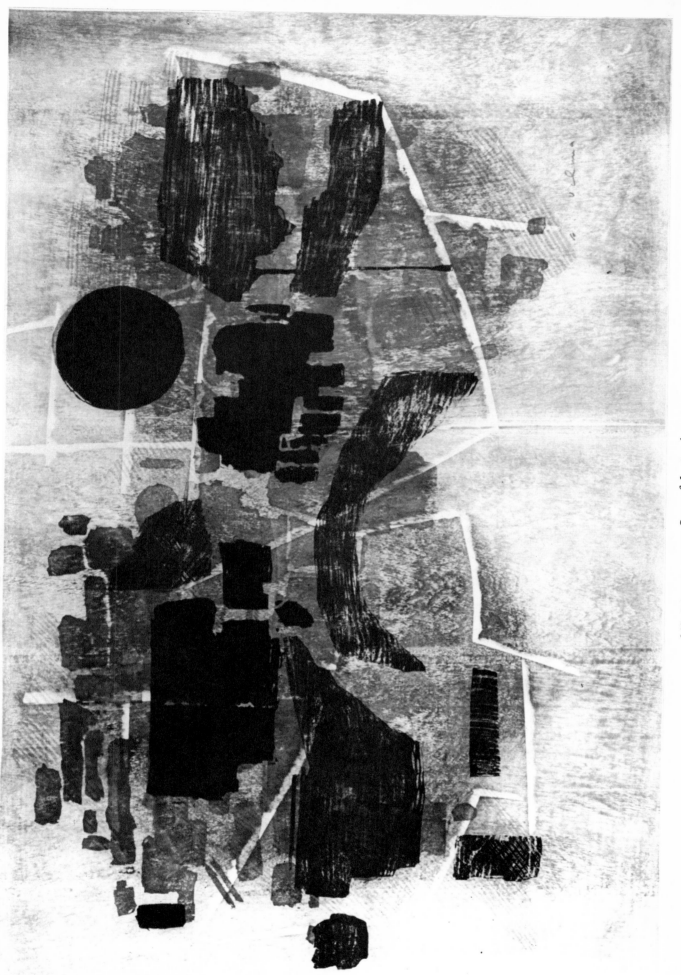

251. UCHIMA ANSEI: *Song of the Seashore.* Page 281

252. SHINAGAWA TAKUMI: *Here Everything Was Alive.* Page 281

253

253. HATSUYAMA SHIGERU: *Flowers, Birds.* Page 281

254. HIRATSUKA UN'ICHI: *Horyu-ji in Early Autumn.* Page 281

255. MUNAKATA SHIKO: *Ubari*. Page 281

256. MUNAKATA SHIKO: *Kasen'en*. Page 282

257. MORONOBU: *Stroll by the Bay* (detail).
Page 254

NOTES ON THE PRINTS

by Richard Lane, ph.d.
RESEARCH ASSOCIATE
HONOLULU ACADEMY OF ARTS

WITH THE injunction "describe 257 prints in thirty pages," brevity has necessarily been the first consideration in the following notes. Where a brief notation on subject matter would suffice to clarify a print, I have always tried to include such. With the numerous Kabuki prints, however, simply recording the names of the actors, their roles, and the name of the play itself has used up my allotted space, making unfeasible any thought of outlining the plays, or even the scene in question. Actually, every detailed book on ukiyo-e must comprise in itself a full encyclopedia of Japanese history, folklore, and manners as mirrored in the prints. In that sense the present volume must admit to aiming itself more at simple identification, and fostering appreciation, than to presenting an advanced guide to the prints herein displayed.

There has, perhaps fortunately, been no space to comment on the often curious translations and comments of earlier cataloguers who were unfamiliar with the Japanese language and customs of the Edo period. Sexes are frequently confused, Japanese names are misspelled as often as not, and translations are sometimes but ill-inspired guesses, like that in the Wright Catalogue description of Print 228: "Two voices over Gomosaki. (The voice of the cuckoo and the voice of the rain.)" It will be another forty years, doubtless, before ukiyo-e studies may be expected to reach any generally sound, scholarly basis either in Japan or in the West, and it would be as unkind to correct connoisseurs still living as it would be ungrateful to criticize the pioneers of sixty years ago. We are still not too far removed from the era when a personable connoisseur of European art plus the most sociable Japanese student available were considered the perfect combination for compiling a study or catalogue of Japanese prints.

Several innovations of this volume should be noted. It is the first book on ukiyo-e to follow modern Japanese romanization throughout, including, in the notes, all diacritical marks. (Thus instead of the archaic spellings "Kwaigetsudo," "Yeisho," "ukiyo-ye" – even worse, Ficke's misspelling "ukioye" – we have Kaigetsudō, Eishō, ukiyo-e.) One innovation that may perhaps be thought a retrogression will be seen in the dating. When there is no positive manner of dating a print, but on the basis of style and technique I think it dates from, say, 1743–47, I write "mid-1740's." I do not record "ca. 1745" – or worse, "1745." This is not done to free myself from the embarrassment of later correction, but rather to indicate that I know no way of more exact dating at the moment. All too often the "exact guesses" of early scholars have been treated as fact by later students. The great pioneer Fenollosa, for example, on the basis of style dated Print 51 in this book as "ca. 1751" – and later students have assumed he had some secret, perhaps oracular, source of data. My own Kabuki research would indicate an exact month in 1756 for this print: had it been labeled "early 1750's" from the beginning, would it not have been, contrary to expectations, a service and a warning to later students that the matter was by no means settled? (The great Art Institute of Chicago *Primitives* catalogue, which I reviewed for the *Harvard Journal of Asiatic Studies* in 1957, is but one example of how pernicious this mania for "exact guessing" has been on museum personnel.) Of course, I do not deny that a gifted student may, through prolonged study of a particular artist or period, come to know his special field well enough to ascertain dates as close as a year or two; but the total field of ukiyo-e studies is too complex to be known that well in less than a lifetime, and during the first decade or so of study it is best to be humble before the vast mountain of material that must be learned and assimilated – while at the same time maintaining a rigid skepticism of all earlier theories and supposed facts that do not stand up under detailed scrutiny.

And a warning should be given regarding Kabuki dating in general – including that in these notes. I have seen the greatest Kabuki experts in Japan make errors of as much as twenty years in Kabuki dating when they happened to find a role that seemed to fit the print in question. Often the only method of verifying a date after the general combinations of actors and roles have been pinned down, is to read the entire play and find the exact scene represented. Yet a majority of the early Kabuki texts were never published, and of those that were, a considerable percentage have been lost; even the extant works have seldom been reprinted. In effect, then, even if given ideal conditions for study – continued presence in Japan, with twenty hours available for each print – a tenth of the Kabuki prints would still remain mysteries to the most skilled researcher.

The only advice I can give to the serious student of ukiyo-e is this: rely on no one, base opinions on original sources, and make first editions of dated prints and illustrated books your bible when you seek to determine the date of an undated print – for in such cases stylistic dating is the only reasonably accurate method I know.

These notes have been written in Japan, far from the actual prints they describe, and I must note with profound gratitude the continued cooperation of Mr. Michener, Mr. Griffing, Miss Morse, and other personnel of the Honolulu Academy of Arts in providing me with all the photographs and information I required – even sending the originals in a few cases where authenticity was in doubt. Data on size, condition, provenance and number of colors are entirely the work of these devoted people. In Japan, friends Tsuihiji Nakasuke and Kikuchi Sadao have lent helpful suggestions, and Yoshida Teruji was kind enough to recheck much of the Kabuki dating. At the publishers', thanks are due to Meredith Weatherby and Ōgimi Kaoru, who have seen to the backbreaking work of editing, make-up, and bookmaking. While most of the material of this section is original with the writer, notes for the modern prints incorporate many suggestions by Mr. Michener (his comments will be readily distinguished by their more colloquial style) and have also been kindly checked over by Oliver Statler. However, final responsibility for the print captions and notes as a whole necessarily rests with the present writer. I may add that, unlike some such projects, I think this one has proved a joy and an education to all concerned.

Tokyo, Summer, 1959

Key to the Notes

1. THE ARTISTS. All Japanese names, whether ancient or modern, are given in their original form, surname first, art-name last. (Note that Sugimura, No. 13, is the only important ukiyo-e artist known by his surname rather than his art-name; with a few artists, like Chōki, the surname is either unknown or seldom used, and the studio name is given instead.) For what they may be worth, very brief biographical notices have been included for each of the artists represented, featuring, most often, his work as it relates specifically to the prints illustrated. At the present stage of ukiyo-e studies even the most elementary statements may involve highly complex problems, but such have only been hinted at here. The notes are grouped under the respective artists, and the artists are in general arranged in the same roughly chronological order of the text. For the convenience of the reader, an alphabetical list of artists, together with their prints, will be found beginning on p. 6.

2. TITLES. Few of the earlier Japanese prints were given titles by the artists, and those devised by Western students have uniformly reflected prevailing Occidental tastes rather than Japanese. Thus Nos. 11 and 13 have, even in modern times, often retained such mildy titillating, but inaccurate, titles as "Spying on Lovers" and "An Interrupted Embrace." Once one is aware of the naturalistic Japanese view of sex and, moreover, of the fact that these prints were originally frontispieces to albums containing the most frank depictions of 17th-century sex life, this Victorian coyness seems somewhat ridiculous. Nearly all prints in this book have been newly titled, with emphasis on the main idea of the print rather than its secondary features. Intrusive poetry has been eschewed in titles: to call Hokusai's great print of Mt. Fuji at dawn "The Breezy Call of Incense-breathing Morn" seems to me a hindrance rather than a help to direct perception of the beauty of the work. With the Kabuki prints, there has not been much choice but to give the names of the actors as the title; even here, however, in the few cases where the drama is well known in the West I have sometimes given, instead, the names of the roles portrayed. For the moderns, of course, the title chosen by the artist has been followed so far as possible.

3. DATES. To conserve space, for detailed dating I simply give the month in roman numerals; thus XI/1715 signifies "Eleventh Month in the lunar year 1715/16." (Old Japanese dates were recorded in the lunar calendar, which varied from year to year but was generally two to five weeks later than the Gregorian year. Thus most of the Twelfth Month, and sometimes the end of the Eleventh Month, in the Japanese calendar would fall in January or early February of the following Gregorian year. For our purposes here it has seemed sufficient simply to record the Japanese month with the roughly equivalent year; dates are seldom precise enough to warrant more involved calculations.) The order of the plates was largely settled before these notes were written (the determining factor often being layout considerations) and hence sometimes bears little relation to chronological order. In such cases I have occasionally added a note to the biographical data, commenting on the artist's chronological development in relation to the prints illustrated.

4. DESCRIPTIONS. These expand upon the title and aim at pointing out and explaining matters significant, but not readily apparent to persons unfamiliar with Japan. There was no space to go into detail on the numerous literary allusions in the prints, but cross-references to other prints in the volume (see, for example, Print 101) will usually make the general idea clear to the persistent reader.

5. LEGENDS OR TRANSLATIONS. Verses, whether good or bad in the original, have been translated as literally as possible, but with a view to making their relation to the print apparent. At the same time I have avoided over-translation, and when the original is subtle or obscure, I have tried to make the translation conform. With a print like No. 110, of course, I have gone a bit deeper into the literary significance than the average Edoite of Harunobu's day would have fathomed, but this was an example of particular interest. Like the verses, legends inscribed on the prints have been given in translation only, except when they consist primarily of Japanese proper nouns.

6. ALTERNATE VERSIONS. Much work remains to be done in the comparative study of alternate impressions of many of the prints shown here. My own notes are necessarily limited in this respect, for they were prepared from small monochrome photographs, without having access either to the originals or to such publications as Ledoux, Hirano, and many of the great Occidental catalogues.

7. SIGNATURES AND SEALS. Data on signatures, seals, and publishers' inscriptions are given in romanization rather than translation as they will be principally of interest to specialists. Publishers' names and seals are often cited literally, in abbreviated form, when their identity would be apparent to the student, but in fuller form when they represent some

difficulty in deciphering. Unsigned works are so indicated; when no external evidence of authorship is noted, the attribution is simply my own opinion, though I have been careful to indicate all cases (e.g., Nos. 3, 4, 52) where a definite attribution seemed unwarranted at the present time. Note that the recurrent terms *hitsu, shōhitsu, zu,* and *ga* appearing after artists' names signify "painted by"; *hammoto* means "publisher"; *kiwame* (later *aratame*) is the censor's seal found on many prints after 1790; *-za* means "Theater." Owner's seals on the front or back of a print are generally not recorded in these notes other than the mention under provenance.

8. CONDITION. The present evaluations of condition are generally conservative. Note that line-cuts often, and color plates sometimes, do not reproduce the slight defects in a print. The background tones of the color plates in this book approximate, so far as possible, the paper colors of the prints as they appear today, often including the natural darkening of age. The notation "holes" refers generally to minor wormage. Whether a print is trimmed or not is sometimes difficult to determine, since minor differences sometimes date back to impressions originally made on

slightly odd sizes of paper. "Oxidation" refers to the phenomenon seen when chemical change partially darkens a color; mineral red often turns blue-gray, but more crucial is the occasional change of mineral white to gray; this phenomenon may be studied in the following prints, notice of which is accordingly omitted from the notes proper: 5, 16, 65, 118, 126, 127, 128–29, 130, 139, 143, 145–46, 180.

9. PROVENANCE AND PRIOR PUBLICATION. Under provenance, following the citation "From," are listed the names of all known previous owners of the particular print, beginning with the latest and, when earlier owners are unknown, sometimes including date of acquisition. A bibliographical citation following "In" signifies that the particular print shown in this book was the one illustrated in that publication. If readers know of other appearances of these prints, or of additional former owners, the Honolulu Academy of Arts would greatly appreciate correspondence. A key to the abbreviations of book and catalogue titles will be found in the Bibliography. Following is a list of former owners of the prints, including their full names, where available, and print numbers:

Adachi Toyohisa (Tokyo ukiyo-e printer), 231
Ainsworth, Mary E., 62, 113
Anderson Coll., 238, 254
Appleton, Col. Henry, 199
Baker, Kington, 46, 101, 103–4, 112
Bateson Coll., 24, 26, 112
Berès, Huguette (Paris dealer), 43
Bing, Siegfried, 168
Blanchard, Mrs. John Osgood, 115, 190
Brussel, Jack (N. Y. dealer), 19, 212
Bullier Coll., 78, 184, 205
Cartier Coll., 29
Chandler, Charles H., 1, 3, 4 ff.
Church, Frederick Edward, 37
Cox, Warren (N. Y. dealer), 9, 64, 68–70, 116, 119, 153, 186
Crist Coll., 153
Cutter, Marian, 186
Doi Coll., 136, 160
Fenollosa, Ernest Francisco, 15, 23(?), 33, 116(?), 119(?), 142(?)
Ficke, Arthur Davison, 58, 78, 100, 118, 180, 257
Field, Hamilton Easter, 187
Ford, Tod, 1, 5, 143, 162, 189
Forman, Georgia, 229
Freer, Charles Lang, 1, 5, 143, 189
Fukuda Bunko (Fukuda Coll.), 102
Gonse, Louis, 158, 170, 175, 177–78
Gookin, Frederick W., 58, 257
Grabhorn, Edwin, 156, 201
Gunsaulus, Helen C., 229
Happer, John Stewart, 10
Hartnett, William C., 236, 238, 254

Haviland, Charles, 157, 193
Hayashi Tadamasa, 65–67, 68–70, 107, 150, 182, 184, 200, 223, 226–27
Hillier, J., 36, **211**
Hubert Coll., 57
Itō Tokumatsu, 7, 99
Jacquin, Charles, 151, 203, **215**
Jaeckel Coll., 13
Kane, Louisa Langdon, 45, 76, 86–88
Kegan Paul (London dealer), 12, 14, 176, ⌊211
Kellogg Coll., 24, 26, 85
Ketcham, W. H., 15, 23, 33, 51, 116, 119, ⌊142
Kobayashi Bunshichi, 29, 108, 156
Koechlin, Raymond, 149
Kondō Toyotarō (Kyoto dealer), 28, 114
Koscherak, Raymond (N. Y. dealer), **126**,
Kuki Saburō, 2, 35 ⌊177–78, 180, 183
Lane, Richard, 2, 35
Ledoux, Louis V., 92, 126, 177–78, 183
Lewis, Robert E. (San Francisco dealer), 24, 26, 85, 112
Litchfield, A. M., 101, 103–4, 109
Longweil, Mme., 92
Mansfield, Howard, 222
Manzi, Michel, 38, 42, 72
Matsuki Bunkio, 1, 5, 74, 208
Matsuki Kihachirō, 25, 126, 138
May, Frederic, 110, 164
Mayuyama & Co. (Tokyo dealer), 20, 30, 49, 130, 139, 144, 152, 181, 206
Metzgar, Judson D., 58, 61, 100, 209, 223, ⌊236, 257
Mihara, A.S., 184
Morse, Charles J., 9, 15, 23, 48, 51, 64, 68–70, 116, 119, 142, 145–46
Murata Kimbei, 82

"Nadeshiko-sono," 102
Nail, Harry (Palo Alto dealer), 121, 238,
Orange, James, 49 ⌊254
Ōshima Kano, 110, 164
Ōya Shobō (Tokyo dealer), **171**
Packard, Harry, 121
Rouart, Alexis, 100, 154–55
Ruth Coll., 112
Sakai Tōkichi (Tokyo dealer), 18, 230
Salomon, Charles, 154–55, 227
Samuel Coll., 112
Schraubstadter, Carl, 105–6, 197, 217
Shōbisha (Tokyo dealer), 17, 39, 40, 96, 97, 137, 140–41, 163, 184, 232, 234–35
Shūgyō Hiromichi, 96
Sotheby & Co. (London auction house),
Stark Coll., 36 ⌊27, 111
Statler, Oliver, 235, 240, 244, 250, 255–56
Straus-Negbaur, Tony, 16, 59, 107, 126, 131, 167, 169, 174, 185
Thornicraft, T. C., 49
Tikotin, Felix (Dutch dealer), 13, 29, 36, 197
Tomita Gisaku, 10
Tomoda Coll., 47, 127
Tregaskis, James, 46, 101, 103–4, 109, 112
Tuttle, George, 229
Vignier, Charles, 72
Von Heymel, Walter, 46
Wakai Kanesaburō, 21, 65–67, 169
Walpole (N. Y. dealer), 192
Wright, Frank Lloyd, 41, 73, 79, 82, 123, 133–35, 161, 205 ⌜38, 42, 85, 92
Yamanaka & Co. (Kyoto-Osaka dealer),
Yōseidō (Tokyo dealer), 239, 245–46, 248

10. TECHNIQUES. Data concerning techniques and dimensions are made available for ready reference by placing them at the end of each note. The traditional Japanese techniques of printing are summarized briefly below. Examples of each

are cited from the plates, which will often provide a better idea of the method and result than words can.

Sumizuri-e: printed from one block, in black. (11, 21)
Tan-e: a sumizuri-e handcolored in orange (red lead),

yellow, sometimes mineral green or gray. (16, 22)

Beni-e: a sumizuri-e handcolored in vegetable colors such as orange or red, yellow, blue, green. (In older books sometimes confused with benizuri-e; in the 18th century almost synonymous with urushi-e; due to its ambiguity, not used here.)

Urushi-e: a beni-e characterized by the addition of glue to the pigments, giving a lustrous appearance; "gold" dust (generally bronze or brass) or powdered mica was sometimes sprinkled on the wet pigments. (24, 27)

Ishizuri-e: a rare form consisting of a sumizuri-e with the outline in white on black, after the manner of Chinese stone-rubbings. (36, 50)

Benizuri-e: a true color-print in red and green, sometimes yellow, blue, gray, all printed from blocks, sometimes with overprinting to produce three colors from two blocks. (73, 98)

Nishiki-e: A full-color print, a natural extension of the technique of the benizuri-e to a full scale of colors. Most of the prints from Harunobu on employ nishiki-e techniques. Among the more unusual devices found in nishiki-e is that of gaufrage; as its Japanese name karazuri ("empty-printing") indicates, it consists of heavy embossing with a block to which no color is applied. Karazuri is particularly effective in giving dimension to snow, waves, and kimono patterns, but of course is hardly susceptible to ordinary reproduction methods. (1, 103–4)

Modern creative-print artists employ some of the above methods (particularly sumizuri-e and nishiki-e), but also many new devices peculiar to themselves, as well as some borrowed from the Dadaists.

The number of colors shown for a given print is only a rough guide to the complexity of the printing. It includes neither related shades of a single color nor the color of the key block, although black is counted if applied other than by the key block. Nor is this number a guide to the number of blocks used, since a single color may be printed several different times from different blocks to achieve numerous shade variations, or, on the other hand, different colors may be applied at different times by printing from portions of a single block. See No. 189 for an example. The notation "gradation" indicates that a gradation of coloring has been achieved by wiping portions of the wet block before printing.

11. DIMENSIONS. Measurements are given in centimeters and take in the entire paper area, including margins. (As a handy comparison, the pages of this book are about 31×23 cm. or $12\frac{1}{4} \times 9$ in.) Common Japanese print sizes mentioned in the text are roughly as follows:

Chūban:	25.5×19 cm.	$10 \times 7\frac{1}{2}$ in.
Hashira-e:	73×12 cm.	$28\frac{3}{4} \times 4\frac{3}{4}$ in.
Hoso-e:	33×14.5 cm.	$13 \times 5\frac{5}{8}$ in.
Kakemono-e:	76.5×23 cm.	30×9 in.
Ōban:*	38×25.5 cm.	15×10 in.
Tanzaku:	38×13 cm.	15×5

*Many early ōban were originally issued as album sheets.

The Notes

Moronobu

Hishikawa Moronobu (d. 1694). The first great consolidator of the ukiyo-e style worked from the early 1670's to shortly before his death in 1694. His dynamic early work is seen in No. 12, the supple power of his peak years in No. 11, and the graceful style of his last years in No. 257.

11. LOVERS WITH ATTENDANT. Early 1680's. At the right, the lover reclines upon the bedding, his elbow on an armrest. Before him sits his paramour, probably a courtesan. Above them is mosquito-netting, indicating the season is summer. At the left, the courtesan's attendant. Such prints were usually frontispieces to erotic series. Unsigned. Condition good (two ink stains, horizontal creasing, backed). From Chandler, 1910. Sumizuri-e. 29.9×35.1.

12. GROUPS OF TRAVELERS. Mid-1670's. At the right, a samurai with his two servants and baggage, possibly on a journey. To the left, going in the opposite direction, a group of five ladies with their servants. The latter group is doubtless returning from cherry-blossom viewing, for one of the ladies bears a branch of cherry blossoms and the servants carry picnic utensils. Unsigned. Condition fair (tears in margin, stains, scuffing, backed). From Kegan Paul. Sumizuri-e, with late handcoloring. 28.3×42.3.

257. STROLL BY THE BAY (detail). 1695. A lady takes a summer stroll beside a bay. In the original her maidservant follows with a fan and above the illustration appears the biography of the poetess se, with the famous love verse that the design illustrates: "Bay of Naniwa: must I spend my life without meeting him. even for an interval as brief as these reed-nodes?" Detail from an illustration appearing in Vol. I of *The Hundred Poets Illustrated*, Edo, IV/1695. This book records the death of Moronobu in its preface and, like several of Moronobu's signed works of the 1690's, shows evidence of having been redrawn for publication, most probably by the master's son Morofusa. Condition poor (smudged, trimmed, corner damaged). From Metzgar, Gookin, Ficke. Sumizuri-e. Detail from book page measuring 19.3×14.3.

Sugimura

Sugimura Jihei (worked 1680's to 1690's). The most impressive of Moronobu's immediate followers, Sugimura specialized in love scenes and erotica. Much of his unsigned work was formerly attributed to Moronobu.

13. LOVERS BY A SCREEN. Mid-1680's. A young samurai, seated while practicing with a small hand-drum, is interrupted by the embrace of a maiden. At the right a young girl peeks from behind the screen. Poem: "My longings ere we met are as naught: parting is indeed the beginning of love." Unsigned. Condition good (some general spotting,

backed). From Tikotin, Jaeckel. In Hillier, Pl. 3; Ostier, No. 13. Sumizuri-e. 27.2×39.6.

Sukenobu

Nishikawa Sukenobu (ca. 1671–1751). Even more than Moronobu's, Sukenobu's work lay primarily in the field of book illustration, and only a few independent prints are known. A quiet grace was the ideal of the Kyoto ukiyo-e artists, of whom Sukenobu was the most prominent.

3. [Style of Sukenobu.] COURTESANS IN PROCESSION. 1710's. The procession of a leading courtesan; she is followed by two girl attendants and a manservant, who carries her large umbrella. Although the print seems closest to the style of the Kyoto master Sukenobu, it might possibly be an early work of Masanobu's done under strong Sukenobu influence. Unsigned. Condition good. From Chandler. Sumizuri-e. 26×36.5.

14. HAIRDRESSING. *Ca.* 1730's. A young man sits before a mirror playing the samisen, while a girl coifs and perfumes his hair. The printed signature appears to be a late addition, possibly applied by a publisher or dealer to an unsigned album sheet. Signature: Yamato-eshi Nishikawa Sukenobu hitsu. Condition fair (patched, heavy general scuffing, trimmed?). From Kegan Paul. Sumizuri-e. 26.2×17.5.

Kaigetsudō Dohan

Kaigetsudō Dohan (worked 1710's). In his paintings Dohan was the least inspired member of the Kaigetsudō school, but in his prints he ranks among the ukiyo-e greats. Like the other members of his school, he treated the gorgeous Japanese kimono as sufficient raison d'être for his work, and rather consistently avoided other means of creating atmosphere. It is with good reason that the prints of the Kaigetsudō school have come to symbolize the spirit of ukiyo-e, and of the period which bore them: they are the most powerful manifestation we have of the Japanese courtesan, arbiter of taste and of love in an age when these were a cultivated man's principal concerns. More than anything by Moronobu, Sugimura, Kiyonobu, Kiyomasu, or Masanobu – all masters of the strong black line – the Kaigetsudō prints manage to stand alone in their massive contours as eternal symbols of Japanese womanhood.

7. COURTESAN. 1710's (late impression). A young courtesan pauses in her promenade to gaze at something or someone, her right sleeve lifted in feigned modesty. On the back of the present print appear both the Happer and Watanabe seals and the following notation in Happer's handwriting: "Print made from a genuine old block engraved not later than 1705, on paper of the same period, with ink over 300 years old. Tokyo, Oct. 1916. Printer: S. Watanabe. Certified as a true statement: J. S. Happer." Signature: Nippon giga Kaigetsu matsuyō Dohan zu; Dohan seal. Publisher's seal: Moto-hama-chō, Igaya, hammoto. Condition good. From Chandler. Sumizuri-e. 58.1×28.6.

15. COURTESAN. 1710's. The courtesan lifts her long skirts and swings her left under-sleeve as she prepares to walk. On her kimono we see a New Year's design of battledore, shuttlecock, pine branches, and other festive decorations; while her outer robe shows a rich rhythm of cursive calligraphy against black and white cloud patterns. Signature: Kaigetsu matsuyō Dohan zu; Dohan

seal. Publisher's seal: Moto-hama-chō, Igaya, hammoto. Condition fine (several patched worm holes in background, minor tears in margin, backed). From Morse, Ketcham, Fenollosa. [The first adequately presented U.S. exhibition of ukiyo-e was held in the Fine Arts Building, 215 West 57th Street, New York, January 1896. All prints not otherwise attributed were presumed to belong to the art auctioneer, W. H. Ketcham, but it has always been confidently believed that most of them were actually the property of Ernest Francisco Fenollosa, then Curator of the Department of Oriental Art, Boston Museum of Fine Arts, who compiled the trail-blazing catalogue. In the present collection appear more than a dozen choice prints from that first major American exhibition, but only two, this and No. 33, are specifically traced to Fenollosa.] Sumizuri-e. 57.5×31.7.

Kiyonobu I

Torii Kiyonobu I (ca. 1664–1729). (There is some doubt that the exact dates and relationships of the early Torii artists will ever become clear, but it seems best for the moment to assume that the names Kiyonobu and Kiyomasu each represent two generations of artists working under the same name.) Kiyonobu I began his work as an illustrator in the Moronobu style in 1687, and had illustrated a number of novels and dramas by the end of the century, when he began issuing albums and independent prints. Pl. 2 is a good example of the linear power that characterizes Kiyonobu's middle period; Nos. 24, 29, and 31 show the more refined grace of his later years, a style that was to dominate most of the subsequent Torii work, and is often, as here, difficult to distinguish from the early work of his pupils.

2. SEATED COURTESAN. Early 1700's. The right half of an erotic album plate; the courtesan exposes her thigh while her lover, at the left, is suggestively depicted in the nude. Unsigned. Condition good. From Lane, Kuki. Sumizuri-e. 22.2×21.5.

24. FUJIMURA HANDAYŪ. Late 1710's. The Kabuki records would indicate this print represents Handayū II, probably in the female role of Umegae in *Chūjō-hime Kyō-hiina*, performed II/1715, Nakamura-za. Stylistically, however, the print would seem to date from several years later, and the Binyon-Sexton guess of "1719" is probably not far off. Signature: Torii Kiyonobu hitsu. Publisher's seal: Hammoto, Moto-hama-chō, Igaya. Condition fine (inconspicuous center fold); this print suffered foxing after leaving England, but the colors are unusually well preserved. From Lewis, Kellogg, Bateson. In Binyon, Pl. XX, Fig. 2. Urushi-e: 5 colors by hand. 34×16.

29. KANTARŌ AND TAKENOJŌ. 1721. Sanjō Kantarō in the female role of Shōshō, and Ichimura Takenojō as Soga Gorō in *Tsurugame wakayagi Soga*, performed I/1721, Ichimura-za. Signature: Torii Kiyonobu hitsu. Publisher's seal: Sakai-chō, Nakajimaya, hammoto. Condition good (center fold, tear in right margin, trimmed on right, backed). From Tikotin, Cartier, Kobayashi. In Ostier, No. 37. Urushi-e: 3 colors by hand. 28×15.6.

31. ICHIKAWA KUZŌ. 1718. Kuzō as Miura Arajirō in *Zen kunen yoroi-kurabe*, performed XI/1718, Morita-za. Signature: Torii Kiyonobu hitsu. Publisher's seal: Emiya,

Shimmei-mae, yoko-chō. Condition good (creased, stained, backed). From Chandler, 1905. Urushi-e: 2 colors by hand. 29.5 × 15.8.

Kiyomasu I

Torii Kiyomasu I (worked mid-1690's to early 1720's). Little is known of Kiyomasu's early work, but during the 1710's his signed prints far outnumber those by Kiyonobu, who may have been his elder brother. Kiyomasu's style is somewhat more graceful than Kiyonobu's in his middle years, but the two are often difficult to tell apart. Nos. 17–20 are part of a series issued by two publishers during 1715 and 1716 to celebrate the famous Kabuki roles of Ichikawa Danjūrō II. No. 22 includes an interesting portrayal of the handsome actor Ikushima Shingorō, most famous for his role in the notorious Ejima-Ikushima scandal of but two years later, which ended his career (cf. Michener, The Floating World, p. 68; Lane, Kaigetsudō, pp. 29–30).

16. NAKAMURA SENYA IN THE ROLE OF TOKONATSU. 1716. Senya played this female role in XI/1716 at the Nakamura-za in the drama *Mitsudomoe katoku-biraki.* Legend: "Nakamura Senya, arrived from Kyoto." Signature: Torii Kiyomasu; Kiyomasu seal. Publisher's seal: Komatsuya, Yushima Tenjin, Onnazaka no shita. Condition good. From Chandler, Straus-Negbaur. In Einstein, Pl. 36; Frankfurt, No. 14; Straus-Negbaur, No. 13; *Kunstwanderer*, p. 467; Benn, Pl. 8. Tan-e: 3 colors by hand. 58.4 × 32.9.

17. GORŌ, SHŌSHŌ, AND ASAHINA. 1715. A scene in the Yoshiwara. At the left, Ichikawa Danjūrō II as Soga Gorō rising from hiding in a cauldron; to the right, Nakamura Takesaburō as the courtesan Shōshō, and Tomizawa Banzaburō as Asahina. A young girl is serving saké as Shōshō plays the samisen. From *Bandō ichi kotobuki Soga*, performed I/1715, Nakamura-za. Legend: "Great Cauldron in the House of Assignation." Signature: Torii Kiyomasu; Kiyomasu seal. Publisher's seal: Moto-hama-chō, Igaya, hammoto. Condition fair (worm holes, paper soiled and creased). From Shōbisha; Tokyo sale, 1927. In *UT* III, 220; Tokyo sale, 1927, No. 3. Sumizuri-e. 30 × 37.7.

18. SAINT NARUKAMI AND PRINCESS TAEMA. 1715. A scene at the saint's hermitage. Ichikawa Danjūrō II as Saint Narukami, with Nakamura Takesaburō as Princess Taema, in *Narukami shōnin*, performed V/1715, Nakamura-za. Legend: "A Stylish Narukami." Signature & seals: same as No. 17. Condition fair (two ink stains). From Sakai. Sumizuri-e. 29.3 × 40.3.

19. AGEMAKI AND SUKEROKU. 1716. A scene at the entrance to the Yoshiwara. Ichikawa Danjūrō II as Sukeroku, with Nakamura Takesaburō as the courtesan Agemaki, in *Shikirei yawaragi Soga*, performed II/1716, Nakamura-za. A servant girl is at left. Legend: "Agemaki and Sukeroku." Signature & seals: same as No. 17. Condition fair (trimmed at bottom). From Brussel. Sumizuri-e. 26.9 × 42.5.

20. FUWA AND OKUNI. 1715. A scene at the entrance to a Kabuki theater. Ichikawa Danjūrō II as the samurai Fuwa Banzaemon, with Nakamura Takesaburō as Okuni, the girl who began Kabuki, in *Mimasu Nagoya*, performed VII/1715, Nakamura-za. A servant girl is at the left. Legend: (at left) "Okuni Kabuki: Women's Dance, Men's Dance. Okuni's Kabuki Performance"; (at right) "Chōzō

of the Wet Hair [a noted wrestler]." Signature & seal: same as No. 17. Publisher's seal: same as No. 16. Condition good (worm holes, stains). From Mayuyama. Sumi-zuri-e. 28.5 × 41.4.

21. WARRIORS IN COMBAT. 1710's. This print depicts not Kabuki but a scene of historical combat from the wars of the Taira and Minamoto; Taira no Kagekiyo rips the armor off Miho no Tanishirō as the latter's sword splinters. Signature: Torii uji Kiyomasu zu. Seals: same as No. 17. Condition good (mended tears, stained along right side, thin spots, scuffed). From Chandler, Wakai. [This collection contains about two dozen prints marked with the oval seal of the early Japanese collector Wakai Kanesaburō. He was the Tokyo vice-president of a firm that exported ukiyo-e to Paris, but he always maintained that he held back the choice examples for his personal collection, stamping each with his seal, which can be seen on Pl. 21, 67, and 169. The present collection also contains about six dozen prints marked with the circular seal of Hayashi Tadamasa, 1853–1906, who served as Paris agent for Wakai's firm. Hayashi acquired most of the Wakai prints, and also assembled a handsome collection of his own, which was the subject of a detailed sales catalogue published in Paris in 1902, listing 1,797 items, many with illustrations. Collectors have always prized Wakai and Hayashi prints, but the presence of their seals on a print does not automatically insure authenticity, for dealers have found them easy to forge; nor do the seals insure quality, for judging merely from some of the poorer prints in this collection which bear both Wakai and Hayashi cachets, the artistic judgment of the owners must have been quite elastic. In this book the Hayashi seal appears on Pl. 65, 68–70, 107, 150, 182, 184, 200, 223, 226, and 227. Of these, four are listed in the Paris catalogue, 65, 107, 184 and 227 – the first and third being illustrated.] Sumizuri-e. 54 × 31.5.

22. TAKIE, SHINGORŌ, AND DANJŪRŌ. 1712. From top to bottom, Kirinami Takie as Takiguchi's younger sister, Ikushima Shingorō as Yorimasa, and Ichikawa Danjūrō as Hayata, in the drama *Fukuwara yunzei Yorimasa*, performed I/1712, Yamamura-za. The legend gives the names of the three actors. Unsigned, but probably by Kiyomasu I. Publisher's seal: Sakai-chō, Nakajimaya, hammoto. Condition good (some stains, hat of standing figure painted purple by later hand). From Chandler, 9/11/1918. Tan-e: 3 colors by hand. 30.4 × 15.6.

23. HEIKURŌ AND TAKESABURŌ. Stylistically one would tend to date this print *ca.* 1710; the Kabuki records, however, indicate that it may depict Yamanaka Heikurō as Sadatō, and Nakamura Takesaburō as a page, in *Yoroi-kurabe Ōshū no kogane*, performed XI/1716, Ichimura-za. Signature: Torii Kiyomasu; Kiyomasu seal. Condition fine (folded, slightly scuffed, backed; lower third of print employs darker shade of paper). From Morse, Ketcham, Fenollosa(?). Sumizuri-e. 65.2 × 32.5.

25. COURTESAN. *Ca.* 1705–10. A lone courtesan walking. Signature: Torii Kiyomasu; Kiyo seal. Condition good (mended tear lower right, some stains). From Chandler, K. Matsuki. Tan-e: 2 colors by hand. 31.5×15.2.

Kiyonobu II

Torii Kiyonobu II (worked 1720's to ca. 1760) probably collaborated in the late work of Kiyonobu I, making it difficult to distinguish the artist involved in "Kiyonobu" prints of the 1720's. Like Kiyomasu II, he never attempted prints on the scale of the great work of the first generation of the Torii, but his small handcolored prints are impressive in their own quiet way, as are his later color prints and illustrations.

26. FUJIMURA HANDAYŪ. 1727. Handayū II as Kikusui, wife of Kusunoki, in *Hōnen Taiheiki*, performed XI/1727, Morita-za. She is disguised as a vendor of bamboo articles. Signature: Torii Kiyonobu hitsu. Publisher's seal: Komatsuya. Condition good (weather spots, repaired worm hole left margin); like No. 24, suffered foxing after leaving England, but colors unusually well preserved. From Lewis, Kellogg, Bateson. In Lewis, cover. Urushi-e: 2 colors by hand, gold dust. 34.6×16.

27. SEGAWA KIKUNOJŌ. 1737. Kikunojō, in the role of the fox-spirit Kuzunoha, dances before a fox-trap, baited with a rat, in the drama *Ōuchi kagam Shinoda-zuma*, performed III/1737, Nakamura-za. Legend: "Shinoda Dance; Segawa Kikunojō." Signature: Torii Kiyonobu hitsu. Publisher: hammoto, Murataya. Condition fine (double fold, slight breaks right margin, possibly trimmed). From Chandler; Sotheby, 10/18/1920. In *UT* II, 93, trimmed. Urushi-e: 3 colors by hand, gold dust. 32.1×15.2.

Kiyomasu II

Torii Kiyomasu II (worked 1720's to early 1760's). His work is uneven, but at his finest he represents one of the quiet peaks of ukiyo-e. Like Kiyonobu II, he is at his best in his handcolored lacquer-prints; the firmer lines of color printing tend to emphasize a certain awkwardness of composition inherent in both these artists.

28. THE MAIDEN TAMAMUSHI. 1730's. She stands in the prow of a ship beside the fan at which the archer Nasu no Yoichi will bend his bow – signaling the commencement of the Battle of Dannoura. Signature: Torii Kiyomasu. Publisher: Sakai-chō, Nakajimaya, hammoto. Condition fine (urushi on woman's haori is rough). From Kondō. Urushi-e: 4 colors by hand, gold dust. 31.9×16.1.

30. DANJŪRŌ AND HIROJI. 1720's. Ichikawa Danjūrō II stripped to the waist in the role of Soga Gorō, with Ōtani Hiroji as the warrior Asahina, probably in the "Kusazuribiki" scene of the same drama noted in No. 19. Unsigned, but in the style of Kiyomasu II. The style and lacquer technique would indicate a date somewhat later than that of the first Kabuki performance. Publisher's seal: Shimmei-mae, Izutsuya. Condition fine (trimmed right?). From Mayuyama; Tokyo sale, 1933. In Tokyo sale, 1933, No. 8. Urushi-e: 3 colors by hand, gold dust. 31.9×15.2.

32. SEGAWA KIKUJIRŌ. 1746. Kikujirō as Okiku in *Fuji no yuki mitsugu Soga*, performed I/1746, Nakamura-za. Signature: Eshi Torii Kiyomasu hitsu. Publisher: Urokogataya hammoto. Condition good (center fold, small patches, urushi upper right possibly retouched). From Chandler,

1/5/1927. Urushi-e: 3 colors by hand, gold dust. 31.4×14.8.

Masanobu

Okumura Masanobu (ca. 1686 to 1764). Masanobu's work covers the whole range of early ukiyo-e, from sumizuri-e and tan-e through urushi-e, ishizuri-e, and beni-e, on down to the benizuri-e that just precede the development of full-color prints. Masanobu's prints abound in the wit and Edo verve that typified the best in eighteenth-century popular art. He was often his own publisher, and thus exercised a greater control over the final printed result of his designs than most ukiyo-e artists. In his early work he shows a great fondness for parody and novel designs (Nos. 9, 34, 35). With maturity – and with the increasing importance of coloring in the success of a print – he concentrates his attention more on design and harmony of composition. Some critics speak of a "decline" in his later work; but I think they are simply expressing a preference for the strength of the earlier ukiyo-e. Certainly I know no more satisfying print in ukiyo-e than No. 51, one of Masanobu's last designs, and the only example of his work in color printing which we show here.

4. [Style of Masanobu]. COURTESANS IN PROCESSION. 1710's. Two courtesans, at left, with three attendants. Unsigned. Condition good. From Chandler. Sumizuri-e. 27×37.

8. ONOE KIKUGORŌ. 1744. Kikugorō as Kichisa, in *Nanakusa wakayagi Soga*, performed early spring 1744, Ichimura-za. The young page holds a love letter partly concealed by his sleeve – intended, doubtless, for his paramour, the maiden Oshichi. Signature: Hōgetsudō shōmei Okumura Bunkaku Masanobu shōhitsu; Tanchōsai seal. Condition good (worm holes left margin, slight tear upper corner, backed). From Chandler. Urushi-e: 3 colors by hand 66.9×16.2.

9. LADY MURASAKI. 1720's. The Lady Murasaki is depicted in modern dress, samisen at her feet, in a pastiche on the famous scene showing her composing the *Tale of Genji* at Ishiyama Temple. In the distance to her right is a scene from classical legend, a parody on the exile of the courtier Yukihira and his affair with the salt-water carriers (cf. Nos. 1, 219) Matsukaze and Murasame. The cartouche at the upper right reads "A Stylish Suma," referring to a chapter in the *Tale of Genji* wherein the hero is, in imitation of Yukihira's story, exiled to Suma. Signature: Okumura Masanobu zu; Masanobu seal. Publisher's seal (lower left): Kikuya, Asakusa Komagata-chō. Condition good (marginal tears and stains, backed). From Cox, Morse. Sumizuri-e. 29×44.5.

33. YOUNG SAMURAI ON HORSEBACK. Mid-1740's. A stylish young samurai is seated upon an elaborately bedecked mount. Above his head bloom cherry blossoms, and through a window two girls peek at him admiringly. Poem: "To the breeze of love the cherry blossoms fall, beside the viewing-window." Signature: Hōgetsudō shōmei Okumura Bunkaku Masanobu shōhitsu; Tanchōsai seal. Condition good (signs of framing). From Chandler, Ketcham, Fenollosa. Urushi-e: 4 colors by hand. 60× 25.6.

34. CUTTING UP THE FLUTE FOR FIREWOOD. 1710's. At the left the host, a gay blade now come down in the world, chops up his treasured *shakuhachi* for firewood to prepare tea for the fair young samurai visitor. The ornaments of the room and their inscriptions bear witness to the man's former station: (left to right) "Though somewhat cracked, the *inrō* owned by Kenkō [famous 14th-century writer]"; "Though somewhat damaged, a courtesan-painting by Hishikawa [Moronobu]"; "Though somewhat worn, the Hachijō-silk cloak of Narihira [9th-century poet and lover]." The title of the print is given as "A *shakuhachi* version of *Hachi no ki*" – referring to the famous Noh drama in which an impoverished samurai, visited by the Shōgun incognito, chops up his treasured potted trees to provide firewood. The ukiyo-e version bears vaguely pederastical implications. The painting in the alcove has the signature "Hishikawa hitsu," and it is interesting to note that Moronobu was already now recognized as the founding genius of the new ukiyo-e style. This print is the last of a series of twelve parodies on Noh plays. Signature: Okumura Masanobu zu; Masanobu seal. Condition good (paper thin on lower left corner and crudely repaired). From Chandler. Sumizuri-e. 26.2×36.5.

35. Lovers Playing Checkers. 1720's. A courtesan and her lover play checkers with silver pieces, employing for checkerboard the man's patterned jacket, which is thrown over his knees. The man's pocketbook lies open at the lower right. The word *Kyō* written to the upper left may indicate this represents one of a series of three prints dealing with amusements in the gay quarters of the three metropolises, Kyo[to], Osaka, Edo. Unsigned. Condition fair (damage at centerfold repaired). From Lane, Kuki. In Shibui, Series II, 43. Sumizuri-e. 26.6×36.7.

36. [19th-century imitation of Masanobu.] Courtesan Walking. This problem print dates stylistically from about the 1710's, but the hardness of the lines and the distortions (for example, the over-large head and, even more, the dwarfed hips) cast rather conclusive doubts upon its authenticity. The girl's face, too, is rather closer to the Kaigetsudō style than to Masanobu's, and the paper seems clearly of the 19th century. Japanese critics assume the print to be a Meiji-period production for export purposes; however, the synthetic style and odd technique make me wonder if it may not represent, rather, an amateur "antiquarian" print of the late Edo period. Signature: Okumura Masanobu; Masanobu seal. Condition fine (three thin spots patched and reblackened). From Tikotin, Hillier, Stark. In Hillier, Pl. 6; De Gruyter, cover and No. 36. Ishizuri-e. 40.3×29.

37. Girl with Mirror. Mid-1740's. A girl walking as she applies rouge with the aid of a hand mirror. Signature: Hōgetsudō shōmei Okumura Bunkaku Masanobu shōhitsu; Tanchōsai seal. Condition good (small holes patched). From Chandler, Church. Urushi-e: 3 colors by hand. 71×25.4.

38. Onoe Kikugorō. 1744. Kikugorō as Soga Gorō in the same drama as No. 8. He holds the reed hat and flute of the wandering *komusō*. Signature: Hōgetsudō shōmei Okumura Bunkaku Masanobu shōhitsu; Tanchōsai seal. Con-

dition fine. From Chandler, Yamanaka, Manzi. In Manzi, No. 10; V&I, I, 128; *UT*, III, 153. Urushi-e: 3 colors by hand. 62.5×14.2.

39. Ichikawa Ebizō. 1749. Ebizō as Sukeroku, in *Otokomoji Soga monogatari*, performed I/1749, Nakamura-za. Poem: "Become young again, with plum branches for arrows Ebizō enters second youth." Signature: Hōgetsudō hashira-e kongen Okumura Bunkaku Masanobu shōhitsu; Tanchōsai seal. Condition poor (backed). From Shōbisha. Urushi-e: 3 colors by hand. 67.6×24.8.

40. Courtesan Walking. Mid-1740's. A courtesan walks lifting her long skirt with her right hand. Poem: "The courtesan's procession: he loses his powers of levitation— the cuckoo-bird." Signature: Hōgetsudō shōmei Okumura Bunkaku Masanobu shōhitsu; Tanchōsai seal. Condition poor (backed). From Shōbisha. Urushi-e: 3 colors by hand. 69×25.

41. Sanokawa Ichimatsu with Puppet. Mid-1740's. The actor Ichimatsu is seen handling a puppet representing the courtesan Matsuyama. Poem: "She wends her way on through the tears of rain at dusk, and then at last Matsuyama." Signature: Hōgetsudō shōmei hashira-e kongen Okumura Bunkaku Masanobu shōhitsu; Tanchōsai seal. Condition good (worn spot along right margin, repaired). From Chandler, Wright. In Wright, No. 4. Urushi-e: 2 colors by hand. 71×24.9.

42. Courtesan with Love Letter. Mid-1740's. A courtesan stands reading a love letter, probably soon after rising in the morning, for her kimono and sash are but summarily arranged. A lenient critic might suggest the courtesan's sloppy appearance represents a realistic depiction of a decadent scene; such realism is seldom seen prior to Utamaro, however, and I would, rather, suggest this as simply a rare example of hasty design and poor execution on Masanobu's part. A comparison with the other fine prints shown here from the same period (No. 40, for example, which is in equally bad condition) will show how far this print falls short of Masanobu's ideal. Signature & seals: same as No. 40. Condition fair (horizontal creasing, spotting, scuffing, backed). From Chandler, Yamanaka, Manzi. In V&I, I, 127; *UT* III, 157. Urushi-e: 4 colors by hand. 70×16.7.

43. Evening Cool by Ryōgoku Bridge. 1740's. A large "perspective-print" showing the interior of a teahouse, the guests, geisha, and courtesans amusing themselves at backgammon, music, dancing, drinking – or just resting. (For the same subject with significant variations, cf. *UT* III, 163). Title at upper right: "Evening Cool at Ryōgoku Bridge: Large Perspective-print." Publisher: Tōri-shio-chō akaki hyōtan-jirushi Okumuraya Genroku hammoto. Signature: Tōbu Yamato gakō Hōgetsudō Tanchōsai Okumura Bunkaku Masanobu shōhitsu; Tanchōsai seal. Condition fine (inconspicuous center fold, wormage, two crudely patched holes), colors almost as originally painted. From Berès. Urushi-e: 10 colors by hand. 47.7×67.

44. Sanokawa Ichimatsu. Mid-1740's. The actor is seen

not in a role, but as he enters the stage-door, holding his reed hat in his hand. Signature: same as No. 40. Condition good (center fold). From Chandler. Urushi-e: 3 colors by hand. 69.4 × 14.7.

45. SHIDŌKEN THE STORYTELLER. Mid-1740's. The famous but eccentric 18th-century storyteller Shidōken is seated at his podium. An open volume of the classic *Tsurezure-gusa* is before him, and in his hand he holds his trademark, a wooden phallus used to "pound home" the climax of a recitation. The tablet by his head reads "Tales of Ancient Battles. Lecturer: Shidōken." Verse: "The over-ripe persimmon is shaped like Daruma: its bottom rotten." A hint of the later realism of Sharaku's prints may be discerned in such satirical early prints as this. Signature: Hōgetsudō Okumura Bunkaku Masanobu shōhitsu; Tanchōsai seal. Condition good (worn spots roughly patched). From Chandler, Kane. Urushi-e: 4 colors by hand. 69.3 × 17.

46. KUO CHÜ THANKS HEAVEN. 1720's. Kuo Chü (in Japanese Kakkyō), the filial son, thanks heaven for the pot of gold; beside him are his wife and baby. For the full story see No. 215. Legend: "Twenty-four Filial Paragons: Kakyo [the name is given in a facetious misspelling]." Signature: Nippon gakō Okumura Masanobu shōhitsu, Tōri-shio-chō Okumuraya: Tanchōsai seal. Condition fine (worm holes through cartouche, patched and recolored). From Chandler, Baker, Tregaskis, Von Heymel. In Baker, No. 30. Urushi-e: 3 colors by hand. 31.2 × 15.2.

47. ACTOR IN SNOW. Mid-1720's. An unidentified actor in female role (the robe bears the crest later used by Osagawa Tsuneyo) is walking in the snow with a small dog. The role is clearly from a drama based on the *Hachi no ki* story (cf. No. 34), possibly that of Sano's wife in *Matsu-kazari Kamakura-biraki*, performed I/1724, Nakamura-za. (The Kabuki authority Yoshida Teruji suggests Tsuneyo in the role of Kōtō no Naishi in *Gaijin Taiheiki*, performed XI/1750 at the Ichimura-za; but this date is stylistically difficult to reconcile with the print.) Legend: "Winter; Pictures of the Four Seasons: Plum Blossoms in the Snow." Signature: Ukiyo-e Nippon gakō Okumura Masanobu shōhitsu, Tōri shio-chō beni-e toiya ezōshi oroshi akaki hyōtan mejirushi itashisōro Okumuraya. Condition fine (backed). From Tomoda. Urushi-e: 4 colors by hand, gold dust. 33.8 × 15.3.

48. SŌJŪRŌ AND KANTARŌ. 1721. Sawamura Sōjūrō as Soga Jūrō plays the hand-drum, while Sanjō Kantarō in the female role of Shōshō stands behind him. From the same drama as No. 29. Signature: Nippon gakō Okumura Masanobu shōhitsu, Tōri-shio-chō edoiya beni-e ezōshi oroshi akaki hyōtan mejirushi tsukamatsuri sōro Okumura; Tanchōsai seal. Condition fair (trimmed, several holes and tears, backed). From Chandler, Morse. Urushi-e: 5 colors by hand, gold dust. 31.4 × 16.

49. ICHIKAWA MONNOSUKE. 1723. Monnosuke dances beside his horse in the role of Hōjō Tokimune. From *Hachi no ki onna mikyōsho*, performed XI/1723, Ichimura-za. Signature: same as No. 48. Condition good (trimmed,

glue stain right margin, backed). From Mayuyama, private apanese collector, Orange-Thornicraft. In Orange, Pl. 1. Urushi-e: 4 colors by hand, gold dust. 30 × 15.5.

50. HSÜ AND CH'AO RESIST TEMPTATION. 1740's. The ancient Chinese sage Hsü Yu was offered the throne of China by the Emperor Yao; he hurried to a waterfall to cleanse his ear of the taint of worldly ambition. His friend Ch'ao Fu went a step further and hastened to stop his ox from drinking of the contaminated waters. A Zen story popular in Japan, it well illustrates the spirit of resistance to worldly temptation. Legend: "Hsü Yu washes his ear; Ch'ao Fu leads his ox and goes home." Signature: Hōgetsudō Okumura Masanobu ga; Tanchōsai seal. Condition good (backed). From Chandler, 12/26/1907. Ishizuri-e. 31.2 × 14.9.

51. SANOKAWA ICHIMATSU. 1756. Ichimatsu plays the flute before a gate, in the role of Uga no Rangiku-maru. From *Masakado shōzoku no enoki*, performed XI/1756, Nakamura-za. Legend: title of play and name of actor. Signature: Hōgetsudō Okumura Bunkaku Masanobu ga; Tanchōsai seal. Condition fair. From Morse, Ketcham. In Wadsworth, No. 27. Benizuri-e: red, green. 31 × 14.1.

Wagen

Hanekawa Wagen (Chinchō?). The name Wagen, which appears on a few rare prints of the 1720's, is usually considered to represent an obscure pupil of Hanekawa (Hagawa) Chinchō's (ca. 1679–1754). The recent discovery, in an illustrated book by Chinchō, of the same hand-seal as that on our print, makes me wonder if "Wagen" should not be added to Chinchō's several noms de plume. There is a certain "rough" element in the Chinchō-Wagen prints which lends them a unique flavor. Although Chinchō's remaining works are few, he is famous among ukiyo-e artists as being of samurai stock, and working at his artistic calling only when the spirit moved him.

53. YAMASHITA KINSAKU. 1723. Kinsaku as Naniwazu, a woman peddler of tooth blackening. She carries her wares in a box on her back and holds a sample package in her left hand. The text of the actor's speech advertising the wares is given at the top of the print. From the same drama as No. 47. Signature: Hanekawa Wagen hitsu, with hand-seal. Publisher's seal: Murataya hammoto. Condition fair (stained, backed). From Chandler. Urushi-e: 3 colors by hand, gold dust. 33.5 × 15.5.

Kiyotomo

Torii Kiyotomo (worked 1720's to 1740's) was probably a late pupil of Kiyonobu I; his work greatly resembles that of his fellow-pupil Kiyonobu II, both in its strong points and its weaknesses.

54. YAMAMOTO KOHEIJI WITH PUPPET. Ca. 1732. The puppeteer Koheiji is shown manipulating a female puppet. Legend: "Ōsaka Dewa; Yamamoto Koheiji at the puppet." No detailed records seem extant for the Osaka Dewa troupe, but they are known to have been performing at the Sakai-chō theater district of Edo in 1732. Signature: Torii Kiyotomo hitsu. Publisher's seal: Nakajimaya. Condition fair (numerous small patches, general discoloration). From Chandler. Urushi-e: 2 colors by hand, gold dust. 31.8 × 15.9.

Terushige

Katsukawa Terushige (worked late 1710's to early 1720's). Nothing is known of this rare artist, who may perhaps have been a gifted amateur. The publisher's seal is notable in that it includes the claim that he is the inventor of the beni-e genre.

55. MANGIKU AND DANJŪRŌ. 1718. Sanokawa Mangiku as the maiden Sanada, and, in the background, Ichikawa Danjūrō II as Kawazu Saburō. From *Hiragana yomeiri Izu nikki* performed XI/1718, Nakamura-za. Signature: Katsukawa Terushige. Publisher's seal: Asakusa-mitsuke Dōbō-chō, beni-e kongen Gonshirō. Condition: fair (discolored because of framing, general fading from exposure to light). From Chandler. Urushi-e: 3 colors by hand, gold dust. 29.7 × 15.9.

Kiyotada

Torii Kiyotada (worked 1720's to 1740's), like Kiyotomo, seems to have been a pupil of Kiyonobu I. In his fusion of the Kiyonobu and Masanobu styles he impresses one as being possessed of more talent than either Kiyotomo or Kiyonobu II; it is unfortunate that so little of his work is now known.

56. OSOME AND HISAMATSU. *Ca.* 1720. The maiden Osome tends her toy garden while her lover Hisamatsu stands behind her, a love letter protruding from his kimono. Though not a Kabuki print, this probably dates from shortly after the first Edo performance of the story of these two lovers in 1719. Legend: *Aburaya Osome utasaimon*, with part of the text of the long ballad. Signature: Torii Kiyotada. Condition good (stained at top). From Chandler. Urushi-e: 3 colors by hand, gold dust. 31.8 × 16.1.

Toshinobu

Okumura Toshinobu (worked ca. 1717 to 1740's), possibly an adopted son of Masanobu's, principally designed small lacquer-prints featuring one or two figures of actors or girls. Within this limited field, however, he often excelled all but the finest work of his master, and in sustained performance maintained a remarkable standard of quality.

52. [Style of Toshinobu.] GIRL PLAYING SAMISEN. *Ca.* 1720. A girl is seated playing the samisen with a practice-book open on her lap. The song is Edo Handayū's "Matsu no uchi," acted by Sanjō Kantarō as part of the drama *Keisei Fuji takane*, performed I/1718, Ichimura-za. The print, unsigned, has usually been attributed to Masanobu, but the pose seems a bit stiff for that master. (Stylistic differences are apparent, but notice should be made of a signed Toshinobu print [*UT* II, 114] depicting the same figure, position reversed, with samisen and the same "Matsu no uchi" practice-book. Our print may well represent an alternate version of this Toshinobu print, redrawn by an anonymous artist of considerable skill.) Condition fine (stains along left). From Chandler, 6/22/1919. Urushi-e: 3 colors by hand, gold dust. 32.8 × 15.8.

57. ICHIKAWA GENNOSUKE. 1729. Gennosuke as Ushiwaka, from *Yahagi no chōja kogane no ishizue*, performed XI/1729, Morita-za. Signature: Okumura Toshinobu hitsu. Publisher's seal Igaya. Condition fine. From Chandler, Hubert. In Hubert, No. 3. Urushi-e: 2 colors by hand, gold dust. 33.3 × 15.6.

58. SANJŌ KANTARŌ. 1724. Kantarō as Okuni, the girl who began Kabuki. She is performing the tea ceremony under cherry blossoms. Poem, written on a card hanging from the branch: "The early flowers of Yoshino: cherry blossoms that support the snow." From *Taiheiki Okuni Kabuki*, performed XI/1724, Nakamura-za. (Note that Torii Kiyoshige's similar design of the same actor [*UT* II, 202; Hayashi, opp. p. 70] may well derive from this print.) Signature: Yamato gakō Okumura Toshinobu hitsu. Publisher's seal: Izutsuya. Condition good (slight stains, holes, rubbing). From Chandler, Metzgar, Ficke, Gookin, Metzgar. Urushi-e: 5 colors by hand, gold dust. 30.4 × 15.2.

59. MONNOSUKE AND WAKANO. 1723. Ichikawa Monnosuke as Tokimune carries on his back Arashi Wakano as the Princess Tokoyo. From the same drama as No. 49. Signature: Okumura Toshinobu hitsu; Okumura seal (this seal is rather oddly inscribed; for more accurate examples, cf. Buckingham, p. 182, Nos. 21–22, where it is misread "Mitsuoki"). Publisher's seal: Shiba shimmei-mae yoko-chō, hammoto, Emiya. Condition fine (wormage). From Chandler, Straus-Negbaur. In Einstein, Pl. 23; Frankfurt, p. 23, No. 42; Straus-Negbaur, No. 79, Pl. 12; *UT*, II 116; *Kunstwanderer*, p. 467. Urushi-e: 4 colors by hand, gold dust. 31 × 14.3.

60. SANJŌ KANTARŌ. 1725. Kantarō as the Princess Nao. From *Semimaru onna-moyō*, performed XI/1725, Ichimura-za. Signature: Okumura Toshinobu hitsu. Publisher's seal: Hasegawa-chō hammoto, Ōmiya. Condition good. From Chandler, 1908. Urushi-e: 4 colors by hand, gold dust. 33 × 16.2.

Shigenaga

Nishimura Shigenaga (ca. 1697–1756), though not one of the artistic geniuses of ukiyo-e, was one of the great teachers and innovators, and his name deserves to be better known. He experimented with perspective and was the earliest ukiyo-e artist to work extensively in the landscape-with-figures genre shown in No. 61. He popularized the triptych form, and, taking hints from Chinese art, developed the ishizuri-e ("stone-print," cf. No. 50) and mizu-e ("water-print," employing blue pigment) genres. His own style was an individual one based on Kiyonobu, Sukenobu, and Masanobu; his pupils Toyonobu and Harunobu were to prove the leaders of the following generation.

61. DESCENDING GEESE AT KATATA. 1720's. No. 7 in a series celebrating the famous "Eight Views of Lake Biwa" (cf. No. 144). In the right foreground a peasant and his son carry firewood, while a townsman, a priest, and a servant approach from the left. In the background is the "Floating Shrine" of Katata with a flock of wild geese landing. Poem: "Many the peaks they have crossed on their journey; near to the Northland they now pause en route and descend at Katata, the wild geese." (For Masanobu's version of the same subject, including the same verse, see Noguchi's *Ukiyoye Primitives*, Pl. 54.) Signature: Eshi Nishimura Shigenaga; Shigenaga seal. Publisher: Shiba Shimmei-mae yoko-chō Emiya hammoto. Condition fine. From Chandler, Metzgar. Urushi-e: 3 colors by hand, gold dust. 33.3 × 16.

62. SHŌKI THE DEMON-QUELLER. 1740's. Shōki, originally a Chinese benign god, was adopted by the Japanese and became associated with Boy's Day, when his picture was displayed. Besides being a queller of bad devils, he was traditionally a woman-hater; hence his frequent depiction by facetious ukiyo-e artists in rather compromising situations (cf. No. 101). Signature: Senkadō Nishimura Shigenaga hitsu; Shige seal. Condition fair (tear left margin, discolorations). From Chandler, who received it as a wedding present from the distinguished collector of early prints, Miss Mary E. Ainsworth. Urushi-e: 2 colors by hand. 66.6×10.2.

63. SHŌKI THE DEMON-QUELLER. 1740's. Verse: "Driving out each and every evil demon, Spring comes to our house." Signature: Senkadō Nishimura Shigenaga hitsu; Shigenaga seal. Publisher: Bakuro-chō itchōme Shōkakudō Yamashiro; Fuji seal. Condition fine (browned). From Chandler. Urushi-e: 2 colors by hand. 65.2×23.7.

64. SANOKAWA ICHIMATSU. *Ca.* 1743. Ichimatsu as the young man Hisamatsu; under his sleeve he conceals a folded love letter. Ichimatsu played this role at the Nakamura-za I/1743 in *Kadomidori tokiwa Soga*, and again IX/1745 in *Higashiyama-dono takara no ishizue*. This print (and a similar one by Toyonobu) is generally supposed to date from the first performance. Signature: Senkadō Nishimura Shigenaga hitsu; Urokogataya seal. Condition good. From Cox, Morse. Urushi-e: 2 colors by hand. 68.5×16.

Mangetsudō

Mangetsudō (worked 1740's). All of the rare prints bearing the name Mangetsudō are done in late Masanobu style, and among them are several which are simply pirate editions of Masanobu's work (e.g., Nos. 68–70). This makes one wonder if Mangetsudō was really an individual artist, or simply a name used by the publisher for his pirating activities. Whatever the ethics of his business, however, the Mangetsudō publisher printed with care, and his prints are only inferior to Masanobu's originals in a certain hardness of the facial features.

65–67. YOSHIWARA KOMACHI. Late 1740's. An uncut triptych entitled "Three Scenes of a Yoshiwara Komachi." The left panel is entitled "Komachi Washing the Booklet" and shows a standing courtesan with the verse: "Komachi now washes away her bitterness: the shaded vines." The center panel is entitled "Komachi the Parrot" and shows a courtesan whispering in her maidservant's ear, with the verse: " 'Tell him this,' the parrot repeats, 'Let's meet in October.' " The right panel is entitled "Visiting Komachi" and shows a forlorn young man, lantern in hand, with the verse: "The bleak winter wind, and toward the Yoshiwara embankment, surge unknown the seaward breakers." Each section displays a small inset with a scene symbolic of that episode in the life of the ancient poetess Komachi; each is signed "Mangetsudō," with the seal "Kōrin" (Benibayashi). Interestingly enough, the words "right" and "left," found, respectively, at the tops of the cartouches for the left and right panels, are the reverse of their actual position. This is a phenomenon to be found in about two-thirds of extant uncut triptychs; in some cases the panels were clearly meant to be reordered after cutting, but in most

such, as here, the composition demands that the notations be interpreted as "stage right" and "stage left," i.e., as seen by the characters within the picture. Condition fair (folded, generally scuffed, poems which were originally printed in red badly faded, greens and blacks still good, backed). From Chandler, Hayashi, Wakai. In Hayashi, p. 42, No. 325; *UT* III, 114. Benizuri-e: red, green. Uncut triptych: 30.6×43.

68–70. LOVERS UNDER UMBRELLAS. Late 1740's. The three sheets, which are divided, bear the title "Triptych of Lovers under Umbrellas," with the order noted: left, center, right. Each is signed "Mangetsudō," with the seal "Kōrin." The verses originally printed beside the figures have faded beyond recognition. (Pl. 68–70 reproduce the panels in the order in which they are currently mounted. Compositionally, the sequence 70–69–68 is obviously preferable and was doubtless that originally intended, for, as I note under Nos. 65–67, a majority of the early triptychs are similarly "mislabeled." A glance at the Buckingham catalogue, for example, reveals some thirteen uncut triptychs with the order noted; of these, four – pp. 219, 221, 233 – are labeled left to right; one – p. 72 – is labeled in reverse but with the obvious intention of being corrected after cutting; and the other eight – pp. 85, 92, 169, 197, 198, 220 – are labeled in reverse but, as in our own Nos. 65–67, with no intention of later adjustment.) This triptych seems to be a direct copy of a work by Masanobu, the "right sheet" (actually, left) of which may be seen in Buckingham, p. 168. Condition fair. From Cox, Morse, Hayashi. Benizuri-e: red, green. Rejoined triptych: 31.4×43.6.

Shigenobu

Nishimura Shigenobu (worked 1730's to early 1740's). This is generally considered the early name of Ishikawa Toyonobu, but the matter is by no means certain. Shigenobu's work follows in the direct style of his teacher Nishimura Shigenaga during the 1730's and early 1740's; the prints signed Toyonobu appear in the early 1740's in a quite new style. It would seem best to treat Shigenobu as a separate entity for the time being. With this problem in mind it is interesting to note the Shigenobu-Toyonobu influence recorded under No. 71. Toyonobu is either copying Shigenobu (who may well, then, have been his teacher rather than Shigenaga), or is copying an earlier work of his own.

71. ICHIKAWA EBIZŌ. 1736. Ebizō as the warrior Shinozuka Gorō, in *Hobashira Taiheiki*, performed IV/1736, Ichimura-za. (For Toyonobu's version of this print, done two decades later, see the left panel of *UTS* IV, part 2, No. 34.) Legend: the name of the role and the actor. Signature: Nishimura Shigenobu hitsu. Publisher: hammoto, Tōri-abura-chō, Murata. Condition good (paper brown, worm holes). From Chandler (E.T.S. 12/26/1922). Urushi-e: 2 colors by hand, gold dust. 32.2×15.4.

72. GIRL SELLING FLOWERS. 1730's. A girl flower-vendor walks along bearing her wares. To the larger branches are tied *tanzaku* (poem cards). (Note the similar design by Toshinobu in No. 60.) Signature: Yamato-eshi Nishimura Shigenobu hitsu. Publisher: Izutsuya, Shimmei-mae yoko-chō. Condition good (trimmed left, right, bottom; worm-age, tears along right margin, backed). From Chandler,

Vignier, Manzi. Urushi-e: 2 colors by hand, gold dust. 30.4×14.5.

Toyonobu

Ishikawa Toyonobu (1711–85) owed as much to Masanobu as he did to his teacher Shigenaga (or Shigenobu). Again, in the grand impassivity of his girls there is something of the Kaigetsudō manner. Toyonobu's relation to Shigenobu is discussed under that artist. Following the lead of Shigenaga, Toyonobu experimented in the depiction of the nude. Such prints of his as No. 10 are almost sexless in their formalism, yet are interesting as an early ukiyo-e attempt to escape from the domination of the kimono in depicting female beauty.

10. GIRL AFTER BATH. Late 1750's. The girl has just come from the bath, her bathrobe pulled over one shoulder. Poem: "Well formed young breasts bloom like a pair of chrysanthemums." (For a version with different publisher and coloring, cf. *UTS* IV, part 2, No. 18.) Signature: Ishikawa Toyonobu zu; Toyonobu seal. Publisher's seal: Kyōichi, Hei; Dōsei(?). Condition good. From Chandler, Tomita, Happer. In Happer, April 1909, No. 200. Benizuri-e: red, green, blue. 69.3×10.8.

73. ICHIMATSU AND KIKUGORŌ. 1756. Two wandering *komusō* with their basket-hats: Sanokawa Ichimatsu as Soga Gorō, and Onoe Kikugorō as Kyō no Jirō, in *Umewakana futaba Soga*, performed III/1756, Ichimura-za. Signature: Tanjōdō Ishikawa Shūha Toyonobu zu; Toyonobu seal. Publisher: Urokogataya. Condition fine (two tears right margin). From Chandler, Wright. In Ficke, *Chats*, Pl. 7: Wright, No. 9. Benizuri-e: red, green. 44.8×31.9.

74. ICHIMATSU AND KIKUNOJŌ. 1747. Sanokawa Ichimatsu as Kōsuke, and Segawa Kikunojō as Onatsu, in *Unohana nise no aikago*, performed IV/1747, Ichimura-za. Signature: Tanjōdō Ishikawa Shūha Toyonobu zu; Ishikawa uji; Toyonobu seals. Publisher: Urokogataya. Condition good. From Chandler, B. Matsuki. Benizuri-e: red, green. 43.6×28.1.

75. MAIDEN. Mid-1740's. A young girl stands holding in her right hand a samisen plectrum, and in her left a practice-book for the Tokiwazu ballad "Ochiyo Hambei ukina no mōsen," first performed VIII/1744, Nakamura-za. (For another version of the same subject by Toyonobu, cf. *UT* III, 135.) Signature: Tanjōdō Ishikawa Shūha Toyonobu zu; Ishikawa uji, Toyonobu seals. Publisher's seal: Izumi. Condition fine (paper browned). From Chandler, 1/8/1905. Urushi-e: 4 colors by hand. 61.5×24.

76. GIRL HOLDING UMBRELLA. 1740's. A girl in a rain-cape and high clogs walks under an umbrella, possibly in light rain. Poem: "Though she hides her love, it comes out in her face: the cuckoo-bird." Signature: same as No. 75. Publisher's seal: Mura, hammoto. Condition good (tears on margin). From Chandler, Kane. Urushi-e: 3 colors by hand. 68.9×14.8.

77. GIRL WITH FLOWERS. 1740's. In her right hand she holds a pail filled with blossoms, and in her left, a poem-card. Signature: same as No. 75. Publisher's seal: Mura. Condition fair (thin spots, toned). From Chandler. Urushi-e: 2 colors by hand. 69.5×16.1.

78. GIRL WITH UMBRELLA. 1740's. She is dressed in a rain-cape and high clogs, and is closing or opening her umbrella. Signature and publisher the same as for No. 74. Condition fair (water stains, folds). From Chandler; Ficke; Hakone sale, 1919; Bullier. In Ficke cat., 1925, No. 20; Hakone sale, 1919, No. 6; *UT* III, 11; *UTS* IV, part 2, 20; V&I, I, 212. Urushi-e: 3 colors by hand. 70×15.6.

79. GIRL WITH LANTERN AND FAN. 1740's. Dressed in negligee, she is doubtless retiring on a summer night. Signature and publisher the same as for No. 74. Condition good (browned). From Chandler, Wright. In Wright, No. 3. Urushi-e: 3 colors by hand. 67.3×15.9.

80. COURTESAN AND MAIDSERVANT. Late 1740's. A courtesan walks holding a samisen while her little maidservant carries her Tokiwazu practice-book. Poem: "Her form so resilient, like the pale-cherry tree." Legend upper left: "Triptych, Edo, right." This is one of a series of three prints showing, respectively, the beauties of Osaka, Kyoto, and Edo. The three are illustrated in the *Bulletin of the Worcester Art Museum*, April 1915, p. 8. Signature and publisher the same as for No. 74. Condition fair (apparently framed without glass, therefore exposed portions soiled). From Chandler. Urushi-e: 4 colors by hand. 65.4×24.7.

81. ICHIMATSU AND KIKUGORŌ WITH PUPPETS. 1749. Manipulating the marionettes representing Agemaki and her lover Sukeroku are the actors Sanokawa Ichimatsu and Onoe Kikugorō, in the roles of Ushiwaka and the Princess Go-ō. From *Hatsu-tora Kurama Genji*, performed I/1749, Ichimura-za. Signature and publisher the same as for No. 73. Condition fair. From Chandler, 2/11/1921. In *UT* III, 22. Benizuri-e: red, green. 37.4×44.7.

82. YOUNG MAN WITH FLOWER-CART. Late 1750's. A young samurai carries a hanging flower arrangement done in the manner of a flower-cart. Poem: "The cherry blossom blooms but a moment: so too the flowering days of fair young lads." Signature: Ishikawa Toyonobu hitsu; Ishikawa uji, Toyonobu seals. Publisher: Urokogataya. Condition fine (slight discoloration). From Chandler, Wright, Murata. In *UTS* IV, 17. Benizuri-e: red, green, yellow. 38.8×17.4.

Kiyoshige

Torii Kiyoshige (worked late 1720's to early 1760's). A late pupil of Kiyonobu I, Kiyoshige often lends a rather stiff, angular note to his figures. His large pillar-prints in the Masanobu manner, however, rank among the masterpieces of the Torii school.

83. SANOKAWA ICHIMATSU. Early 1740's. The actor is seen in the role of a samurai, carrying a branch of cherry blossoms. (Yoshida Teruji suggests the role may be that of Yoriie in *Ainoyama onna katakiuchi*, performed III/1761, Nakamura-za; but stylistically the print would seem to date from nearly two decades earlier.) In an unsigned version this print has always been given to Masanobu; cf. *UT* III, 154 and V&I I, 133. Signature: Torii Kiyoshige hitsu; Kiyoshige seal. Publisher: Urokogataya. Condition fine (small worm holes, backed.) From Chandler. Urushi-e: 3 colors by hand. 71.2×16.

85. ICHIKAWA YAOZŌ. 1754. Yaozō in the role of Soga Gorō, from *Satsuki-matsu Soga tachibana*, performed I/1754, Ichimura-za. Poem: "They bloom in two colors: the flowering azaleas of Matsushima." Signature: Torii Kiyoshige; Kiyoshige seal. Publisher: Yamamoto. Condition good. From Lewis, Kellogg, Yamanaka. Benizuri-e: red, green, gray, overprinting. 39.1×17.5.

Kiyomitsu

Torii Kiyomitsu (ca. 1735–85), son of Kiyomasu II, represents the final period of glory of the traditional Torii school. His output was extensive, and many of his actor prints are dull, but in such imaginative scenes as that of No. 92 he displays a dreamlike grace that equals the best of Harunobu.

84. BANDŌ HIKOSABURŌ II. *Ca.* 1760. The actor is shown in the role of Akaneya Hanshichi, probably from *Furiwakegami suehiro Genji*, performed I/1760, Ichimura-za. Poem (by Jōa): "The face of first love: pale blush of early maples." Signature: Torii Kiyomitsu hitsu; Kiyomitsu seal. Condition good (small section of upper left corner missing, folded, toned). From Chandler, 11/12/1912. Benizuri-e: red, green, gray. 48.8×19.5.

92. MAIDEN DREAMING. 1760's. In the center, a maiden of the nobility dreams of being frightened by a large cat which leaps from amidst the peonies as butterflies scatter about. At the left a maidservant holds a lantern while to the right another maidservant with lantern enters with a samurai, possibly the maiden's lover. Signature: Torii Kiyomitsu ga; Kiyomitsu seal. Publisher: Tōri-abura-chō, Hōsendō, Yamamoto Kohei. Condition fair (folded). From Chandler, Longweil, Ledoux, Yamanaka. In London, No. 41. Benizuri-e: red, yellow, gray, overprinting. 31.3×43.5.

93–95. DANCERS. 1760's. Three girl dancers are depicted in roles derived from the Noh drama. Each panel is signed the same as No. 92. Publisher: Yamamoto. A cut triptych with original sheets rematched. Condition good (each sheet is folded along the center, the two outside sheets with vertical folds, indicating that the triptych was once backed). From Chandler, 4/5/1927. Benizuri-e: red, green, blue. Rejoined triptych: 31×43.7.

97. ICHIKAWA EBIZŌ. 1758. Ebizō II sharpens an arrowhead in the role of Yanone Gorō, from *Kyūjūsanki ōyose Soga*, performed I/1758, Ichimura-za. Signature is the same as for No. 92. Publisher: Yamamoto, Iwatoya. Condition fair (trimmed). From Shōbisha. Benizuri-e: red, yellow, blue, gray. 41.8×28.7.

Kiyohiro

Torii Kiyohiro (worked 1750's to 1760's). His figures are patterned closely after those by Kiyomitsu and Toyonobu, but in his overall compositions Kiyohiro reveals a special genius of his own. Nos. 87 (central panel) and 96, for example, rank among the masterpieces of the late Torii style.

86–88. COUPLES UNDER UMBRELLAS. 1750's. Left: A man holds the umbrella for a courtesan under plum blossoms Poem: "Spring rain: the plum blossoms not only fra-

grant, but the roads also muddy." Center: A young man holds the umbrella for a maiden, her pose reminiscent of Komachi praying for rain with a verse. Poem: "Heavy evening showers: thus we feel the force of poetry again." Right: A maidservant holds the umbrella for a maiden who is imitating the manner of a samurai. Poem: "First showers of autumn: in the dress of a man she's really lovable." A noted actor's crest appears on the umbrella above each figure: (l. to r.) Ichimura Uzaemon IX, Nakamura Kumetarō, Sanokawa Ichimatsu II, Nakamura Tomijūrō, Arashi Wakano, Segawa Kikunojō. They are placed in accordance with the type role each actor specialized in, but the actual figures do not represent actors. Each panel is signed: Torii Kiyohiro hitsu. Publisher: Tōri-abura-chō, Yamamoto (Maruya Kohei). Condition good (trimmed, stained, water spot on left umbrella, small crease). From Chandler, Kane. Benizuri-e: red, 2 shades of green. Uncut triptych: 28.7×43.6.

89–91. YOUNG PEOPLE BY THE WATERSIDE. 1750's. A triptych. Left: Two girls playing with fireworks by the river. Poem: "To Ishigake, the fireworks of Nawate float." Center: Two young lovers eloping. Poem: " 'The fireflies light'– thus he answered at Akuta River." Right: A young traveler gazes at the morning sun. Poem: "The first dream of the year: even Master Yuriwaka must cut his forelocks." Each panel is signed: Torii Kiyohiro hitsu. Publisher: Urokogataya. Condition fine (coloring smeared, some wear at corners, backed). From Chandler, 2/10/1920. In *Ukiyo-e Kabuki gashū*, Pl. 28. Benizuri-e: red, green. Uncut triptych: 31.4×44.4.

96. HIKOSABURŌ AND KICHIJI. 1753. Bandō Hikosaburō II as Sōchōden and Segawa Kichiji II as Jikokuden in the dance "Akutagawa momiji no shigarami." This was performed as part of the drama *Kammuri-kurabe yawaragi Kuronushi* XI/1753, Ichimura-za. An alternate version of this print (*UT* III, 73; Buckingham, p. 239) omits the upper right set of boxes carried by the noodle-vendors, changes the actors' names and crests, and fills the background with a dialogue concerning noodles from another play. On the noodle-boxes are the shop-advertisements "Ippachi, sobakiri" and "Yamatojiya," and between the actors the legend: "This scene, a great hit." Signature: Torii Kiyohiro hitsu; Kiyohiro seal. Publisher: Tōri-abura-chō, Hōsendō, Maruya, with seal. Condition good (patched along left margin and lower right corner, some smearing of black lettering, blue registry imperfect lower left and upper right). From Shōbisha, Shūgyō. In *UT* III, 74. Benizuri-e: red, blue. 42.5×30.2.

Fujinobu

Yamamoto Fujinobu (worked 1750's to 1760's). His prints are rare and the name may well be but a nom de plume of the well-known ukiyoe-publisher Yamamoto Kohei (Maruya), employed for his occasional essays in the creative field.

98. SANOKAWA ICHIMATSU. 1758. The actor is seen in the role of the courtesan Umegawa, from the same drama as No. 97. The verse is apparently by Ichimatsu: "Umegawa – with the ferryman of love, at Sano." Signature:

Yamamoto Fujinobu ga; Yamamoto, Fujinobu seals. Publisher: Yamamoto. Condition fine (small discolorations). From Chandler. Benizuri-e: red, green, blue, overprinting. 38×18

Harunobu

Suzuki Harunobu (ca. 1725–70). Although Harunobu's role in the technical development of full-color prints has been often exaggerated, there is no doubt that he ranks among the great geniuses of ukiyo-e. He studied first under Shigenaga, but his early prints are in the Torii and Toyonobu styles. By 1762, however, he had already developed his own unique style, which was soon to dominate the ukiyo-e world. Toward the end of 1764, Harunobu was commissioned to execute a number of designs for calendar prints for the coming year. Various noted literati of Edo contributed designs and ideas, and the printers outdid themselves to produce technically unusual work. From this combination of talents was born the nishiki-e ("brocade-picture"), or full-color print, where formerly only two or three colors had been featured. Among the prints thus produced at New Year's, 1765, were Nos. 101, 103, and 109. The designs are a bit harsher than the more supple work of Harunobu's maturity, but we can already see here the spirit of parody, and lyricism, that was to characterize his later work. Though we know nothing of Harunobu's formal education, he was certainly one of the most literate of the ukiyo-e designers. In such prints as Nos. 100, 110, and 111, verses and design are wedded in a happy combination seldom seen before or after. But whatever the literary or legendary implications of a Harunobu print, it is his color and his wonderful ideal of femininity that remain after all else is forgotten.

1. GIRL WITH CRANES. Mid-1760's. A girl walks past two cranes, carrying pails of seawater. Possibly a New Year's print with an implied parody on depictions of the god Fukurokuju with cranes. (The straw apron draped on the pail at the right may be supposed to represent Fukuroku-ju's bald head and long white beard.) The girl carrying sea-water (for making salt) was a favorite subject of ukiyo-e artists; see also Nos. 9 and 219. Signature: Suzuki Harunobu ga. Condition fine (slight scuffing lower left, backed). From Chandler, B. Matsuki, Ford, Freer. Nishiki-e: 6 colors, overprinting, gaufrage. 28.5×21.1.

5. GIRL WITH OX. Mid-1760's. A girl, possibly Harunobu's favorite model Osen, is shown in a parody on the standard Far Eastern "Ox-herd Boy" theme. She is depicted beneath a pine tree with broom in hand, sweeping up love letters (possibly written to Osen herself) while the docile ox follows her with baskets for their disposal. The coincidence of the broom and letters suggests the possibility of another parody – on depictions of Kanzan and Jittoku. In this case the ox must be assumed a substitute for one of the Zen monks! Unsigned. Condition fine (stain along left margin). From Chandler, B. Matsuki, Ford, Freer. Nishiki-e: 5 colors, gaufrage. 28.4×21.8.

100. GIRL BY VERANDA. Late 1760's. A girl, just come from an afternoon bath, stands by the veranda watching the falling paulownia leaves. A towel hangs on a rack, and the girl's sash is draped over the screen at right. The verse is by Fujiwara Toshiyuki, from the *Kokinshū:* "Though nothing said too clearly to my eyes that fall had come, yet was I startled by the sound of autumn's wind." In an alternate version of this print (Tokyo National Museum), all of the greens are replaced by mustard-yellow, with an effect more warm, but less suggestive of impending autumn. Signature: Harunobu ga. Condition fine. From Chandler, Ficke, Metzgar, Rouart. Nishiki-e: 5 colors, overprinting. 27.7×21.

101. SHŌKI CARRYING GIRL. 1765. The Chinese demon-queller Shōki is shown carrying a girl on his back (cf. No. 62). Several parodies on classical legend may be implied here: the elopment scene in the *Tales of Ise* (cf. No. 90), Ōmori Hikoshichi carrying the sorceress on his back, and Komachi praying for rain (No. 87). First issued as a calendar print (*UT* IV, 154; V&I, II, No. 24), which bore the date 1765, and in addition to Harunobu's name, that of Takahashi Rosen as *kō* (designer, artisan). Unsigned. Condition good (general staining, backed). From Chandler, Baker, Tregaskis, Litchfield Album. In Baker, No. 62. Nishiki-e: 5 colors. 26.7×20.8.

102. PRINCESS NYOSAN. Mid-1760's. She is shown with her cat on a leash, in a famous scene from the *Tale of Genji*. Signature: Suzuki Harunobu ga. Condition fine (some fading). From Chandler, "Nadeshiko-sono," Fukuda Bunko (the latter two represented by seals at lower right). Nishiki-e: 4 colors, gaufrage. 29×21.7.

103–4. TWO GIRLS BY STREAM. 1765. A summer scene of two girls relaxing beside a stream. The girl at left has dropped one of her clogs, and the girl at right is retying her sash. The left panel also appears as a calendar print with the date 1765 on the fan (*UTS* V, 6). Unsigned. Left panel: Condition good. From Chandler, Kington-Baker, Tregaskis, Litchfield Album. In Baker, No. 61. Right panel: Condition good (shows signs of having been washed, slight staining, backed). From Chandler, 1919. Nishiki-e: 5 colors, gaufrage. Diptych: each 26.8×20.9.

105–6. GIRL GREETING LOVER. Mid-1760's. In a pastiche on the famous legend of Ōta Dōkan (founder of Edo) and a rustic maiden, we see at the left a girl advancing from her flowered gate to greet a stylish young man who appears accompanied by a boy carrying a cricket-cage. The girl proffers a love letter on her open fan. A stream flows between the pathway and the fence. (The scene is also reminiscent of the "Yūgao" chapter in the *Tale of Genji*.) Unsigned. Condition good (some staining, backed). From Chandler, Schraubstadter. In Schraubstadter, 1921, No. 46; Noguchi, Pl. 33, where it is wrongly attributed to another collection. Nishiki-e: 6 colors. Diptych: each 26.3×19.3.

107. THE EMPEROR'S LADIES AT BACKGAMMON. 1766. The T'ang emperor Hsuan-tsung watches while two of his court ladies play backgammon, two maidservants in attendance. The lady to the left is presumably the famous beauty Yang Kuei-fei, who was to prove Hsuan-tsung's downfall. This design is found also as a calendar print, with the date 1766 and the inscription of the artisan, or designer, Toyoko *kō* – a girl's name (Tokyo National Museum). Unsigned. Condition good (backed). From Chandler, Straus-Negbaur, Hayashi. In Frankfurt, 1909, No. 85; Kurth, *Harunobu* (1910 and 1923), Pl. 9; Straus-Negbaur, No. 149; *UT* IV, 91; Yoshida, No. 246. Nishiki-e: 4 colors. 24.3×35.5.

108. LOVERS READING LETTER. Late 1760's. On a snowy morning a girl and her lover read a letter – possibly one he had sent when they first knew love. Two pastiches are suggested by this scene: the deity Fugen seated on an elephant (here suggested by the *kotatsu* brazier) reading a letter; and the famous letter-viewing scene in the *Chūshingura* drama (cf. Nos. 121, 124). Signature: Harunobu ga. Condition fine. From Chandler; Kobayashi, whose square seal shows through at the lower left corner. Nishiki-e: 7 colors, overprinting, gaufrage. 27.3 × 21.

109. LOVERS READING LETTER. 1765. A calendar print which follows the same general design as No. 108. The first part of the letter notes the "long months" with their poetic names, and the second part gives the "short months," together with the year in question, 1765. Unsigned, the print is sealed "Hakusei" (designer of the Harunobu print shown in Hillier, Pl. 16). Quite possibly the present print represents the first version, done by Harunobu after a design by Hakusei. No. 108, which is far more skilled, may then represent a freer version done by Harunobu in his maturity. Condition fine (backed). From Chandler, Tregaskis, Litchfield Album. Nishiki-e: 7 colors. 28.1 × 20.9.

110. CHINESE SCHOLAR AND JAPANESE GEISHA. Late 1760's. On the surface, this print would seem to be an interesting comparison of Chinese and Japanese civilizations: the Chinese scholar at left displaying a subdued painting of orchids in his hand while he rides in a boat elaborately decorated in the Chinese manner; to the right a Japanese girl, probably a geisha, displaying a stylish kakemono print by Harunobu as she rides in a Japanese boat which features the natural wood. These elements alone are enough to interest cultural historians – but not an ukiyo-e artist, to whom a picture of a man and a woman naturally evoked thoughts of love, rather than culture. With this in mind we note the scholarly books at the man's feet, and the samisen at the girl's: he was perhaps sent to apan to study and instead found love, which he must now renounce. The verse, appropriately enough, is from the chorus of the Noh drama *Haku Rakuten* (the poet Po Chü-i, who, in the play, was sent by the Chinese emperor to "subdue" Japan with his verse but failed – just as here ukiyo-e may be interpreted as conquering Chinese art). It is adapted here to a new situation: "The moss-grown rock is not all that it seems: does it not now wear the sash of dawn parting?" (In its original context the verse might be translated: "The rock which bears a cloak of moss wears not a sash; where, strangely enough, the bare mountain does wear one [of clouds]!") Signature on both print and scroll: Harunobu ga. Condition fine (scuffing lower right, blue on man's robe faded). From Chandler, Ōshima, May. Nishiki-e: 6 colors. 28.9 × 20.8.

111. LOVERS AND PLUM TREE. Late 1760's. "The Second Month: Plum Tree by the Stream" from a set, *Stylish Poems of the Four Seasons*. A young man climbs a fence to break off a plum branch for his ladylove, who reclines against an old stone lantern. The night is black but the stream reflects the moonlight. Poem: "Even the hand of him who ties the knot of love will be fragrant: how then

the stream that flows beneath the plum!" Signature: Harunobu ga. Condition fine (the black is a little thin in spots; trimmed at bottom?). From Chandler, Sotheby. In Sotheby, 4/17/1918, Pl. 1. Nishiki-e: 4 colors. 27.6 × 20.6.

113. LOVERS IN THE SNOW. Late 1760's. Two lovers walk through the falling snow holding a snow-laden umbrella. We may suppose the scene to represent the morning after a night of love: the man looks in the girl's eyes as she modestly averts her face from his ardent gaze. The contrast of the man in black and the girl in light garments reflects the pairing of the raven and the heron in classical art. For an alternate version of this famous pr nt, see Ledoux, II, No. 29. Signature: Suzuki Harunobu ga. Condition good (small worm holes, backed, slightly trimmed at top). From Chandler, Ainsworth. Nishiki-e: 5 colors, gaufrage. 32.7 × 19.9.

116. YOUNG MAN PLAYING KICK-BALL. Late 1760's. A young man is playing the aristocratic game of *kemari* ("kick-ball"); the ball flies above his head, and in the background is the bamboo enclosure of the kick-ball court. Signature: Harunobu ga. Condition fair. From Cox, Morse, Ketcham, Fenollosa(?). Nishiki-e: 4 colors, gaufrage. 68.7 × 12.8.

Harushige

Suzuki Harushige (worked mid-1760's to 1770's). Harushige was the ukiyo-e nom de plume employed by the well-known painter and student of occidental matters Shiba Kōkan (ca. 1738–1818). He was a skilled imitator of Harunobu's style and, as he himself confessed, after Harunobu's sudden death in his prime, designed a number of prints to which he affixed Harunobu's signature, and which were accepted as genuine by his contemporaries. Harushige's style is characterized by greater use of Western-style perspective, and his figures are often less delicate than Harunobu's.

112. [Style of Harushige.] GIRLS WITH SNOWBALL. Early 1770's. A courtesan stands watching her two maidservants warm their hands after making a large snowball. In the background a river scene with boatmen. Although it would be unwise to ascribe all Harunobus with perspective-technique to Harushige, this print, with its stiffness and exaggeration, and its typically odd signature, would seem to fall among the forgeries – albeit one of the finest of such. The design may have been suggested by a Harunobu book illustration (*Ehon chiyo no matsu*, 1767, pp. 7–8). Cf. also various early Tosa illustrations to Ch. XX ("Asagao") in the *Tale of Genji*. Signature: Harunobu ga. (At the Ruth sale in London in 1911 and at the (Kington Baker sale in 1916 this particular print was catalogued as by Harunobu.) Condition good. From Lewis, Bateson, Baker, Tregaskis, Ruth, Samuel. In Ruth, No. 59. Nishiki-e: 6 colors, gaufrage. 27.4 × 20.7.

Koryūsai

Isoda Koryūsai (worked mid-1760's to 1780's). Though possibly a pupil of Shigenaga's, Koryūsai was influenced most by his friend Harunobu, and in his first works employed the derivative name Haruhiro. The best of his early prints (e.g., Nos. 99 and 118) almost reach the level of Harunobu, and some critics consider Koryūsai's work in this large pillar-print category one of the glories of ukiyo-e. Koryūsai's later prints (e.g., Nos. 112–13) are more massive and feature the elaborate coiffures then developing in the gay quarters. With the 1780's Koryūsai abandoned popular prints and devoted himself to production of the more prestigious ukiyo-e paintings.

99. YOUNG MAN WITH HAWK. 1770's. A boy samurai holds his hawk upon his gloved hand as two sparrows fly past overhead. The hawk regards the little birds with more than passing interest, for sparrows are his favorite food. This print displays an interesting combination of natural innocence (the boy and the sparrows) and predatory cruelty. Signature: Koryūsai ga; Masakatsu seal. Condition fine (thin spot at top, has been framed). From Chandler, Itō. Nishiki-e: 6 colors. 64.2×12.3.

114. THE COURTESAN MICHINOKU WITH ATTENDANTS. Late 1770's. The courtesan Michinoku, of the Tsutaya House, is reading the *Hundred Poets* while her little attendants play at "poem cards." From the series *First Designs of Model Young Leaves*. Signature: Koryūsai zu. Publisher: Eijudō. Condition fine. From Kondō. Nishiki-e: 5 colors. 38.9× 25.9.

115. THE COURTESAN MICHIHARU WITH ATTENDANTS. Late 1770's. The courtesan Michiharu, of the Tsutaya, is on procession with three attendants. From the same series as No. 114, with the subtitle "White garments of the Eighth Month." Signature and publisher: same as No. 114. Condition fine. From Chandler, Blanchard. In Blanchard, Pl. 8. Nishiki-e: 5 colors. 39.4×26.7.

118. GIRL WITH MOUSE. Early 1770's. A girl – possibly a courtesan – in dishabille plays with a mouse. The subject matter might suggest dating the print in the zodiacal Year of the Rat, 1768, but the style seems a bit later. Signature: Koryūsai ga; Koryū seal. Condition fine. From Chandler, Ficke. In Ficke, 1920, No. 91. Nishiki-e: 5 colors. 72.3× 13.3.

Kuninobu

Kuninobu (worked 1770's to early 1780's). Kuninobu's work is typical of several obscure but skilled artists in the Harunobu style who attempted to fill the gap caused by that great master's early death in 1770.

117. LOVERS WALKING AT NIGHT. Early 1770's. A man and girl are seen walking beneath a willow tree late at night; the man carries a lantern. The print may well represent the michiyuki travel scene of some famous pair of lovers. Signature: Kuninobu ga. Condition good. From Chandler, 3/17/1906. Nishiki-e: 3 colors, overprinting. 66.4×12.6.

Masunobu

Masunobu (worked 1770's) produced a number of delicate prints in the style of Harunobu. Nothing is known of him, but he may possibly be the same artist as Tanaka Masunobu, who designed prints and illustrated books in the Masanobu manner during the 1740's and 1750's.

121. CHŪSHINGURA PARODY. Early 1770's. The famous seventh act of the *Chūshingura* features a scene in which Yuranosuke, leader of the Forty-seven Rōnin, reads an important and highly secret letter on the veranda of a Gion teahouse; he is overseen by two people: the courtesan Okaru, who covertly reads the letter in her hand-mirror,

and a spy of the enemy, who is hiding under the porch. In Masunobu's parody the courtesan and warrior are replaced by a maiden and a fair young man, and the spy by a dog – a pun on the Japanese word *inu*, which means both "dog" and "spy." Signature: Masunobu ga. Condition fine. From Nail, Packard. Nishiki-e: 9 colors. 70.8×12.7.

Bunchō

Ippitsusai Bunchō (worked 1760's to 1770's) combined the lyricism of Harunobu with the realism of Shunshō to produce some of the most uniquely individual prints in ukiyo-e. His speciality was actors, but some of his greatest work lay in the depiction of girls and courtesans. The nervous, haunting brilliance of Bunchō's work led one critic (Ficke) to imagine "an intangible spiritual abnormality" about him; perhaps so, but it is the same quality that compels us in Memling, Grünewald, El Greco.

125. ŌTANI HIROJI III. 1769. The actor as Shirobei in *Edo no hana wakayagi Soga*, performed I/1769, Ichimura-za. He poses menacingly beside a pine tree in a storm, lifting his rain-cap from his head. Signature: Ippitsusai Bunchō ga; Mori uji seal. Condition fine (flaw near right foot from defect in block). From Chandler. Nishiki-e: 5 colors. 31.2×14.3.

126. OSEN. *Ca.* 1770. The famous waitress and beauty Osen is depicted in front of her tea-shop, the Kagiya, which stood beside the torii of the Kasamori Inari Shrine in Edo. She holds a tray of cakes in her hand, and behind her we see teacups and utensils, a cherry-blossom flower arrangement, a sign with the name of the shop, and the gateway to the shrine. Signature & seals: same as No. 125. Condition good (slight stains). From Koscherak, Ledoux, K. Matsuki, Barnes, Straus-Negbaur. In Ledoux, III, 5; OAZ, n.f.2:152; Straus-Negbaur, No. 190; *UT* V, 267 (rephotographed from Straus-Negbaur). Nishiki-e: 4 colors. 32.7×14.9.

127. OSEN. *Ca.* 1770. The same subject and scene as in No. 126. Osen poses with a fan in her hand and a small towel grasped in her teeth. The season here is summer, where in No. 126 it was doubtless early spring. Poem: "At Kasamori the rain ceases, and Osen stands in the summer shade." Signature & seals: same as No. 125. Condition fine (slight discoloration at top). From Tomoda. Nishiki-e: 4 colors. 33×15.2.

Shunshō

Katsukawa Shunshō (1726–93) was trained in the genre-painting schools of Chōshun and Itchō but from the late 1750's began to develop a more realistic style of his own. He learned much from the color harmonies of Harunobu and Shigemasa, and in his special field, the actor print, soon overshadowed the hitherto dominant Torii school. Though no startling innovator, Shunshō ranks with Kiyonobu and Sharaku in his influence upon Kabuki depiction; his pupils were very numerous, not the least of them being Hokusai. Like several other ukiyo-e greats, Shunshō devoted his final years more to paintings than popular prints.

128–29. KIKUNOJŌ AND SANGORŌ. 1775. Segawa Kikunojō III as Kawazu Saburō, and Arashi Sangorō II in the female role of Tagasode. The actors are shown here in the "Mandarin-duck Dance" featured in the drama *Hanazumō Genjibiiki*, performed XI/1775, Nakamura-za. (Mandarin duck › are the customary symbol of marital felicity in Far Eastern art and rhetoric.) Signature: Shunshō ga. Condition fine (small holes). From Chandler, 1/6/1927. Nishiki-e: (No. 128) 4 colors; (No. 129) 7 colors, overprinting. Diptych: each 32.3×15.

130. KOJŪRŌ, TSUNEYO, AND SŌJŪRŌ. 1785. In the center, Nakayama Kojūrō as Hotoke Gozen; at the left, Osagawa Tsuneyo II as the courtesan Naniwazu; at the right, Sawamura Sōjūrō as Komatsu Shigemori. The actors are posed before a flower-viewing pavilion. From the drama *Yuki-mochidake furisode Genji*, performed XI/1785, Nakamura-za. Unsigned; Hayashi [Shunshō] jar-shaped seal. Condition fine (slight stains). From Mayuyama. Nishiki-e: 5 colors. 39×26.1.

131. SUKEGORŌ AND NAKAZŌ. 1768. Nakamura Sukegorō III, as Danshichi Kurobei, and Nakamura Nakazō as Giheiji, quarrel in a scene from *Natsu-matsuri Naniwa kagami*, performed V/1768, Nakamura-za. Signature: Shunshō zu; Hayashi seal. Condition good (stains, some rubbing). From Chandler, Straus-Negbaur. In Straus-Negbaur, No. 212; *UT* V, 176. Nishiki-e: 4 colors. 28.9×21.5.

132. NAKAZŌ AS HOTEI. 1780. Nakamura Nakazō is seen in the role of Hotei, one of the Seven Gods of Fortune, in a scene from *Kite kaeru nishiki no wakayaka*, performed XI/1780, Nakamura-za. Signature: Shunshō ga; Matsu seal. Condition good (marginal stains, scuffing). From Chandler, 6/23/1919. Nishiki-e: 4 colors. 43.3×14.8.

Shunkō

Katsukawa Shunkō (1743–1812). Of Shunshō's pupils who devoted their work to the theater, Shunkō ranks first; in his finest prints he is fully the equal of his master. Shunkō's work extends from the early 1770's through his final years; in the late 1780's his right arm became paralyzed, but, switching to his left hand, Shunkō worked on to produce the type of large actor heads (No. 137) which were one of his main contributions to ukiyo-e.

120. ICHIKAWA DANJŪRŌ V. Mid-1780's. The actor is shown on the street, outside a Kabuki theater, but probably in an individual portrait rather than a role. Behind him, through the window, we see the theater musicians practicing. Signature (partially cut off): Shunkō ga. Condition fair (trimmed, slight repairs). From Chandler. Nishiki-e: 3 colors. 64.3×11.5.

133–35. SUKEROKU, AGEMAKI, AND IKYŪ. 1784. Ichikawa Yaozō III as the hero Sukeroku, Nakamura Rikō as the courtesan Agemaki, and Ichikawa Danjūrō V as the aged suitor Ikyū, in a scene from *Soga musume chōja*, performed III/1784, Nakamura-za. The series may possibly be made complete by the addition, at left, of the print showing a saké-merchant – actually Soga Jūrō in disguise (Wright Cat. 1927, No. 102); or yet another panel may have existed to the left or right of Ikyū. Signature on each print: Shunkō ga. A seal is faintly visible at the lower right of No. 135. Condition fine (No. 135: minor holes, slight stains). From Chandler, Wright. In Wright, No. 154. Nishiki-e: (No. 133) 4 colors; (No. 134) 5 colors, gaufrage; (No. 135) 4

colors. Three sheets of a pentaptych(?): left, 32.1×16.3; center, 32.2×14.6; right, 32.2×15.

136. MOKUEMON, YAMAUBA, AND KINTOKI. 1785. Ichikawa Danjūrō V as Shibakari Mokuemon (in reality the god of Mt. Ashigara), Segawa Kikunojō III in the female role of Yamauba, and Ichikawa Monnosuke as the herculean boy Kintoki. A scene from *Shitennō Ōe no yamairi*, performed XI/1785, Kiri-za. Signature: Shunkō ga. Condition fine (slight stains and holes, partly backed). From Chandler, Doi, Kawaura. In *UT* VIII, 193; Kawaura, No. 167. Nishiki-e: 6 colors, overprinting. 38.5×25.4.

137. ICHIKAWA MONNOSUKE. 1789. Monnosuke II as the maiden Osome, from *Edo Fuji wakayagi Soga* (cf. No. 152), I/1789, Nakamura-za. Signature: Shunkō ga. Condition good. From Shōbisha. Nishiki-e: 5 colors. 36.7×25.3.

Shun'ei

Katsukawa Shun'ei (ca. 1762–1819). Another great pupil of Shunshō's, Shun'ei adds a modern touch to the Katsukawa school, as well as a pronounced element of facial exaggeration which adds to the individuality and dramatic force of his actor prints, but in lesser hands was to lead to the decline of figure work in the 19th century. Sharaku and, most of all, Toyokuni, were among those influenced by Shun'ei's style. He was somewhat eccentric in his behavior but had a wide circle of friends, among them Shunchō, Utamaro, and Toyokuni, with each of whom he sometimes collaborated on prints such as No. 179 below.

138. ICHIKAWA EBIZŌ. 1795. Ebizō (cf. No. 168) as Yokizō (in reality Mita no Tsukau), from a scene in *Fuku-botan Azuma dairi*, performed XI/1795, Kawarazaki-za. Signature: Shun'ei ga; kiwame, Uemura seals. Condition good. From Chandler, K. Matsuki. Nishiki-e: 6 colors. 38.6×25.9.

139. ICHIKAWA EBIZŌ. 1795. Ebizō as the samurai Kakogawa Honzō, from *Kana-tehon chūshingura*, performed V/1795, Kiri-za. (Cf. No. 206 below.) Signature: Shun'ei ga; Iwa seal. Condition fine (imperfection in paper causing white spot at left knee of kimono; oxidation of white). From Mayuyama. Nishiki-e: 6 colors. 39.4×26.4.

140. NAKAYAMA TOMISABURŌ. 1795. Tomisaburō as the courtesan Okaru, from the same drama as No. 139, with same signature and seal. Condition fine. From Shōbisha. Nishiki-e: 6 colors. 38.4×25.7.

Masanobu (Kitao)

Kitao Masanobu (1761–1816) was the most precocious of Shigemasa's several brilliant pupils and might well have developed into the stature of a Kiyonaga had he continued to work in the print field. But the rewards of the print designer were seldom financial, and Masanobu chose to devote most of his later life to novel-writing under the name Santō Kyōden and running his shop, which sold tobacco-pouches and pipes with great success. Masanobu produced few prints but his remarkable album of Yoshiwara beauties, of which one plate is shown in No. 141, has served to win him a place in any selection displaying the wonders of the Japanese color print. (His name is written differently from that of the pioneer Okumura Masanobu; to distinguish the two in romanization, the form K. Masanobu is sometimes used for the later artist.)

141. COURTESANS AT LEISURE. *Ca.* 1783. To the left a high-ranking Yoshiwara courtesan stands and inscribes a poem on a card as her attendant holds the writing utensils. In the center another courtesan is seated reading a ballad; before her sits an attendant with samisen in hand; and to the right a young attendant stands holding a saké-container. The scene is of courtesans at leisure, probably on the second floor of a courtesan house; the season is spring and cherry blossoms are seen blooming from the garden below. The verses and calligraphy are supposedly from the courtesans' own hands; that to the right is by Utagawa; that to the left is by Nanazato and reads: "Enfolded in impending rain, the fragrance of the still plum tree!" This is one of a series of seven large prints by Kitao Masanobu published together in album form by Tsutaya Jūzaburō early in 1784. Each print features two leading courtesans with their attendants and two autographic verses. The prints are thought first to have been issued separately during 1782 and 1783, and one bears the date II/1783. Two of the series are signed, "Kitao Rissai Masanobu ga," with the seal "Soseki," and the title "Autographs of Famous Beauties of the Greenhouses." The later title of the series as a whole is *Yoshiwara Courtesans: A New Collection of Beauties, An Autographic Mirror.* Unsigned. Condition fine. From Shōbisha. Nishiki-e: 9 colors in many shades. 37.3 × 50.4.

Shigemasa

Kitao Shigemasa (1739–1820) was the son of an Edo publisher and, in his prime, was considered one of the ukiyo-e greats, though today he is little known even among collectors. The reasons for this are that his signed work is rare and that his prints, though always distinguished by fine draftsmanship, frequently reflect more the general artistic fashions of his time rather than the individual personality of the artist. Shigemasa, like his good friend Shunshō, was one of the great teachers of his age, and his pupils have eclipsed him in fame, if not in native genius: Shumman, Masanobu, Masayoshi, as well as such unofficial pupils as Utamaro and Hokusai. Shigemasa's finest prints were probably his rare geisha series, of which two examples are described below; characteristically, they are unsigned.

142. TWO GEISHA. *Ca.* 1776. Two geisha – entertainers rather than straight courtesans – are shown in a standing pose. They are identified by name as Oshima and Onaka. Legend: "Beauties of the Four Directions: Beauties of the East." ("East" here probably refers to the Fukagawa gay quarter.) The Tokyo National Museum copy of this print has the manuscript notation "An'ei V" (1776). Unsigned. Condition good (holes crudely repaired, backed). From Chandler, Morse, Ketcham, Fenollosa(?). Nishiki-e: 5 colors, gold dust. 39.2 × 26.

143. GEISHA WITH MAIDSERVANT. Late 1770's. A geisha walks to the left, followed by a maidservant carrying a samisen box. The samisen has always been a necessary accouterment of the geisha, and there was a special class of male or female servant, called the *hakoya*, who carried this musical instrument for the geisha and helped with clothing changes. Shigemasa seems to have been particularly sensitive to fashions in kimono design, and we note in Nos. 142 and 143 the careful attention he has given to such foreign materials as velvet and calico, which were then enjoying a considerable popularity. Unsigned. Condition fine (holes). From Chandler, Ford, Freer. Nishiki-e: 6 colors. 39.1 × 26.8.

Toyoharu

Utagawa Toyoharu (1735–1814) is best remembered today as the founder of the Utagawa school and the teacher of Toyokuni and Toyohiro, but he is an artist of considerable interest in his own right. His early prints, such as No. 119, are in the Harunobu manner, but display a delicacy that almost borders on weakness. Toyoharu's greatest achievement was the development of the uki-e, or perspective-print, as shown in No. 144. Forming a kind of bridge between ukiyo-e and Western art, these prints have been strangely neglected by Western students. Few subsequent ukiyo-e artists failed, however, to be influenced by Toyoharu's view of landscape and background; Hokusai's work would be difficult to imagine without it.

119. LOVERS WITH KITE. Early 1770's. A young man holds a spool of kite-string as a girl ascends a ladder within the garden to disentangle his kite, to which a love letter is attached. Signature: Utagawa Toyoharu ga. Condition good. From Cox, Morse, Ketcham, Fenollosa(?). Nishiki-e: 5 colors. 68.3 × 9.5.

144. EIGHT VIEWS OF LAKE BIWA. Late 1770's. The famous "Eight Views of Lake Biwa" (see Nos. 61 and 229) are here encompassed in a single "perspective print," which combines the traditional Japanese techniques with the concept of perspective as lately adapted from Western art. Each of the set scenes is labeled; in the foreground (left to right): Evening Glow at Seta Bridge, Clear Day at Awazu, Returning Sailboats at Yabase; in the background: Autumn Moon at Ishiyama Temple, Evening Bell at Mii Temple, Lingering Snows on Mt. Hira, Night Rain at the Karasaki Pine, Descending Geese at Katata. Legend: "Perspective-print: Scenic Views of Japan: Eight Views of Lake Biwa." Signature: Utagawa Toyoharu ga. Publisher: Eijudō Nishimuraya. Condition fair (backed). From Mayuyama. Nishiki-e: 3 colors. 26 × 38.8.

Kiyonaga

Torii Kiyonaga (1752–1815), son of an Edo bookseller, was a pupil of Kiyomitsu's, last of the great figures in the traditional Torii line. Although Kiyonaga maintained his responsibilities as "Torii IV," his genius led him far beyond the limits of this school of Kabuki artists, and even in treating the theater Kiyonaga devised quite new forms and approaches, such as we see in Nos. 152 and 156–57. His special field, however, was the depiction of stylish young men, graceful girls and courtesans, against broad and fully realized backgrounds of the Edo he knew so well; the other prints we show are of this type: they utilize elements that had been standard in ukiyo-e since its origins, but combine them on a grand scale, with a solid, realistic draftsmanship that is withal poetic and evocative, a style that was to dominate ukiyo-e for twenty years or more. It was Kiyonaga's vision that formed Utamaro's style, but when the latter's star rose to predominance in the early 1790's Kiyonaga returned to his original work of theater posters and paintings, designing few prints during the last two decades of his life.

122. MAIDEN WATCHING A YOUNG MAN. Early 1780's. From her window a maiden admiringly watches a fair young man pass by. Signature: Kiyonaga ga. Condition fair (backed). From Chandler, 10/20/1906. In Hirano, Pl. 94(?). Nishiki-e: 3 colors. 69 × 12.3.

145–46. EVENING SCENE AT SHINAGAWA. Mid-1780's. Early evening in the gay quarter of Shinagawa, south of Edo. At the left a woman carrying a lantern guides a young male guest; they are followed by a geisha and two girls, the last of whom pauses to converse with another geisha whose servant carries her samisen-box and lantern. Upper right, a lantern of the Sentai Kōjin Shrine. (For an alternate version with sky printed lighter and signature at lower right of No. 145 in white, see Noguchi, *Torii Kiyonaga*, Pl. 12.) The Seventh Month in a famous series of diptychs entitled *Minami jūni-kō*, "Twelve Months in the South," devoted to the customs of the Shinagawa gay quarter. Each sheet is signed "Kiyonaga ga," with the title of the series. Condition fine (pasted to form a single print, creased, inconspicuous worm holes, some fading of colors). From Morse. In Morse, No. 80; Wadsworth, No. 102. Nishiki-e: 6 colors, gradation. Joined diptych: 38.1×50.7.

147–48. SNOWY MORNING IN THE YOSHIWARA. Late 1780's. At the left the young male guest reclines against the bedding, composing a letter; behind him a young girl attendant looks out over the snowy Yoshiwara embankment while another girl sits before him at the brazier. The principal courtesan stands to the right of her lover, in dishabille, while two lesser courtesans look at the fish a girl has just brought in. Legend: "Snowy Morning in the Greenhouses." Each sheet is signed: Kiyonaga ga. Condition good (holes crudely patched; prints pasted together along center margins, some scuffing, colors excellent). From Chandler, 2/20/1928. In Hirano, Pl. 68. Nishiki-e: 5 colors, overprinting, gaufrage. Joined diptych: 38.3×50.4.

149–50. NEW YEAR'S SCENE AT NIHOMBASHI. Mid-1780's. Left, a maidservant carrying plum blossoms and a child's kite, then a matron and a girl whose large hat bears the legend "Enoshima, Monthly Pilgrimage." Right, a maiden of quality accompanied by two maidservants and a boy. Beyond the pillars of the bridge are seen warehouses, Edo Castle, and in the distance Mt. Fuji. Each sheet is signed "Kiyonaga ga," with the publisher's seal of Eijudō. Condition fine. (This fairly well-matched diptych was assembled by Chandler. Left sheet backed, right unbacked. Blue ink notation on back of left sheet shows below foot of the girl with pilgrim's hat.) No. 149 from Chandler, Koechlin; No. 150 from Chandler, Hayashi. Nishiki-e: 6 colors. Diptych: left, 38×25.2; right, 38.3×25.8.

151. RIVER COOL AT DUSK. Mid-1780's. Two women of the Floating World cool off on a summer evening at Hama-chō by the Sumida River. A waitress stands at the left. This print is the left side of a diptych, the other half of which shows two geisha and a servant walking toward the right. Signature: Kiyonaga ga. Condition fair (folded, holes, stain lower center, fading at right; bottom slightly trimmed?). From Chandler, Jacquin. In Jacquin, No. 282; V&I, III, 125. Nishiki-e: 5 colors. 37×25.5.

152. KOMAZŌ AND MONNOSUKE. 1789. Ichikawa Komazō II as the lover Hisamatsu, and Ichikawa Monnosuke II as the maiden Osome, in the "Yukari no hinagusa" scene of *Edo Fuji wakayagi Soga*, performed I/1789, Nakamura-za (cf. No. 137). The lovers stand beneath cherry blossoms. Signature: Kiyonaga ga. Publisher: Eijudō. Condition

good. From Mayuyama. Nishiki-e: 6 colors, overprinting. 38.9×26.

153–55. SUDDEN SHOWER AT THE MIMEGURI SHRINE. Mid-1780's. Left, two men and two women take shelter from the shower under the gateway to the shrine; center, a hotel maid carries umbrellas and clogs for the use of marooned guests, while behind her a girl runs for shelter, her hair protected by a kerchief; right, two girls, skirts pulled up, share an umbrella, followed by another running girl, whose head is bare and sash in disarray. In the heavens are seen the forces of rain and thunder personified as stylish Edoites: the deity at left dangles his leg over the cloud, smokes his pipe, and surveys the rain-drenched confusion that has resulted below; the next three deities are discussing the merits of a calligraphic poem-card; the two deities at the right are listening to suggestions from one of their minions regarding, perhaps, further shower-attacks in the direction of the Yoshiwara, across the river to the west. The Mimeguri Shrine has long been associated with the poet Kikaku, who in 1693 composed a famous verse there, supplicating the gods to end the current drought – a request which was immediately granted. It is perhaps Kikaku's verse that the chief gods seem to be admiring in Kiyonaga's version. To this conceit has been added a fanciful rendition of the idea of "cherry-blossoms scattered by the storm" – with, as is customary in Japanese metaphor, young girls replacing the petals. A substantial essay could be written on the allusions involved in this one print. Each panel is signed "Kiyonaga ga." Condition good. (Although these prints come from two different sources, they have fortunately aged at about the same rate. The ground color, however, was originally more yellow in No. 153, more green in Nos. 154–55. The green of the shrubbery and red of the buildings are well matched. Some scuffing and small stains.) No. 153 from Cox; Crist; Ōiso sale, 1914; in Ōiso, No. 184. Nos. 154–55 from Chandler, Salomon, Rouart; in Salomon (No. 26), Rouart. Nishiki-e: 6 colors. Triptych: left, 38×25.7; center and right (joined), 38×49.9.

156. IWAI HANSHIRŌ IV WITH MANSERVANT. Mid-1780's. Rather than a scene from a play, this is simply a "candid" view of the actor walking along the street accompanied by a manservant. Such prints met a natural desire among Kabuki devotees for scenes from the private lives of their favorites. Hanshirō IV was noted as a master of female roles, and Kiyonaga's portrait records clearly the delicate grace that pervaded the actor's manner even offstage. Signature: Kiyonaga ga. Condition good (stains). From Grabhorn, Kobayashi. Nishiki-e: 5 colors, overprinting. 33.4×15.

157. MATSUMOTO KŌSHIRŌ IV WITH GEISHA. Mid-1780's. Like No. 156, this print supposedly represents a scene from the actor's daily life. Kōshirō is depicted in the snow under a willow tree, his hands kept warm inside his sleeves. Beside him stands an immaculate Edo geisha, her stylish femininity nicely balancing the actor's masculine stance. Kiyonaga produced a number of prints of this type and they rank among his most interesting work, forming, as they do, an arresting combination of the two staple subjects of ukiyo-e: girls and actors. Signature: Kiyonaga ga. Condition good. From Chandler, Haviland. In Hirano, Pl. 8. Nishiki-e: 4 colors. 33.2×15.3.

Utamaro

Kitagawa Utamaro (1753–1806), pupil of the minor painter Toriyama Sekien, owed his greatest artistic debt to Kiyonaga, to whose graceful, lifelike women he added a strong element of eroticism, flavored, moreover, with an intuitive grasp of the nature of female psychology. It is these elements that have made Utamaro best-known in the West of the dozens of skilled Japanese portrayers of womanhood: his girls and women speak directly to the viewer in personal terms of frankly sensual beauty; and, behind this surface attraction, in Utamaro's finest works we sense the mind of the "eternal female," seemingly oblivious to her own charms, yet all too well aware of their effect upon her male audience and of their profound influence upon her own life and her particular concept of happiness. Harunobu and Utamaro are the great masters of ukiyo-e in the portrayal of femininity and love – but what a difference in their ideals!

123. AGEMAKI AND SUKEROKU. Mid-1790's. The famed lovers Agemaki, courtesan of the Yoshiwara, and Sukeroku, the Japanese Robin Hood. Signature: Utamaro hitsu; Murataya seal. Condition poor (backed). From Chandler, Wright. Nishiki-e: 5 colors. 65.3×15.

158. GIRL WITH GLASS PIPE. Early 1790's. A girl in gaily patterned kimono blows a toy glass pipe. One of a series entitled *Ten Studies in Female Physiognomy,* of which the present print shows the only younger woman represented in the series. Though only six of the series are known, another group of five prints with slightly variant title exists; the print illustrated here is common to both series, however, so that the total number of subjects is ten. Signed "Physiognomist: Utamaro ga"; kiwame and Tsutaya seals. Condition fine. From Chandler, Gonse. In Gonse, No. 40. Nishiki-e: 6 colors, white mica. 38.7×25.7.

159. OKITA CARRYING TEACUP. Early 1790's. The famous beauty Okita, waitress in the Naniwaya teahouse at Asakusa, is seen carrying a cup of tea on its tray. Like Osen of a generation earlier (Nos. 126–27), the beauties Okita and Ohisa (Nos. 165–66) were the major attractions of their respective shops, and both girls appear frequently in prints by Utamaro and his contemporaries. The poem-card at the upper left is signed with the fanciful pen-name "Katsura Mayuzumi" and reads: "(While resting at the teahouse called Naniwaya.) Like the port of Naniwa, ceaseless the wayfarers, and none do not stop here." In other versions of the print the verse appears further to the left, or is omitted. Signature: Utamaro hitsu; kiwame, Tsutaya seals. Condition fine. From Chandler, 1910. Nishiki-e: 4 colors, overprinting, white mica. 38.2×25.

160. THE COURTESAN WAKAUME WITH MAIDSERVANT. Early 1790's. The Yoshiwara courtesan stands in ceremonial costume with her little maidservant half-hidden behind her. The cartouche gives the name and address of her house (the Tamaya, Edo-chō itchōme), the courtesan's name (which means "young plum-blossom"), and the names of her two attendants, Mumeno and Iroka. The poem-card at left is signed Hō Nankō and reads: "Bloom-

ing from amidst the linen-white snow, her name likewise fragrant, the young plum-blossom." For another version of this print, see V&I IV, 30, and *UT* VII, 33. Signature & seals: same as No. 159. Condition good. From Chandler, Doi. Nishiki-e: 4 colors, overprinting, white mica. 39.1×26.1.

161. A MAIDEN OF THE UPPER CLASSES. Early 1790's. At the right stands a maiden of the cultivated class, summer fan in hand; at the left an older woman is seated before a koto (zither), adjusting a plectrum on her finger. In the foreground are seen the plectrum-box and a small cage with a singing insect inside. Legend: "Customs of the Three Classes of Maidens: A Picture of the Cultivated Class." Signature: Utamaro hitsu; Wakasaya seal. Condition fine. From Chandler, Wright. Nishiki-e: 6 colors, overprinting. 38.4×25.5.

162. COURTESAN AFTER BATH. Mid-1790's. A Yoshiwara courtesan is seen refreshed after her morning bath, half-clothed in a bathrobe and drying her face with a towel. The little maidservant, also in dishabille, offers her mistress a cup of tea. The cartouche, designed in the shape of an old-style clock, reads: "Hour of the Serpent [9–11 A.M.]. The Twelve Hours of the Day in the Greenhouses: A Series." In old Japan the day was divided into twelve hours, and each of the two-hour intervals was identified with an animal of the zodiac. One of a series of twelve prints devoted to intimate Yoshiwara scenes. Signature & seals: same as No. 159. Condition fine (pasted down along the edges, minor holes, stains). From Chandler, Ford. Nishiki-e: 7 colors, gold dust. 36.4×24.2.

163. [UTAMARO II(?)] THE COURTESAN HANAŌGI. Ca. 1806–07. The famous Yoshiwara courtesan Hanaōgi (Kasen) is depicted with paper and writing-brush in hand, composing a letter to a lover. Note the kimono design, which reflects her name ("Blossom-fan"). The flowered cartouche gives the name and address of her house (Ōgiya, Edo-chō itchōme), her name, and that of her attendants, Yoshino and Tatsuta. The problem of distinguishing late Utamaro I from early Utamaro II is complicated by the fact that the pupil is thought to have assisted the master in several of his late works. I would, however, tentatively assign this to Utamaro II, *ca.* 1806–07. (For a very similar portrait of Hanaōgi by Utamaro I, but dating from a decade earlier, see Michener, *The Floating World,* Pl. 53.) Signature: Utamaro hitsu; seal of Enjudō. Condition fair. From Shōbisha. Nishiki-e: 3 colors. 36.8×24.1.

164. FESTIVAL TRIO. Early 1790's. In the front, two geisha masquerade as Buddhist priests for a Niwaka dance-performance in the Yoshiwara. The girl at left carries a display of the whisks employed in the tea ceremony; the girl at right holds a hollow gourd, which she taps with a stick. Behind the two geisha stands a high-ranking Yoshiwara courtesan. Legend: "Three Fair Beauties of the Greenhouses." Signature: Utamaro hitsu; seal of Tsuruya. Condition fine (folded, some fading). From Chandler, Ōshima, May. In May, No. 387. Nishiki-e: 4 colors, overprinting, gray mica. 38.8×26.

165–66. OHISA, FRONT AND BACK. Early 1790's. Ohisa, like Okita of No. 159, was one of the reigning beauties among Edo girls during the 1790's. She was the daughter of a prosperous cake merchant near Ryōgoku Bridge and was only about fourteen when, around 1791, she began to attract favorable attention at her father's shop. The present print, together with a similar one depicting Okita, is among the most unusual of Utamaro's works: it is printed front and back on one sheet of paper, with perfect registry even when viewed against a strong light. These prints must have been a great novelty to the connoisseurs of the time; the technical difficulties involved were doubtless what prevented widespread use of the ingenious form. Ohisa is depicted in summer kimono, apron at waist and fan in hand, with the legend "Takashima Ohisa." Signature: Utamaro ga; kiwame and publisher's seals. Condition good (some scuffing). From Chandler, 4/9/1911. Nishiki-e: 3 colors. Each 32.4×14.8.

Sharaku

Tōshūsai Sharaku (worked 1794–95). Sharaku's extant prints date almost entirely from a ten-month interval in 1794–95; but whatever his native genius, whatever the skilled guidance provided by his publisher, the great Tsutaya Jūzaburō, Sharaku's tremendous, evenly-balanced output cannot be explained as the sudden inspiration of an untrained amateur. Attempts to identify Sharaku with other contemporary masters (Maruyama Ōkyo, Kabukidō Enkyō, for example – and Chōki has occurred to me as an intriguing if equally wild hypothesis) have so far proved abortive, but I have a suspicion that somewhere in the vast mass of uncatalogued eighteenth-century paintings and prints the key will some day be found. One print, datable as 1799, has already come to light to confuse the issue, as have one or two dated fan-paintings, which would suggest either that Sharaku did occasional later work or that another of the men who employed that nom de plume also dabbled in art. Although Sharaku's genius is universally recognized today, in his own time the new element of sharp realism and psychological caricature was hardly appreciated by the Edo populace, which doubtless accounts for his short career. Sharaku's earliest prints were among his greatest and most original – the large actor portraits such as are shown in Nos. 167–70. Here we see an individuality of expression and a psychological probing of a depth hitherto unknown in ukiyo-e – though Utamaro's intuitive perception of female vanity in the years just preceding this may well have been Sharaku's immediate spur to creation. In dynamic group composition Sharaku also excelled, as in No. 172; in his panels of single, standing figures, however, such as No. 171, he reveals his basic debt to the school of Shunshō and fails to find the opportunity to wield his incisive brush either in creative character portrayal or sinuous theatrical composition. To point out the limitations of Sharaku's genius at least serves to make more believable the riddle of his existence.

167. TANIMURA TORAZŌ. 1794. Against a striking background of dark-mica pigment we see the Kabuki actor portraying a tense moment as Washizuka Yaheiji, secondary villain of *Koi-nyōbō somewake tazuna,* performed V/1794, Kawarazaki-za. Torazō, who had migrated from the Kyoto-Osaka theater world to Edo, was never noted as a great actor, and even this fact has been captured in Sharaku's masterly portrait, which reveals a supporting player exerting his utmost in a villainous role, bereft of that reserve of strength and character that makes a really superb actor. Signature: Tōshūsai Sharaku ga; kiwame and Tsutaya

seals. Condition good (top of head retouched). From Chandler, Straus-Negbaur. Nishiki-e: 4 colors, gray mica. 37.8×25.

168. ICHIKAWA EBIZŌ. 1794. The great Ebizō (Danjūrō V) in the role of Takemura Sadanoshin from the same drama as No. 167. Some confusion surrounds the identity of this role, but it seems most likely to represent Sadanoshin, Noh player and father of the heroine of the drama. It is the evil deeds of Yaheiji (cf. No. 167) and his villainous brother which force Sadanoshin to harakiri during the course of the play. (The controversy over whether the actor is Ebizō III or IV would seem to be based on a confusion in the ideographs for the name. Danjūrō V would have been Ebizō IV except that he changed the "spelling" of his name while retaining the same pronunciation. Thus we should have to employ some such odd designation as "II Ebizō I" in the absence of Japanese characters.) Signature & seals: same as No. 167. Condition good (center folds, rubbing, backed). From Chandler, Bing. Nishiki-e: 3 colors, gray mica. 36.8×24.4.

169. ARASHI RYŪZŌ. 1794. The actor is seen as the money-lender Ishibe Kinkichi in *Hanaayame Bunroku Soga,* performed V/1794, Miyako-za. Signature & seals: same as No. 167. Condition good (rubbed; patched hole on right shoulder). From Chandler, Straus-Negbaur, Wakai. In Frankfurt, No. 212; Kurth, *Sharaku,* p. 170; Straus-Negbaur, Pl. 32; *UT* VIII, 39 (rephotographed after Straus-Negbaur); *Kunstwanderer,* p. 469. Nishiki-e: 4 colors, gray mica. 37.7×25.

170. SAWAMURA SŌJŪRŌ III. 1794. The actor appears in the role of the samurai Ōgishi Kurando from the same drama as No. 169. Signature & seals: same as No. 167. Condition good (holes; stains and fading at bottom). From Chandler, Gonse. In Gonse, Pl. 4. Nishiki-e: 3 colors, gray mica. 38.8×25.7.

171. ICHIKAWA DANJŪRŌ VI. 1794. The actor is seen as the young samurai Fuwa Bansaku, son of the villain in *Keisei sambon karakasa,* performed VII/1794, Miyako-za. The print probably represents the left panel in a set of three devoted to leading actors in the drama. Signature & seals: same as No. 167. Condition good (some stains, slightly trimmed at bottom). From Ōya shobō, Danjūrō family (?). Nishiki-e: 4 colors. 31.7×14.9.

172. ONIJI AND OMEZŌ. 1794. Ōtani Oniji II as Ukiyo Tohei and Ichikawa Omezō as the sumō wrestler Ikazuchi Tsurunosuke in *Nihommatsu Michinoku-sodachi,* performed VII/1794, Kawarazaki-za. Since the same actors appeared in more than one role during the course of the play there is still some controversy regarding the exact roles portrayed, but the above surmise seems most probable. This print is one of the most dynamically executed of all Sharaku's group compositions. Signature & seals: same as No. 167. Condition good (holes, some filled and retouched; some stains, rubbing; backed along top and bottom). From Chandler, 6/15/1934. Nishiki-e: 5 colors, overprinting, white mica. 38.8×25.8.

Chōki

Eishōsai Chōki (worked 1760's to early 1800's). Chōki's art is in some respects as baffling as Sharaku's: amidst a quantity of ordinary prints and book illustrations we discover a small number of color prints that rank with the finest ever produced by any ukiyo-e master. Chōki studied together with Utamaro in Sekien's studio, and his work reflects the influence of both artists, as well as something of the Sharaku manner. His idealized girl is more reminiscent of Harunobu than of Utamaro and, with his unique technique of close-up compositions, was his greatest contribution to ukiyo-e. Though Chōki has never achieved the popular renown accorded to some of his contemporaries, a study of Nos. 174–75 makes one wonder if he did not surpass them all in the evocation of poetic atmosphere.

124. CHŪSHINGURA PARODY. Mid-1790's. A parody on the drama of the Forty-seven Rōnin, similar to that noted in No. 121 above. This time the scene is more definitely of the gay quarter, showing courtesan and lover, with the courtesan's little maidservant peeking from beneath the porch. (Note the realistic depiction of the lantern's rays, a concept derived, most probably, from Western art.) Signature: Chōki ga. Condition good (small holes, backed). From Chandler, 3/17/1906. Nishiki-e: 4 colors. 58×11.

173. THE COURTESAN TSUKASA-DAYŪ. Mid-1790's. The Osaka courtesan is shown glancing back over her shoulder, sleeve raised to chin. The legend gives the location and name of her house (Ōsaka Shimmachi, Higashi Ōgiya) and the girl's name. Signature: Chōki ga; seal of Tsutaya. Condition good (folded, slightly soiled). From Chandler, 1928. Nishiki-e: 4 colors, white mica. 38.8×26.3.

174. GIRL IN SNOW. Mid-1790's. A girl in her late teens stands holding a snow-laden umbrella as her manservant bends to clean off her sandal. Note Chōki's skillful employment of the auxiliary figure, at once noticed yet not obtrusive. His achievement in the invention of this type of close-up with secondary figure is only surpassed by his wonderful girl. This print was at one time surmised to represent a portrait of the Genroku poetess Shūshiki, but such appears unlikely; rather is the scene reminiscent of a Chikamatsu puppet-play. The snowflakes seem to have been hand-sifted or stenciled, and thus vary with each copy of this rare print. Signature: Chōki ga; kiwame and Tsutaya seals. Condition good (garment of man possibly re-vamped). From Chandler, Straus-Negbaur. In Frankfurt, No. 190; Kurth, *Masterpieces*, No. 24; *Kunstwanderer*, p. 469; Straus-Negbaur, No. 301; *UT* VII, 452 (rephotographed after Straus-Negbaur). Nishiki-e: 6 colors, gray mica. 38.2×24.4.

175. FIREFLY-CATCHING. Mid-1790's. A woman and a little boy are seen amusing themselves at firefly-catching on a summer evening beside a stream with irises. The boy prepares to grasp at a firefly with fan in hand, and the woman holds a little cage in which to take the insects home. (Firefly-catching is still a favorite summer diversion in rural Japan; city-dwellers can also buy the insects at a penny apiece to scatter in their tiny gardens at dusk.) Signature & seals: same as No. 173. Condition good (inconspicuous holes, stains, backed, woman's neck discolored). From

Chandler, Gonse. In Gonse, No. 55. Nishiki-e: 3 colors, dark-gray mica. 25.7×38.3.

Shunchō

Katsukawa Shunchō (worked late 1770's to late 1790's), though a pupil of Shunshō's and much indebted to that master for his perfect color harmonies, found his ideal in the work of Kiyonaga at its peak and seldom deviated from that style. We are accustomed to judging artists according to their originality, and by this token Shunchō must be relegated to second rank; his actual prints, however, are often quite the equal of Kiyonaga's: they lack the latter's magnificence of concept, but have a peculiar ethereal quality seldom found in Kiyonaga, and a luminous harmony of coloring that is unsurpassed in ukiyo-e.

176. PICNIC PROCESSION. Early 1780's. A wealthy family's cherry-blossom viewing picnic: to the left, in black, the daughter of the family, accompanied by her retinue of servants. The young girls in the center carry utensils for smoking, and a dog, while the manservant at right carries the picnic lunch. A boy, possibly the younger brother, follows. (Cf. Moronobu's version of a similar scene in No. 12.) The influence of Kiyonaga is seen very strongly in this print. Legend: "Stylish Spring Brocade." Signature: Shunchō ga. Condition good (scuffing and some fading, backed). From Kegan Paul. Nishiki-e: 4 colors. 26×39.

177–78. WOMEN BY SUMMER STREAM. Mid-1780's. Six women and a little boy are seen taking their ease variously beside a summer stream. At the left is a footbridge; yellow water-lilies bloom forth from the water, and a willow tree trails its branches overhead. The girl at left is plucking parsley. This design may possibly have been a part of a triptych, but no suitable right panel has yet been found. Each panel is signed: Shunchō ga; seal of Eiyūdō. Condition good. From Koscherak, Ledoux, Gonse. In Gonse, Pl. 1; Ledoux, III, Pl. 25. Nishiki-e: 5 colors in many shades, overprinting. Diptych: left, 38.2×25.9; right, 38.2×26.

179. [Shunchō and Shun'ei.] STREET SCENE. Late 1780's. Two groups pass, regarding each other: at the left a lady and her servant, at the right two firemen. (The two men wear jackets bearing the crests of Onoe Kikugorō and Arashi Ryūzō; such were often presented by actors to the fire brigade.) The scene is probably the Year-end Sale at Asakusa; the head fireman carries the rope decoration used at New Year's. The two women have the signature "Shunchō ga"; the two men, "Shun'ei ga." Such collaboration between two ukiyo-e artists on one print had been seen occasionally before (e.g., Harunobu and Bunchō), but Shunchō and Shun'ei were among the first to employ it with any regularity. Condition good (hole bottom center crudely patched, some scuffing, trimmed, backed). From Chandler, 8/30/1909. Nishiki-e: 5 colors, repeated overprinting. 31.7×22.

180–81 RIVERSIDE SCENE. Late 1780's. The scene is probably Yanagishima, at the eastern edge of Ryōgoku Bridge. At the left a man and his boy servant start across the bridge, glancing at a pair of women, possibly geisha, who have just come from the bath. The man carries a shrine token stuck in his hair – possibly that of the Kameido Shrine, or of Myōken, god of disaster, which was not supposed to be touched by hand. The boy carries some cakes or other souvenir on his back; a kite is flying in the sky and boats ply the river. In the right panel a maiden of quality is seen approaching the bridge, accompanied by two older women. Each panel is signed: Shunchō ga; sealed Chūrin. Publisher's seal: Sen-ichi han. Condition: 180, good; 181, fine. From: 180, Koscherak, Ficke; 181, Mayuyama. Nishiki-e: 6 colors. Diptych: each 39.5×25.5.

Eishi

Chōbunsai Eishi (1756–1829), scion of a high samurai family, had been fully trained in the studio of the official painter Kanō Eisen-in before he turned to the popular ukiyo-e style. It was in the early 1780's that Eishi resigned his official duties for the work he loved; he designed first in the style of Shigemasa but soon took (as did most of his contemporaries) Kiyonaga, and later Utamaro, as his model in the portrayal of beautiful women. It is no accident that Eishi's art ranks as the most aristocratc in ukiyo-e: his was not a strikingly original genius, but neither did he have to cater to the whims of popular taste. His women, whether of the nobility or the demimonde, inhabit a special world untouched by mundane thoughts and passions. During the latter half of his career, with the general decline in print quality, Eishi devoted himself to ukiyo-e paintings, a field in which he reigns supreme for this period.

182. THE DOLL FESTIVAL. Mid-1790's. A young woman sits holding in her hand a doll representing a ceremonially-dressed boy beating a Noh drum. At the lower right is the doll's box and a flower arrangement of peach blossoms, the symbol of this festival of the Third Month. One of a series of five prints, each of which bears the title *The Five Festivals in Modern Style.* Signature: Eishi zu; kiwame and Eijudō seals. Condition fine (trimmed, slight fading). From Chandler, Hayashi. Nishiki-e: 4 colors. 35.8×23.3.

183–84. COURTESAN PREPARING FOR BED (two versions). Late 1790's. The Yoshiwara courtesan Misayama is shown about to retire for the evening; she is removing her perfumed amulet from about her neck. On the floor is a black lacquer box. No. 183, with dark background, probably represents the first impression of this print, while No. 184, with light background, was probably printed later, from different blocks. The different impressions are discussed in detail by Ledoux, who, however, did not realize that the present dark background of his print was the result of extensive hand-retouching, and that the cartouche was probably reprinted later, the original presumably having been defaced when the mica-ground flaked off. Legend: "Selected Beauties of the Greenhouses: Picture of Night-attire: Misayama of the Chōjiya." Signature: Eishi giga; Iwatoya seal. *No. 183:* Condition fair. From Koscherak, Ledoux. In Ledoux, IV, No. 43. Nishiki-e: 4 colors, dark mica (retouched). 37.7×25. *No. 184:* Condition good (slight stains). From Shōbisha; Mihara; Hakone, 1919; Bullier; Hayashi. In Hayashi, No. 695; Mihara, No. 42; Hakone, 1919, No. 87. Nishiki-e: 4 colors, white mica. 38×24.4.

Eishō

Chōkōsai Eishō (worked 1790's). Most impressive of Eishi's pupils, Eishō worked in several forms, but it was only in his large heads of girls that he achieved results both original and on a level with the art of his

master. *Eishō's girls lack the aristocratic refinement of Eishi's, but they are often more human, more lifelike, and we may surmise that the sweetly childish, slightly silly look on the faces of his courtesans mirrors, perhaps unconsciously, one strong element of personality to be found in the Edo gay quarter.*

185. THE COURTESAN SHINOWARA. Mid-1790's. The courtesan is shown adjusting a hair ornament while she reads a love letter. Legend: "Beauties of the Licensed Quarter: Shinowara of the Tsuruya." Signature: Eishō ga. Condition fair (holes, scuffing). From Chandler, Straus-Negbaur. In Frankfurt, No. 146; Straus-Negbaur, No. 290; *UT* VII, 570 (rephotographed after Straus-Negbaur). Nishiki-e: 4 colors, gray mica. 37.3×25.4.

186. THE COURTESAN SOMEYAMA. Mid-1790's. The courtesan is shown removing her perfumed amulet (cf. Nos. 183–84), about to retire for the evening. Legend: "Beauties of the Licensed Quarter: Someyama of the Matsubaya." Signature: Chōkōsai Eishō ga. Condition good (trimmed, stains). From Cox; Cutter; Hakone, 1917. In Hakone, 1917, No. 98. Nishiki-e: 5 colors, gray-white mica. 37.1×24.9.

Shūchō

Tamagawa Shūchō (worked 1790's to early 1800's) is one of several minor artists of the Kansei period who followed in the wake of the great Utamaro. It might even be suggested that the lack of signature on this type of print was a device of the publisher to capitalize on Utamaro's tremendous success, the idea being that an unsigned "Utamaro" was more saleable than a signed Shūchō. Although Shūchō was no great artist, he had a readily recognizable style of his own, rather between those of Utamaro and Chōki, but lacking the erotic vitality of the one, the refinement of the other.

187. GIRL WITH WHITE MOUSE. Late 1790's. An informally attired girl, possibly a geisha, is seen playing with a white mouse. The Year of the Rat suggests itself as date of composition, but since this fell in 1792 and 1804 a connection seems unlikely. Unsigned; seal of Ezakiya. Condition good (some stains, scuffing). From Chandler, Field. Nishiki-e: 4 colors. 36.4×25.5.

Hokusai

Katsushika Hokusai (1760–1849). Hokusai's long life embraces much of ukiyo-e history from the late 1770's to the late 1840's: he began as a pupil of Shunshō (employing the nom de plume Shunrō) and did notable prints of actors and wrestlers in the Katsukawa style and girls in the Kiyonaga manner. With the 1790's he developed a remarkable, delicate style of figure drawing that graces his fine surimono (prints employed for greetings, announcements, and the like), book illustrations, and rare prints of the period. By 1810 Hokusai's figure drawing had developed a certain hardness that detracts from its beauty, but his skill as a draftsman, nature-painter, and landscapist had increased to the extent that he was certainly the greatest artist of the time in these fields. Hokusai was already nearly sixty when he produced his great Thirty-six Views of Fuji, but he continued to develop his range and power to the end, some critics considering his series The Poetry of China and Japan the culmination of his style. Hokusai's greatest quality was his passionate interest in all things living, and this included the mountains and trees as well as the variegated people of his native land. His Manga sketchbooks are the fascinating record of his intense curiosity, but practically any of his later prints will reveal the same trait, strengthened and distilled by the discipline of art. In whatever he did, Hokusai's work is so full of humanity as almost to obscure the true quality of his artistic genius.

6. THE POET ABE NO NAKAMARO LONGING FOR HOME (key-block proof). Early 1830's. The poet is seen on the balcony of a Chinese pavilion, declining the food presented him as he gazes out over the moonlit sea. This print doubtless illustrates Nakamaro's famous poem composed in far-off China, where he had been sent from Nara to study: "I gaze up at the Fields of Heaven and wonder: is this the same moon that rose over distant Mount Mikasa at my home in Kasuga?" Key-block proof of one of a series of ten prints entitled *Shiika shashin-kyō,* "The Poetry of China and Japan: A Living Mirror" (usually rendered as "The Imagery of the Poets of China and Japan"). The finished print appears in color in Boller, *Hokusai,* Pl. 24, with significant variations in coloring from the Honolulu finished print. For others in the series, see Nos. 195–96 below. Signature: Zen Hokusai Iitsu hitsu. Publisher: Moriya; kiwame seal. Condition fine. From Chandler. 63.7×27.2.

188. BULLFINCH AND DROOPING-CHERRY. Late 1820's. The inscription gives the names of the bird and flower, and then the following poem by Raiman: "A single bird comes out drenched by the dew: the morning cherry-blooms." Such verses often imply some reference to the human world, in this case, probably, to the picture of a young man returning at dawn from a night of love in the Yoshiwara. One of a series of ten or more medium-size prints featuring birds and flowers and showing strong influence from Chinese painting styles. Signature: Zen Hokusai Iitsu hitsu; kiwame and Eijudō seals. Condition fine. From Chandler. Nishiki-e: 4 colors. 25×18.2.

189. FUJI FROM KAJIKAZAWA. Late 1820's. From a projecting rock the fisherman handles his lines as his boy assistant sits behind him and Mt. Fuji looms in the distance. The scene is at Kajikazawa, on the Fuji River in the province of Kai. Although the fisherman is usually assumed to be handling the lines of a net, he may possibly be employing four cormorants, which are out of sight in their quest for fish. From the series *Thirty-six Views of Fuji.* Signature: same as No. 188. Condition fine (slight marginal stains, some scuffing). From Chandler, Ford, Freer. Nishiki-e or aizuri-e: 1 color, blue, printed in 13 different shades from 9 separate blocks; gradation (cf. No. 218). 25.9×38.8.

190. FUJI FROM HODOGAYA. Late 1820's. A scene on the Tōkaidō highway; left, a palanquin-borne traveler; to the right, a pack-horse driver with passenger, and a mendicant *komusō* priest. Fuji is seen through a row of pine trees that line the road. Signature: same as No. 188. Part of Eijudō seal on saddle blanket. Condition fine (center fold, slight paper defects.) From Chandler, Blanchard. In Blanchard, No. 191. Nishiki-e: 4 colors, gradation. 25.5×37.4.

191. RYŪKYŪ SEASCAPE. Early 1830's. Two islets connected to the mainland by a dragon-shaped causeway and a stone bridge; a boat and small figures. One of a series of *Eight Views of the Ryūkyūs,* the print is subtitled "The Lake's Voice at Rinkai." The quite different mood of this series from Hokusai's other works of this period is probably due to the fact that he was painting from his imagination rather than from direct observation. Signature: same as No. 189;

seal of Moriya. Condition fine. From Chandler, 11/25/1927. Nishiki-e: 4 colors plus brownish-red in cartouche, gradation. 25.2×37.8.

192. THE BRIDGE OF BOATS AT SANO. Early 1830's. Travelers crossing the swiftly-flowing Toné River, the current of which has forced the bridge of boats into an arc. In the foreground are the bridge-warden's cottage and a bare pine; snow covers all. One of eleven prints in the *Famous Bridges* series. Legend: "Rare Views of Famous Bridges in All the Provinces: Old Picture of the Bridge of Boats at Sano in Kōzuke Province." The final word in the cartouche, *kozu* ("old picture"), has generally been misread or omitted in descriptions of this print; it is significant, however, for it means that Hokusai had never seen the bridge in question, for, though famous from ancient poetry, it had long since ceased to exist. Signature & seals: same as No. 188. Condition fine. From Chandler, Walpole. Nishiki-e: 4 colors, gradation. 24.8×37.8.

193. BUTTERFLY AND TREE-PEONY. Early 1830's. One of a series of some eleven large-size prints of the "bird-and-flower" type, more graceful, but less personalized than the smaller series represented in No. 188. Signature & seals: same as No. 188. Condition good (center fold, marginal holes and stains). From Chandler, Haviland. Nishiki-e: 4 colors. 25.3×37.

194. WINTER LANDSCAPE BY THE SUMIDA RIVER. Late 1820's. A snow-covered view at Mukōjima, looking northeast along the Sumida River from an elevation. At the lower right is a small shrine, probably the Umewaka Shrine dedicated to a little boy who was kidnapped and died there in ancient times. The artist would have been standing near the Mokubo-ji, a Buddhist temple erected in the boy's memory. The water in the foreground with boat is an inlet of the river. One of the series *Snow-Moon-Blossoms,* featuring the Yodo River (moonlight), Mt. Yoshino (cherry blossoms), and the present Sumida River (snow). Signature: same as No. 188. (Some impressions of the Yodo River print bear the same seals as No. 188 also.) Condition good (fold at right margin, smoothed out holes at left margin). From Chandler, 5/8/1918. Nishiki-e: 5 colors, gradation. 25.2×38.6.

195. THE POET LI PO ADMIRING A WATERFALL. Early 1830's. The aged T'ang poet is shown leaning on his staff, supported by two frightened boys, as he gazes in admiration at the cataract, probably that of Lo-shan in Kiang-si Province. Li Po's poetic eulogy on the scene includes the famous lines: "Let me be with the things I love, leaving the world of man forever." For an alternate version of this print see Ledoux, V, No. 10. From the same series as No. 6, data identical. Condition fine (slight marginal stains, backed). From Chandler. Nishiki-e: 6 colors in many shades, overprinting, gradation. 51.8×23.2.

196. TRAVELER IN THE SNOW. Early 1830's. A Chinese horseman, followed by his servant, halts his horse on a rocky crag and surveys the snow-clad landscape. In the distance are rustic houses by two old pines; sea gulls float in the chilly water. The name of the poet is omitted in this print and he has been identified variously with the T'ang poets Meng Hao-jan or Tu Fu, or the Sung poet Su Tung-p'o; all three writers have verses suitable to the scene but it is difficult to settle upon one or the other without knowing the immediate source of Hokusai's inspiration. From the same series as No. 6. Condition good (some discoloration). From Chandler. Nishiki-e: 6 colors, gradation. 51.5×22.9.

Hokuju

Shōtei Hokuju (worked late 1790's to mid-1820's). Of Hokusai's pupils Hokuju made the largest contribution as an original landscapist; his cubist landforms, highly stylized clouds, and near-photographic figures and dwellings provide a curiously modern concept of the world. This is not entirely coincidence, for Hokuju was influenced by what little he knew of European art; yet the result must be considered one of the most notable of original Japanese variations upon what were only dimly apprehended concepts of Western forms.

197. MONKEY BRIDGE. Early 1820's. A stylized, draftsman-like view from space of Monkey Bridge, made famous in the West by Hiroshige's print. Legend: "A Newly Sketched Picture of Monkey Bridge in the Province of Kai." Signature: Shōtei Hokuju ga; kiwame and Eikyūdō seals. Condition fine. From Tikotin, Schraubstadter. Nishiki-e: 4 colors, overprinting, gradation. 26×37.9.

Gakutei

Yashima Gakutei (worked mid-1810's to 1830's), who often employed the nom de plume Gogaku, studied ukiyo-e under Hokkei and left a number of skilled surimono and book illustrations, among which his impressionistic landscape scenes are notable. Though a native of Edo, Gakutei lived in Osaka during the early 1830's and the album-plate shown is one of several souvenirs of that sojourn.

198. SQUALL AT TEMPOZAN. 1834. A sailing junk caught in a sudden rainstorm near Tempozan, Osaka; a rough sea, with black clouds overhead. One of a series of six illustrations from Gakutei's album entitled *Famous Views of Tempozan*, published at Osaka in 1834. Legend: "Osaka Tempozan, View of a Squall." Signature: Gogaku; sealed Go. Condition fair (discolored, center fold). From Chandler. Nishiki-e: 4 colors. 25.1×38.

Hokkei

Totoya Hokkei (1780–1850). Best known of Hokusai's pupils, Hokkei had first studied traditional painting under Kanō Yōsen'in. He excelled in elaborately executed surimono and landscape panoramas, such as those illustrated here, which convey well the Hokusai technique and add a vaguely formal yet other-worldly atmosphere seldom found in that earthy master.

199. FOREIGN WARSHIP SALUTING. 1830's. Cannon-smoke blankets a three-masted European warship as she salutes, passing Mt. Inasa near the entrance to Nagasaki harbor. One of a series of some fifteen oblong prints (eight in this collection) entitled *Famous Views in the Various Provinces*; the present print is subtitled "Inasa-yama in Hizen." Signature: Kikō [Aoi-ga-oka] Hokkei ga; kiwame, Shō, and Eijudō seals. Condition fine (slight discoloration). From Chandler, Appleton. Nishiki-e: 5 colors. 17.8×38.4.

200. FERRYBOAT IN RAIN. 1830's. A loaded ferryboat crosses the Sumida River as its passengers try to shelter themselves from the sudden downpour of rain. In the foreground are seen the gulls famous at this spot since ancient times. One of the passengers has dropped his fan into the river. From the same series as No. 199, same signature. Subtitle: "Sumida River in Musashi." Condition fine. From Chandler, Hayashi. Nishiki-e: 5 colors. 17.7×37.1.

201. TRAVELERS AT FUDŌ PASS. 1830's. Three travelers are walking a mountain path, two traders and, in front, a hunter with his gun and dog. The sun is shining between the cliffs and, to the right, two other travelers pause to refresh themselves at a small cataract, above which is seen a personification of the Buddhist deity Fudō, guardian of the pass. From the same series as No. 199, same signature and seals. Subtitle: "Fudō Pass, Mikuni-goe in Jōshū." Condition good. From Grabhorn. Nishiki-e: 5 colors. 17.5×38.2.

202. SUMIYOSHI SHRINE. 1830's. Osaka Bay, seen from the Sumiyoshi Shrine; a drum-bridge and seaside village to the left. From the same series as No. 199, same signature. Subtitle: "Sumiyoshi in Sesshū." Condition fine (backed). From Chandler. Nishiki-e: 5 colors. 18×39.3.

203. NIGHT FESTIVAL AT THE SEASHORE. 1830's. Two Shintō priests are seen dashing for the shore as waves pursue them. It was the yearly ritual at the Sumiyoshi Shrine in Nagato for the priest, late at night on New Year's Eve, to run down with torch to the sea, which parted for an instant while he cut one blade of sea-grass for presentation to the shrine. In this print one priest carries the torch while the other holds a small sickle and his sacred prize. From the same series as No. 199, same signature and seals. Subtitle: "Sacred Rites of Sea-grass Gathering in Nagato." Condition good. From Chandler, Jacquin. In Jacquin, No. 203. Nishiki-e: 4 colors. 17.5×38.

204. WATERFALL AT NIKKŌ. 1830's. The famous "Back-seeing Falls" at Nikkō; travelers stand on a narrow platform beneath the fall and try to see out through the rushing water. From the same series as No. 199, same signature and seals. Subtitle: "Back-seeing Falls at Nikkō in Shimotsuke." Condition fair. From Chandler. Nishiki-e: 5 colors. 17.3×38.3.

Toyokuni

Utagawa Toyokuni (1769–1825). Of the leading ukiyo-e designers Toyokuni was the least original, but succeeded so well in emulating the finer points of his more creative contemporaries that in his best work he is universally accorded a place nearly equal to theirs. Toyokuni's direct teacher was Toyoharu, but he studied successively the styles of Kiyonaga, Shumman, Chōki, Eishi, and Utamaro in the field of girl-prints and Shunshō, Shun'ei, and Sharaku for actor prints. His greatest consecutive effort was the famous series Views of Actors in Role, of which at least forty prints were produced in 1795–96, doubtless under the stimulus of Sharaku's great work of the preceding months but, nevertheless, individual masterpieces seldom surpassed in ukiyo-e. Indeed, though we speak of Toyokuni's predominately imitative talent, we must always add that his work, in whatever style, would never be mistaken for another master's, and often manages to equal or surpass the original model.

205. SAWAMURA SŌJŪRŌ. 1796. Sōjūrō III draws his sword in the role of Ume no Yoshibei, from *Sumida no haru geisha katagi*, performed I/1796, Kiri-za. Signature: Toyokuni ga; Sen-ichi seal. Condition fine. From Chandler, Wright, Bullier. In V&I, VI, 28. Nishiki-e: 6 colors, gradation. 38.6×25.6.

206. MATSUMOTO KŌSHIRŌ. 1795. Kōshirō IV in the dress of a *komusō* as Kakogawa Honzō in that most famous of Japanese dramas, *Kana-tehon chūshingura*, performed V/1795, Kawarazaki-za. (Cf. No. 139 for a rival performance in the same month.) Legend: "Views of Actors in Role: Kōraiya." Signature & seals: same as No. 205. Condition fine (slight scuffing). From Mayuyama. Nishiki-e: 5 colors. 37.7×24.7.

207. ICHIKAWA KOMAZŌ. 1796. Komazō II as the samurai Chōgoku Takumi, from *Hikosan gongen chikai no sukedachi*, performed IX/1796, Kawarazaki-za. Legend: same as No. 206. Signature: Toyokuni ga; kiwame and Sen-ichi seals. Condition fine. From Chandler, 10/18/1920. Nishiki-e: 4 colors, white mica. 36.9×23.9.

208. NAKAMURA NOSHIO. 1796. Noshio II in the role of the courtesan Umegawa, from *Ninokuchi-mura iro no dekiai*, performed IX/1796, Miyako-za. Legend: "Views of Actors in Role: Yamatoya." (For an alternate version lacking cartouche and lantern, see V&I, VI, 34 and *UT* X, 116.) Signature & seals: same as No. 207. Condition good. From Chandler, B. Matsuki. In B. Matsuki, No. 313. Nishiki-e: 6 colors, overprinting, gradation. 37.3×24.7.

209. IWAI HANSHIRŌ. 1795. Hanshirō IV as Sakurai, younger sister of the patriot general Kusunoki Masashige, from *Matsu no misao onna Kusunoki*, performed XI/1795, Kawarazaki-za. (For a slightly alternate version see Hillier, frontispiece, and Ledoux, IV, 52. For Sharaku's version of the same scene see Henderson and Ledoux, No. 78; there is some controversy as to which artist was the imitator.) Legend: same as No. 208. Signature & seals: same as No. 207, with the notation "No. 2" beneath the publisher's seal. Condition good. From Chandler, Metzgar. Nishiki-e: 5 colors, gradation. 37×24.4.

210. ICHIKAWA YAOZŌ. 1796. Yaozō III as Soga Gorō, from *Furiwakegami aoyagi Soga*, performed I/1796, Miyako-za. The actor wears a kimono with butterfly design and holds in his hand the trap used for luring fox-spirits (cf. No. 27). Legend: "Views of Actors in Role: Tachibanaya." Signature & seals: same as No. 207. Condition good. From Chandler, 1920. Nishiki-e: 4 colors. 37.9×25.8.

211. ONOE SHŌSUKE. 1795. Shōsuke as Ōboshi Yuranosuke, leader of the Forty-seven Rōnin, from the same drama as No. 206. Legend: "Views of Actors in Role: Otowaya." Signatures & seals: same as No. 207. Condition fine (slight holes). From Kegan Paul, Hillier. Nishiki-e: 4 colors, gray mica. 37.8×25.1.

Kunimasa

Utagawa Kunimasa (1773–1810) was Toyokuni's earliest pupil, and one of his greatest. He excelled in actor portraits which strove to com- *bine the intensity of Sharaku with the decorative grace of his master Toyokuni. He succeeded in the latter attempt but not the former, and thus it has been his inevitable fate to be treated as a "minor Sharaku." To those who find the biting genius of Sharaku disquieting, Kunimasa may appeal; certainly he gives a more valid portrayal of the actual pageantry of a Kabuki performance, where Sharaku's genius depicts not only an artistic goal seldom achieved by even the greatest performers, but also the human failings of the human actor behind the role.*

212. ICHIKAWA EBIZŌ. 1796. Ebizō as Usui Aratarō (Shibaraku), from *Seiwa nidai ōyose Genji*, performed XI/1796, Miyako-za. The actor is the same "II Ebizō I" discussed at No. 168. Signature: Kunimasa ga; kiwame and Yama-zen seals. Condition good. From Brussel. Nishiki-e: 5 colors. 36.3×24.4.

213. NAKAMURA NOSHIO. 1797. Noshio as the courtesan Shōshō, sweetheart of Gorō (cf. No. 17), from *Hatsukasumi kuruwa no sugomori*, a part of the larger drama *Edo no haru kichirei Soga*, performed I/1797, Miyako-za. Shōshō carries a box on her shoulder like that in No. 12. Signature: Kunimasa ga; kiwame and Ue-yo seals. Condition good. From Chandler. Nishiki-e: 6 colors, gaufrage. 37.3×24.9.

214. ICHIKAWA DANJŪRŌ. 1799. Danjūrō VI as Jirokichi, from *Ōmiura Date no nebiki*, performed I/1799, Nakamura-za. Signature: Kunimasa ga; kiwame and Uemura seals. Condition fine. From Chandler, 12/27/1927. In *UT* X, 203. Nishiki-e: 5 colors. 37×25.4.

Kuniyoshi

Utagawa Kuniyoshi (1798–1861), Toyokuni's second great pupil, was hardly mentioned by the older critics, but is now generally recognized as the outstanding figure designer of the latter days of ukiyo-e, a skilled landscapist, and an interesting experimenter in the harmonious fusion of native and Western styles.

215. KUO CHÜ FINDS THE POT OF GOLD. Mid-1840's. Kuo Chü and his wife are startled at the discovery of a pot of gold; their naked son plays beside them. From the series *The Twenty-four Paragons of Filial Piety: A Mirror for Children*. Legend: "Kuo Chü [Kakkyo] was too poor to take as good care of his mother as he would have liked to. Sometimes he would find good things for her to eat, but the old mother dearly loved her grandson, and would always share the food with the child. The husband and wife were grieved at this and concluded that, in the end, the child was too much of an obstacle to their taking proper care of the mother. They began to dig a hole in the ground, determined thus to dispose of their child; but they dug up, instead, a pot filled with gold. From this time on, their house prospered, and they were able to take care of their aged parent just as they had wished." (Cf. No. 46.) Signature: Ichiyūsai Kuniyoshi ga. Publisher: Shiba Shimmei-mae, Wakasaya. Condition good. From Chandler, Jacquin. Nishiki-e: 6 colors. 21.5×35.

216. TILE-KILNS AT IMADO. Early 1830's. The tile-makers of Imado, in Asakusa beside the Sumida River, tend their smoking kilns; a lone tree breaks the composition and in the dim distance is seen Mt. Tsukuba. Legend: "Famous Sights of the Eastern Capital: Imado in Asakusa." Signature: same as No. 215. Publisher: Ryōgoku, Kagaya. Condition fair (slightly trimmed, small stain in sky). From Chandler, acquired from "S.S.," 4/27/1920. Nishiki-e: 5 colors, gradation. 25×35.

Kunisada

Utagawa Kunisada (1786–1865) was Toyokuni's third notable pupil, and one of the leading artists of his day. The general decline of grace and quality in 19th-century figure work is epitomized in Kunisada's prints, but occasionally in his surimono and his prints of girls or actors he achieves distinction, and in his rare landscapes is to be found some of the most striking work of the period.

217. LANDSCAPE IN MIST. 1830's. Unlike most ukiyo-e landscapes, where the geographical location is exactly recorded (even though the painter may never have been there), here the label is simply "Landscape in Mist"; the scene, however, is doubtless the famous Edo ravine of Ochanomizu, though Mt. Fuji is slightly out of its normal place. A rare work for Kunisada, who specialized in pictures of girls. Signature: Kōchōrō Kunisada ga; kiwame and Yamaguchiya seals. Condition good (backed). From Chandler, Schraubstadter. In Schraubstadter, No. 366. Nishiki-e: 4 colors in many shades, gradation. 26.5×37.9.

Eisen

Keisai Eisen (1790–1848) is best known in Japan for his prints of voluptuous girls and his erotica, in the West for his series of landscapes done in collaboration with Hiroshige. He studied first under a Kanō painter, but later with the ukiyo-e master Eizan, was fond of Chinese painting of the Sung-Ming periods as well as of Hokusai's work, and frequently employed the aizuri-e technique, shown here, of repeated printings in shades of blue, a rather successful attempt to evade the government's austerity-ban of 1842 against nishiki-e. (See No. 189 for an earlier usage – from choice rather than necessity – by Hokusai.)

218. BAMBOOS AND MOON. 1840's. Another rare subject by a specialist in pictures of girls. Verse: "The rain washes, so profoundly clean; the wind blows, so minutely fragrant.' Signature: Keisai; Keisai seal. Kiwame and Echigoya seals. Condition good. From Chandler. Aizuri-e:. 26.4×38.1.

Hiroshige

Utagawa Hiroshige (1797–1858) studied under Toyokuni's more subtle confrere Toyohiro and had produced notable work already before he was twenty. He is the Japanese master par excellence of poetic atmosphere in the landscape print, as Chōki was in figure design. Where Hokusai placed his emphasis on the architectural structure of a landscape, Hiroshige viewed the scene more as a mood to be conveyed. The two masters have in common their reduction of each tableau to a balanced, decorative composition; but where Hokusai is dynamic and restless, Hiroshige is reflective and restful. His prints resemble romantic poetry caught at the peak of inspiration and, unlike the case with many earlier prints, one feels little urge to read the actual verses often inscribed thereon.

219. THE SALT-BEACH AT GYŌTOKU. Late 1830's. A panorama of the beach at Gyōtoku on Edo Bay, famous for its salt-production; on the beach the salt workers are seen carrying seawater or raking the salt-beds. (Cf. Nos. 1 and 9.) One of a rare series of some thirteen panoramas of the environs of Edo. The series is printed in delicate colors without black key-block, and was probably designed for use as letter-sheets, the black calligraphy to form an intricate counterpoint against the landscape, a device remin-

iscent of the days of Sōtatsu and Kōetsu. The style of this series differs considerably from that of most of Hiroshige's prints, but is quite similar to that of his numerous landscape paintings. Legend: "Picture of the Salt-beach at Gyōtoku." Signature: Hiroshige hitsu. No publisher's seal, but thought to be Wakasaya. Condition fine. From Chandler. Nishiki-e: 4 colors, gold dust in cartouche, gradation. 16×51.4.

220. CHERRY BLOSSOMS AT KOGANEI. Late 1830's. Sightseers visit the famed, aged cherry trees of Koganei, west of Edo. From the same series as No. 219. Legend: "View of Koganei." Signature: Hiroshige hitsu. Condition fine. From Chandler. Nishiki-e: 4 colors, gold dust in cartouche, gradation. 16×51.4.

221. SUDDEN SHOWER AT ŌHASHI. 1857. Wayfarers of Edo shield themselves from the sudden shower, caught on the Great Bridge across the Sumida River at Atake. On the river a logger poles his raft, and in the distance are seen dimly the houses and temples of Fukagawa and Honjo. (Both alternate versions are also in this collection, that with two boats near the far shore, and the late version with clouds cut in a straight line. For Van Gogh's fine copy in oils of this print see *Museum*, August 1958.) Legend: "One Hundred Famous Views of Edo: Ōhashi [Great Bridge], Sudden Shower at Atake." (The word "Atake" is almost universally omitted from descriptions of this famous print, doubtless due to the difficult calligraphy; it was the lowest-class red-light district of Fukagawa, and stood just east of the bridge shown here.) Signature: Hiroshige hitsu; aratame seal at top margin, with the date IX/1857. Condition fine. From Chandler. Nishiki-e: 6 colors, gradation. 34×22.

222. MOUNTAIN VILLAGE. Early 1840's. Two peasants toil across a snow-covered bridge, returning to their village; both wear straw raincoats, and the man at left is carrying firewood. The verse is derived from the T'ang poet Po Chü-i and reads: "The snow, like wild-goose feathers, is blown and scattered; the men, in garments as though white cranes, stand and wander about." One of a rare series of some six prints illustrating poems from the Heian-period anthology *Wakan rōei shū* (Japanese and Chinese Verses for Recitation). Signature: Hiroshige hitsu; Ichiryūsai seal. At left, kiwame and Jō-kin seals. Condition good (small holes at bottom right crudely backed). From Chandler, Mansfield. Nishiki-e: 5 colors plus red in cartouche, gradation. 37.4×25.8.

223. BY RYŌGOKU BRIDGE. Mid-1830's. A boatman poles his craft past Ryōgoku Bridge; Fukagawa with its lumberyards is seen in the distance, and a full moon is in the sky. Legend: "Famous Views of Edo in the Four Seasons: Summer, Full Moon at Ryōgoku." Verse: "Upon the bridge, I press through the crowds to view the peep-show fireworks shooting up at Ryōgoku." Signature: Hiroshige ga. Condition fine. From Chandler, Metzgar, Hayashi. Nishiki-e: 5 colors, gradation. 36.9×12.5.

224. AUTUMN MOON OVER THE YOSHIWARA. Late 1830's. In the foreground two coolies carry a palanquin bearing a nocturnal visitor along the slope leading to the Yoshiwara, which is seen in the background beneath the autumn moon and a flight of wild geese. Legend: "Famous Sights of the Eastern Capital: Autumn Moon at Emonzaka by the New Yoshiwara." Signature: Hiroshige ga; kiwame and Shōgendō seals. Condition good. From Chandler, 4/5/1916. Nishiki-e: 6 colors, gradation. 34.1×12.6.

225. MOON THROUGH LEAVES. Early 1830's. In the foreground a cascade of water, beyond it the full autumn moon seen through maple branches shedding their leaves. Legend: "Twenty-eight Views of the Moon: The Moon through the Leaves." The verse is from Po Chü-i: "So sad the maple leaves now fallen on the green moss ground, and the cold autumn breeze at the time of dusk rain." The collection contains another version of this print with less blue in the sky and less color in the leaves. Signature: Hiroshige hitsu; kiwame and Jakurindō seals. Condition good. From Chandler, 10/19/1919. Nishiki-e: 4 colors, overprinting, gradation. 38×17.1.

226. PLOVERS IN FLIGHT. Early 1830's. Two plovers are seen in playful flight across the face of the full moon; beneath them waves break. Verse: "Brother-plovers by the Beach of Keage play kick-ball with the moon." (Cf. No. 116.) Signature: Hiroshige hitsu; Ichiryūsai, Sano-ki seals. Condition fine. From Chandler, Hayashi. Nishiki-e: 4 colors, gradation. 32.2×10.9.

227. WILD GEESE IN FLIGHT. Early 1830's. Three wild geese are seen in flight across the face of the moon, surrounded by a spacious sky. As in many of Hiroshige's bird groups, the last wild goose bends his neck, lending variety to the composition. Verse: "Will there ever be a night like this one! wild geese in the moonlight." Signature: Hiroshige hitsu. Publisher's seal: Shōeidō. The seal seen at the bottom of this print is the most interesting of the several decorative designs employed by Hiroshige. The left figure is the word *ju* (long-life) drawn to resemble a horse seen from the rear; the right is the word *roku* (emolument) designed like a seated deer. The combination "horse-deer" gives the Japanese word *baka*, "fool." We do not know Hiroshige's own interpretation of the seal, but it probably suggests a disdain for longevity and wealth, two of mankind's principal desires. The seal is found on only a few prints of the period *ca.* 1832–33, usually with the design in opposite order from that seen here. Condition good. From Chandler, Salomon, Hayashi. In Salomon, No. 88. Nishiki-e: 4 colors plus red in seals, gradation. 38×12.7.

228. CUCKOO IN FLIGHT. Mid-1830's. The cuckoo cries while in flight over the treetops in a driving rainstorm. Verse: "From one cry to the next he's flown past Iozaki: the cuckoo-bird." (The cuckoo flies swiftly and his cries are widely spaced; from the reference to Iozaki, at Mukō-jima on the east side of the Sumida River, we may assume the bird's first cry to have emanated over the Yoshiwara, across the river to the west.) Signature: Hiroshige hitsu; kiwame and Shōeidō seals. Condition: fair (backed). From Chandler. Nishiki-e: 4 colors plus red in seals, gradation. 37.2×12.8.

229. EVENING BELL AT MII TEMPLE. Mid-1830's. In the distance is seen the towering Mt. Hiei, and before it, nestled among the foothills, the numerous structures of Mii Temple, famed for its evening bell. (Cf. No. 144. The grave of Fenollosa, pioneer of ukiyo-e studies, lies in the cemetery of the abbots of this temple, in the foothills to the right of this print.) Legend: "Eight Views of Lake Biwa: Evening Bell at Mii." Verse: "With one one loves, asleep together until dawn: from the first sound of the dusk bell of Mii." Signature: Hiroshige ga; kiwame and Takeuchi seals. Condition fine (small repair lower left, slight marginal stains). From Forman, Gunsaulus, Tuttle. Nishiki-e: 1 color (gray) in many shades, plus red in seals, and red and blue in cartouche; gradation. 22.8×35.2.

Kiyochika

Kobayashi Kiyochika (1847–1915). Of the small group of Meiji artists who attempted to adapt ukiyo-e methods and styles to the new age, Kiyochika stands preeminent. He sought a fusion of Western and Japanese styles, as Kuniyoshi had before him, and succeeded to a remarkable degree, for he had been trained both in Western photography, oil painting (at Yokohama, under the English artist Charles Wirgman), and Japanese painting (under Kyōsai and Zeshin). Kiyochika's output of prints was large, and many of them are dull; he is at his best in depictions of the Edo-Tokyo he knew so well and sketched so often.

230. PULLING THE CANAL-BOAT. 1876. By moonlight a boatman and his wife tow their craft (out of sight to the right) by hand against the current of the canal at Koume. (The romanized title is an interesting indication that the new name for Edo had not yet been standardized as "Tokyo" at this time.) Dated August, 1876. Signature: Hōensha Kobayashi Kiyochika ga, Wakamiya-chō No. 212. Publisher: Matsuki Heikichi, Yoshikawa-chō No. 2. Condition good. From Sakai. Nishiki-e: 5 colors plus red in cartouche and yellow border, gradation. 22×33.6.

Ryūson

Ogura Ryūson (worked 1880's). Surprisingly, almost nothing is known of this skilled Meiji print-maker. His works are few, but marked by poetic distinction; in imaginative employment of atmospheric affects he often excels Kiyochika, and follows in the line of Hiroshige. Ryūson's prints frequently appeared in two versions, one of them coated with varnish to simulate Western oil painting.

231. MOONLIGHT AT YUSHIMA. 1880. Two citizens of new Tokyo stand on the hill by the Yushima Shrine looking down over the moonlit city; at the left is a tea-shop, at the right a geisha house. Dated Nov. 5, 1880. Signature: Gakō Ogura Ryūson, Tsukiji Odawara-chō, 2–14. Publisher: Arai Hachizō, same address. Condition generally fine. From Adachi. Nishiki-e: 3 colors plus yellow varnish over all. 22.8×33.7.

Yasuji

Inoue Yasuji (1864–89), also known as Yasuharu and Tankei, was a pupil of Kiyochika and before his death at the age of twenty-five gave promise of sufficient genius perhaps to have effected a minor revival of the ukiyo-e style. His works are usually printed with care and display a restrained taste in coloring rather rare for this period.

232. SHOP ON THE GINZA. 1882. At the left, the manager watches the arrival of a shipment; at the right, customers inspect some of the new Western-style canned and bottled goods. The sign above the shop reads: "Canner of Native Fruit, Nakagawa Kōshichi, Tōkyō, Ginza Block 3." The central sign reads "Canned Bamboo-shoots," and that at left repeats the name and address of the shop. Title on the bottom margin: "Night View of Ginza Shop." Dated July, 1882. Signature: Gakō Inoue Yasujirō, Asakusa Namiki-chō No. 19. Publisher: Fukuda Kumajirō, Hasegawa-chō No. 19. Condition fine. From Shōbisha. Nishiki-e: 3 colors in many shades, overprinting, gradation. 35.7×24.

Goyō

Hashiguchi Goyō (1880–1921), though trained in Western oil painting at the Tokyo Art School, soon developed a love for the traditional ukiyo-e and actively engaged in research and writing on the subject. The effect of these studies appeared in creative form during the last six years of his life in the form of a series of impressive studies of women done in modern adaptation of ukiyo-e technique, often printed under the direct supervision of the artist.

233. WOMAN AT TOILETTE. 1918. A young woman in deshabille and holding a small mirror applies cosmetics to her neck with a brush. Dated 1918. Signature: Goyō; sealed Goyō. Condition fine. From two American collectors who wish to remain anonymous, Goyō. [The collection contains ten of the fourteen known prints designed by Goyō; but, following the artist's death, members of his family employed a printer to finish prints Goyō had not completed and in some cases to run off new copies from the old blocks. Also, prints which Goyō had rejected as not up to his standards were rescued. Therefore, the credentials of any Goyō must be questioned, and some coming onto the market now are late printings. It must be assumed that some of this collection's prints are either posthumous or printings which the artist had rejected in his lifetime. The present print, however, one of two copies in the collection, can be traced directly to the artist and may therefore be presumed to have been approved by him.] Nishiki-e: 3 colors, gold dust, gaufrage, white mica. 55.5×39.4.

Shinsui

Itō Shinsui (b. 1896). Pupil of the noted painter of women, Kiyokata, Shinsui still prospers today as a specialist in highly stylized paintings of women in neo-Japanese style. His work in the print field dates back to 1916 and includes a series of Modern Beauties.

234. SAMISEN MINSTREL AT IKENOHATA. 1921. A wandering musician plays the samisen and sings a ballad outside one of the tea-houses of Ikenohata, by Shinobazu Pond in Ueno, hoping for a tip from the revelers inside. Unsigned. Condition fine. From Shōbisha (one of the dealers who commissioned the original print), Shinsui. [This flawless print demonstrates what could be accomplished by using traditional techniques and subject matter. It was commissioned for this purpose by the print-sellers of Tokyo, and the entire edition of about fifty copies went to them directly from the artist.] Nishiki-e: 4 colors in many shades, gradation. 39×24.2.

Yamamoto

Yamamoto Kanae (1882–1946), founder of the Japanese creative-print movement, was early trained as a woodblock engraver in the Western style, later graduating from the Tokyo Art School and studying for several years in Paris.

235. WOMAN OF BRITTANY. 1920. Like Yamamoto's great Moscow prints, this portrait was done in Japan and thus represents the strong recollection of his European travel. Signed. Condition fine. From Statler, Shōbisha, Yamamoto. In Statler, No. 5. [From here on, each print has been designed, carved, printed, and published by the artist. Observe how frequently the signature appears in Roman letters, an article of faith among a group of artists yearning for an international artistic citizenship.] Woodblock print: 4 colors, overprinting. 38.2×29.9.

Sekino

Sekino Jun'ichirō (b. 1914) studied Western art in school briefly, but is largely self-taught. He is well known for his figure-prints and his Kabuki scenes. Recently he has worked in bold, abstract style.

236. LAFCADIO HEARN IN JAPANESE COSTUME. 1953. In portraying the most beloved American ever to reside in Japan, Sekino worked from a full-length photograph in an American edition of Hearn's collected works (Houghton Mifflin, 1910, volume entitled *Japanese Letters*), modifying the composition to suit his own concept and adding the Japanese-style pipe. Signed, sealed. Condition fine. From Metzgar, Hartnett, Sekino, this being the last print sold by Metzgar before his death in 1958. Woodblock print: 6 colors. 60.5×48.

Maekawa

Maekawa Sempan (b. 1888), also self-taught, comes from an old Kyoto family and his prints are among the most conservative of those produced by the creative-print artists.

237. AKITA DANCER. 1954. This distinguished print-maker has stuck closely to Japanese themes and has had a long series of successes, his scenes of industrial life and hot-bath resorts being especially notable. Signed: Senpan (an alternate spelling). Condition fine. From Maekawa. Woodblock print: 4 colors. 38×29.

Saitō

Saitō Kiyoshi (b. 1907) is one of the most productive and popular of the moderns; a native of Aizu, his early work concentrated on the snow scenes of that region.

238. WINTER IN AIZU. 1941. The series of prints thus titled, showing scenes of deep winter in the artist's home country in Fukushima Prefecture, were his first commercially successful work and had much to do with shaping his artistic career. The collection has two copies of this most delightful print in the set; this one is used because of its historical associations. Sealed. Condition fine. From Nail, Anderson, Hartnett, Saitō. In Fujikake, p. 163. Woodblock print: 2 colors plus red in seal. 36.5×44.4.

Kawano

Kawano Kaoru (b. 1916) is a native of Hokkaido; his charming visions of girlhood have recently achieved considerable acclaim.

239. GIRL IN SHELL. 1958. This spectacularly successful print burst upon Tokyo in the winter of 1958 and repeated its triumph wherever it was shown, including Chicago. The artist who designed it has produced a series of enticing prints showing little girls and might be called a modern Harunobu, for the spirit evidenced in his work is similar. Signed. Condition fine. From Yōseidō, Kawano. [Yōseidō is the Tokyo art shop of Abe Yūji and the best single source for modern Japanese prints. While this shop does not serve as publisher, it is the gathering place of artists and their major permanent outlet. Most of the modern prints appearing in this book can be obtained from Yōseidō.] In Mitsukoshi, 1958. Woodblock print: 4 colors, overprinting. 41.8×58.7.

Mabuchi

Mabuchi Thoru (b. 1920) – the "Thoru" is his own romanization of the name Tōru – was taught first by his father, a woodblock engraver, and later studied at the Tokyo Art School under Hiratsuka.

240. AFTERNOON SUN. 1952. This print, which ends the Statler book on modern prints, is a favorite of many connoisseurs. Its mosaic construction is achieved technically by gluing small fragments cut from wooden lunch boxes to the block, but artistically it derives from Seurat's pointillism and from Byzantine mosaic work. This print required three traditional blocks for ground color, and seven mosaic blocks, from which thirty separate printings were pulled. Signed and sealed. Condition fine. From Statler, Mabuchi. In Statler, No. 100. Wood blocks (1 uncarved, 2 carved, 7 mosaic): 6 colors printed in 30 separate stages. 55×75.6.

Hashimoto

Hashimoto Okiie (b. 1899), since graduating from the Tokyo Art School in 1924, has taught art in a Tokyo middle school.

241. GATE AND RETAINER'S HALL, NIJŌ CASTLE. 1957. This artist has specialized in architectural prints showing massive castles depicted in bold line and brilliant color. He has also done several huge prints composed of four segments, each an oversize print in itself. Signed. Condition fine. From Hashimoto. Woodblock print: 5 colors, overprinting. 39.8×55.3.

Onchi

Onchi Kōshirō (1891–1955) early received an aristocratic education but at seventeen entered the Tokyo Art School, where he proved a rebellious student. Dedicated to creative prints from his youth, Onchi made a living by his superlative book-designing. From his middle years he concentrated on the abstract designs that have proved his forte, and is today recognized as perhaps the first master of modern prints.

242. LONELINESS. 1951. Signed Onzi (an alternate spelling). Condition fine. From Onchi. In *Nippon no yūshū*, Vol 4. [Although it is correct to describe the three Onchis shown here as mint, the word has a peculiar significance when used in connection with this artist. A mint Onchi means that it came directly from the artist: dog-eared, rumpled, creased, spotted, and with coloring smeared and edges torn. Onchi kept his finished prints jammed into piles on the floor. Often he walked across one pile to reach

another, jerking forth the print he wanted, slapping it smooth with a rough hand, and shoving it at the would-be customer.] Glass plate for background, cardboard for black line, piece of plywood, paper blocks: 8 colors, overprinting. 72×57.1.

243. CARICATURE NO. 8. 1948. The artist stated that this print reflected the horrors of bombing during the war. Signed: Onzi. Condition fine. From Onchi. In *Nippon no yūshū*, Vol. 4. Woodblock print: 4 colors. 48.7×39.5.

244. POEM NUMBER NINETEEN: THE SEA. 1952. The finest Onchi in the collection and one of his greatest works. Signed: Onzi. Condition fine. From Statler, Onchi. Paper block, wax paper, crumpled cloth: 3 colors. 76.5×57.4.

Yamaguchi

Yamaguchi Gen (b. 1903) led a varied career before being drawn to print-making, in which he was influenced by Onchi.

245. DEEP ATTACHMENT. 1957. This subtle and perfect print has been described by Statler as "a design in which every element seems necessary and in exactly the right place." Signed. Condition fine. From Yōseidō, Yamaguchi. Woodblock print: 4 colors. 63.3×46.5.

Nakao

Nakao Yoshitaka (b. 1910) lives on the island of Shikoku and has experimented with unusual techniques of print-making.

246. FIGURE. 1957. Working largely by himself, Nakao perfected a system of print-making which produced striking, bold figures that looked as if they had been hewn from rock. He achieved this effect by building a wooden form the size of the print, pouring it with concrete, and inscribing the surface as it dried. Later he found that the same effect could be accomplished by using wood blocks properly, and this print was made from such blocks. Nakao is usually associated with Azechi in the minds of Japanese connoisseurs. Signed. Condition fine. From Yōseidō, Nakao. Woodblock print: 7 colors. 83.8×55.8.

Azechi

Azechi Umetarō (b. 1902) is a native of Shikoku, largely self-taught, who has managed to maintain a rough, rustic charm in his works through the years.

247. BIRD IN SAFE HANDS. 1957. This appealing artist is a mountaineer, an essayist, a book illustrator, and a gifted print-maker. He uses bold forms and bright colors and in recent years has achieved wide success with depictions of mountaineers against stark backgrounds. Signed. Condition fine. From Azechi. Woodblock print: 5 colors. 61.2×43.2.

Kinoshita

Kinoshita Tomio (b. 1923) is a new print-maker just beginning to succeed in the art world.

248. MASKS: DESIGN 4. 1957. This is one of a series of such prints issued with striking effect by a new artist hitherto unknown. It is one of the most successful of recent prints, but whether the artist can go on to work of increasing stature remains to be seen. Signed. Condition fine. From Yōseidō, Kinoshita. Woodblock print: 2 colors. 56.4×79.

Yoshida Hodaka

Yoshida Hodaka (b. 1926) became a print artist more or less against his artist-father's wishes; much of his work is abstract.

249. ANCIENT PEOPLE. 1956. Any book on Japanese prints would be incomplete without work of the amazing Yoshida family. Father, mother, two sons, daughter-in-law, and grandsons have all issued prints of distinction. The father, Yoshida Hiroshi (1876–1950), had kept traditional print-making alive largely through his own tremendous effort. He traveled widely and some of his most popular works depicted foreign lands. Even today a blizzard of prints continues to fall from his old blocks and to find a ready market among tourists. His gifted sons have also traveled to many countries, and it is highly appropriate that the Yoshida print shown here should have sprung from Hodaka's travels in Mexico. Recently, in an international competition, a print that seemed to have been plagiarized from this very fine work won first prize and evoked a scandal. Signed. Condition fine. From Yoshida. Woodblock print: 2 colors. 51×68.

Yoshida Masaji

Yoshida Masaji (b. 1917), unrelated to the famous Yoshida family of print-makers, studied at the Tokyo Art School under Hiratsuka and has himself been most successful in teaching print-making to school-children. He was greatly influenced by Onchi's abstractions, but has lately been developing unique styles and techniques of his own.

250. FOUNTAIN OF EARTH NO. 1. 1956. This stark design is not only extremely effective in the large size in which it was issued, but it shows how the sumizuri-e of the early artists can be utilized in modern forms to produce fine prints. Signed. Condition fine. From Statler, Yoshida. In Statler, No. 85. Sumizuri-e. 57×83.

Uchima

Uchima Ansei (b. 1921) is an American of Japanese ancestry who was caught in Japan by the war. He has been active in organizing exhibitions of modern prints, as well as in developing a style of his own.

251. SONG OF THE SEASHORE. 1957. Of this print the artist has said: "It was originally commissioned as a decorative tokonoma piece for the new wing of the Toko-en Inn in Kaike, a hot-bath resort in Tottori Prefecture, by the architect of the inn, Shibaoka Isao. The Japanese-style room in which the first print now rests overlooks the waters of the Japan Sea. In the conception of the design I intended to incorporate something of the atmosphere of the seascape and I had in mind the misty view of the sea towards evening. I started by first laying out the darker grey blotches, painting directly on the board. The size and proportions of the print came about as a result of this first stage. After carving and printing this block I then proceeded to lay out the black forms on a second block. Superimposed printings of the two blocks produced the idea for the background grey and the white lines which took the shapes of ships in the sea. Addition of the light-blue block, which came next,

was meant as an intermediate tone for the greys and black, and also to enhance the idea. Tones were then altered in the background gray, where an extra printing stage was required for the somewhat darker portion in the center, and in some of the black where the technique of 'dry brush' was employed to provide textural variety to the whole. The title was derived from the name of a popular Japanese song. Four shina-faced veneer blocks were used and torinoko paper. The pigment was sumi, forming greys and blacks, plus Prussian blue taken from watercolor tubes. I plan an edition of 100, of which 23 have so far been printed." Signed. Condition fine. From Uchima. Woodblock print: 3 colors plus handcoloring.

Shinagawa

Shinagawa Takumi (b. 1907) is a restless experimenter in new forms and styles, and his work includes mobiles and photography as well as prints.

252. HERE EVERYTHING WAS ALIVE. 1957. Signed. Condition fine. From Shinagawa. Wood blocks, wood impressions, cardboard forms, and crumpled paper: 8 colors, overprinting. 57.5×88.

Hatsuyama

Hatsuyama Shigeru (b. 1897) received his early training in a dyeing shop and has made a living by illustrating books for children in the same mood of fantasy that suffuses his best prints.

253. FLOWERS, BIRDS. 1952. This print is from the same series as the one shown so handsomely in color in Statler, Print 58. Signed. Condition fine. From Hatsuyama. Wood blocks (one progressively carved through various stages, another for circular forms): 4 colors, much overprinting. 53.4×65.

Hiratsuka

Hiratsuka Un'ichi (b. 1895) has been the great teacher and quiet leader of the modern print movement for many years. His own work goes back to the ancient Buddhist prints of Japan, the strong sumi-e of Sesshū, and the black-and-white work of such early ukiyo-e greats as Moronobu (Nos. 11 and 12).

254. HŌRYŪ-JI IN EARLY AUTUMN. 1942. This is probably Hiratsuka's masterwork, combining as it does old forms, old techniques, and strong modern approach. It is a print which grows in stature as one comes to know it. The collection has two versions and reproduces this one, even though the corners are torn, because of its historical associations. Signed & sealed. Condition fine. From Nail, Anderson, Hartnett, Hiratsuka. In Fujikake, p. 145. Sumizuri-e. 78×59.7.

Munakata

Munakata Shikō (b. 1903) goes back to the same simple, traditional techniques as Hiratsuka, but imbues them with a strange power and near-religious intensity. He first achieved some success as a painter in oils, but eventually determined that he could never fully express himself in that alien form.

255. UBARI. 1939. This print and the next come from Munakata's masterpiece, a twelve-print series entitled *Ten Great Disciples of Buddha,* the series being completed by the addition of two prominent Buddhist saints. Ubari, shown here, was a barber from the caste of farmers who became a disciple and compiled the first monastic rules. Signed & sealed. Condition fine. From Statler, Munakata. Like No. 256, the printing from the original blocks may have been done in 1955. Sumizuri-e. 115×42.5.

256. KASEN'EN. 1939. Since this disciple was distinguished for his grasp of the fundamental principles of law, it is not surprising that Munakata says: "He looks exactly like my father. I like this print because of that, but it always reminds me of a scolding he once gave me." For a complete study of this famous series see Statler's essay on Munakata in Vol. 12, Library of Japanese Art. Signed & sealed. Condition fine. From Statler, Munakata. Sumizuri-e. 115× 42.5.

BIBLIOGRAPHY

This bibliography lists the books and catalogues known to contain reproductions of the specific prints appearing in this book, as indicated in the notes, together with a few other items which have been cited. At the beginning of some entries, either in the form of a name followed by a period or of an abbreviation, are shown the space-saving forms which have been used in the notes.

For a detailed bibliography of books on ukiyo-e, the reader is referred to Michener, *The Floating World*, pp. 379–90. Among more recent publications of general interest that should also be mentioned are a reprint of Ficke's *Chats on Japanese Prints* (Rutland, Vermont, 1958), Michener's *The Hokusai Sketchbooks: Selections from the Manga* (Rutland, 1958), Oliver Statler's and Yamada Chisaburō's *Kiyoshi Saitō: His Woodblock Prints* (Tokyo, 1957), Statler's *Umetarō Azechi* (Tokyo, 1959), and volumes in the Library of Japanese Art (Rutland, 1955–59) on individual print artists – *Harunobu, Hiroshige, Hokusai, Kaigetsudō, Kiyonaga, Munakata, Sharaku, Toyokuni,* and *Utamaro.*

Baker. *Catalogue of an Interesting and Varied Collection of Japanese Colour Prints, Original Drawings and Illustrated Books, the Property of Kington Baker, Esq.* Sotheby, Wilkinson & Hodge, London, 1916.

Binyon, Laurence, & Sexton, J.J. O'Brien: *Japanese Colour Prints.* London, 1923.

Blanchard. *Illustrated Catalogue of the Notable Collection of Japanese Color Prints, the Property of Mrs. John Osgood Blanchard.* American Art Association, New York, 1916.

Boller, Willy: *Hokusai.* Stuttgart, *ca.* 1955.

Buckingham. *The Clarence Buckingham Collection of Japanese Prints: The Primitives.* Edited by Helen C. Gunsaulus. Art Institute of Chicago, 1955.

De Gruyter, W. Jos: *Van Moronobu tot Harunobu.* s'Gravenhage, 1952.

Einstein, Carl: *Der Frühere Japanische Holzschnitt.* Berlin, n.d.

Ficke, Arthur Davison: *Chats on Japanese Prints.* London, 1915; reprinted, Rutland, Vermont, 1958.

Ficke. *The Japanese Print Collection of Arthur Davison Ficke.* American Art Association, New York, 1920.

———. *The Japanese Print Collection of Arthur Davison Ficke.* Anderson Galleries, New York, 1925.

Frankfurt. *Japanische Holzschnitte aus der Sammlung Straus-Negbaur in Frankfurt A.M. ausgestellt im Städel'schen Institut, beschrieben von Dr. Julius Kurth.* Frankfurt am Main, 1909.

Fujikake, Shizuya: *Japanese Wood-Block Prints.* Tokyo, 1953.

Gonse. *Collection Louis Gonse. Oeuvres d'art de Japon, choix d'estampes et de livres des principaux maitres de l'ukiyoyé.* Hotel Drouot, Paris, May 11, 1924.

Hakone. (Hakone sale catalogues.) Hakone, November 13–14, 1917, and October 22–23, 1919.

Happer. *Catalogue of the Valuable Collection of Japanese Colour Prints and a Few Kakemono, the Property of John Stewart Happer, Esq.* Sotheby, Wilkinson & Hodge, London, April 26, 1909.

Hayashi. *Collection Hayashi: Dessins, estampes, livres illustrés du Japon.* Paris, 1902.

Hillier, J.: *Japanese Masters of the Colour Print.* London, 1954.

Hirano Chie: *Kiyonaga: A Study of His Life and Works. With a Portfolio of Plates.* Boston, 1939.

Hubert. *Collection Hubert (vente après décès) estampes et livres japonais.* Hotel Drouot, Paris, March 23, 1928.

Jacquin. *Rare and Valuable Japanese Color Prints, the Noted Collection Formed by a Distinguished French Connoisseur of Paris. Catalogue by Frederick W. Gookin.* Walpole Galleries, New York, January 20–22, 1921.

Kawaura Ken'ichi: *Ukiyo-e hanga zenshū* ("Descriptive and Historical Album of Old Japanese Prints of the Ukiyo-ye School"). Tokyo, 1918.

Kunstwanderer, Der. Berlin, June, 1922, pp. 463–70.

Kurth, Julius: *Sharaku* (2nd ed.). München, 1922.

———: *Suzuki Harunobu.* München, 1910; 2nd ed., 1923.

Lane, Richard: *Kaigetsudō* (Library of Japanese Art, No. 13). Rutland, Vermont, 1959.

Ledoux, Louis V.: *Japanese Prints of the Ledoux Collection* (5 vol.). New York and Princeton, 1942–51.

Lewis, Robert E.: *Masterpieces of Japanese Color Prints.* San Francisco, 1954.

London. *Exhibition of Japanese Prints: Illustrated Catalogue, with Notes and an Introduction by Arthur Morrison.* Fine Art Society, London, 1909.

Manzi. *Catalogue des estampes japonaises (première partie) composant la collection du feu M. Manzi.* Galerie Manzi, Joyant & Cie., Paris, February, 1920.

Matsuki. *Japanese Color Prints Including Many Important Prints from the Collection of an Old Samurai Family in Tokio, Brought together by the Well-known Connoisseur, Bunkio Matsuki.* Anderson Galleries, New York, 1920.

May. *Illustrated Catalogue of a Very Important Collection of Rare and Valuable Japanese Color Prints. Formed by the Widely Known Connoisseur, the Late Frederick May.* American Art Association, New York, 1918.

Michener, James A.: *The Floating World.* New York, 1954.

Mihara. *Ukiyo-e hanga tenrankai mokuroku* ("Catalogue of a Special Loan Exhibition of Ukiyoe Prints selected from the collection of Mr. A.S. Mihara to Commemorate the Opening of Viscount Seiki Kouroda Memorial Hall, Uyeno Park, October 17th, 18th and 19th, 1930"). Imperial Institute of Art Research, Tokyo, 1930.

Mitsukoshi. *Gendai mokuhanga shūsaku ten.* Mitsukoshi Department Store, Tokyo, February, 1958.

Morse. *Japanese Prints. Important Primitives & Representative Works by Other Masters . . . From Three Private Collections: The Late Charles J. Morse . . . The Late Helen Fahnstock Hubbard . . . and Mrs. Charles J. Liebman.* Parke-Bernet Galleries, New York, 1927.

Noguchi, Yone: *Harunobu.* Tokyo, 1940.

OAZ. *Ostasiatische Zeitschrift.* Berlin, 18 vols, 1912–43.

Ōiso. (Ōiso sale catalogue.) Ōiso, June, 1914.

Onchi, Kōshirō: *Nippon no yūshū.* Atami, Japan, 1955.

Orange. *Catalogue of an Interesting and Varied Collection of Japanese Color Prints. . . . A Choice Selection of Brilliant*

Surimono; and a Number of Illustrated Books: the Property of James Orange, Esq. and Dr. T.C. Thornicraft. Sotheby, Wilkinson & Hodge, London, 1912.

Ostier, L.: *Primitifs japonais.* Paris, 1954.

Ruth. *Catalogue of the Private Collection of an Importer of Japanese Products Comprising Valuable and Important Japanese Colour Prints Including Works of the Primitives and Early Masters.* Sotheby, Wilkinson & Hodge, London, January, 1911.

Salomon. *Objects d'art du Japon & de la Chine. Laques japonais, bronzes et cloisonnés chinois provenant de la collection Raymon Koechlin. Poteries japonaises, netzuke, gardes de sabres, bronzes provenant des collections Edmond & Marcel Guerin. Estampes, peintures, livres japonais, livres europèens sur l'art provenant de la collection Ch. Salomon.* Hotel Drouot, Paris, June, 1926.

Schraubstadter. *An Exceptionally Important Collection of Rare and Valuable Japanese Color Prints, the Property of Carl Schraubstadter.* American Art Galleries, New York, 1921.

Shibui Kiyoshi: *Catalogue des estampes erotiques primitives du Japon* (2 vol.). Tokyo, 1926, 1928.

Sotheby. *Catalogue of a Valuable Collection of Japanese Colour Prints, the Property of a Parisian Collector.* Sotheby, Wilkinson & Hodge, London, April 17, 1918.

Statler, Oliver: *Modern Japanese Prints: An Art Reborn.* Rutland, Vermont, 1956.

——: *Shiko Munakata* (Library of Japanese Art, No. 12). Rutland, Vermont, 1958.

Straus-Negbaur. *Sammlung Tony Straus-Negbaur. Japanische Farbenholzschnitte des 17. bis. 19. Jahrhunderts. Eingeleitet von Curt Glaser. Beschrieben von Fritz Rumpf.* Berlin, 1928.

Tokyo. (Tokyo sales catalogues.) Ueno, November 18, 1927; Ōmori, May 3, 1933.

Ukiyo-e Kabuki gashū. Tokyo, 1927.

UT. *Ukiyo-e taisei* (12 vol.). Tokyo, 1930–31.

UTS. *Ukiyo-e taika shūsei* (20 vol.). Tokyo, 1931–32.

V&I. Vignier, Ch., & Inada Hogitarō: *Estampes japonaises primitives. . . . Exposées au Musée des Arts Décoratifs en fevrier 1909. Catalogue dressé par M. Vignier avec la collaboration de M. Inada.* Paris, 1909.

——: *Kiyonaga, Buncho, Sharaku, estampes japonaises . . . exposées au Musée des Arts Décoratifs en janvier 1911.* Paris, 1911.

——: *Toyokuni, Hiroshige, estampes japonaises . . . exposées au Musée des Arts Décoratifs en janvier 1914.* Paris, 1914.

Wadsworth. *Japanese Prints: A Selection from the Charles J. Morse and Jared K. Morse Collection, Lent by Mrs. Jared K. Morse.* Wadsworth Atheneum, Hartford, Connecticut, 1951.

Wright. *The Frank Lloyd Wright Collection of Japanese Antique Prints.* Anderson Galleries, New York, 1927.

Yoshida Teruji: *Harunobu zenshū.* Tokyo, 1942.

INDEX